Why had Helena Trescott picked Travis McGee to look after her crazy, suicide-bent daughter?

I think slaying oneself is a nasty little private, self-involved habit and, when successful, the residual flavor is a kind of sickly embarrassment rather than a sense of high tragedy. I am not suited to the role of going around selling the life-can-be-beautiful idea.

So why pick me?

Am I supposed to be the kindly old philosopher, and go set on the girl's porch and spit and whittle and pat her on the hand?

Hang around, kid. See what's going to happen next.

JOHN D. MacDONALD

THE GIRL IN THE PLAIN BROWN WRAPPER

FAWCETT GOLD MEDAL • NEW YORK

THE GIRL IN THE PLAIN BROWN WRAPPER

Published by Fawcett Gold Medal Books, a unit of CBS Publications, the Consumer Publishing Division of CBS Inc.

ISBN: 0-449-14256-6

First Fawcett printing: January 1969

Printed in the United States of America

32   31   30   29   28   27   26   25

1   *IT IS ONE* of the sorry human habits
to play the game of: What was I doing when it happened?

After I heard that Helena Pearson had died on Thursday, the third day of October, I had no trouble reconstructing the immediate past.

That Thursday had been the fourth and final day of a legitimate little job of marine salvage. Meyer made a lot of small jokes about Travis McGee, salvage expert, actually doing some straight-arrow salvage. He kept saying it almost made my cover story believable. But he did not say such things for any ears but mine own.

Actually it was not my ball game. Meyer gets himself involved in strange little projects. Somewhere, somehow he had gotten interested in the ideas of a refugee Cuban chemist named Joe Palacio. So he had talked a mutual friend of ours, Bobby Guthrie, a damned good man with pumps and pressures and hydraulics, into listening to Joe's ideas and going to Joe's rooming house in Miami where Joe had set up a miniaturized demonstration in an old bathtub he had scrounged somewhere.

When Bobby got high enough on the idea to quit his regular job, Meyer put in the money and they formed a little partnership and named it Floatation Associates.

Then Meyer, in one of his mother hen moods, sweet-talked me into donating my services, plus my houseboat, *The Busted Flush*, plus my swift little *Muñequita* boat to the first actual salvage operation. So I had to take the *Flush* down to a Miami yard where they winched aboard a big ugly diesel pump with special attachments rigged by Bobby Guthrie, some great lengths of what appeared to

5

be reinforced fire hose, and several 55-gallon drums of special gunk mixed up by Joe Palacio, plus scuba tanks, air compressor, tools, torches, and so on. Once I had topped off the water and fuel tanks and laid aboard the provisions and booze, the old *Flush* was as low in the water as I cared to see her. Even with all her beam, and that big old barge-type hull, she had to react to what Bobby estimated as seven thousand pounds of extra cargo. She seemed a little discouraged about it.

"If she founders," Meyer said pleasantly, "we'll see if we can raise her with Palacio's magic gunk."

So we took off down Biscayne Bay with the *Muñequita* in tow, heading for the lower Keys. We got an early start and kept waddling along, and by last light we were far enough down Big Spanish Channel to edge cautiously over into the shallows off Annette Key, in the lee of a southwest breeze, and drop a couple of hooks.

The immediate forecast was good, but there was an area of suspicion over near the Leeward Islands, and there was an official half month of the whirly-girl season left. Also the girls are known to come screaming up through hurricane alley after the season is over.

Later I learned that Helena Pearson had written the letter to me that same Saturday, September 28th, the day after she guessed she wasn't going to make it, the letter the attorney mailed, still sealed, with his cover letter. And with the certified check.

That evening at anchor aboard *The Busted Flush* the three Floatation associates were edgy. For Meyer it was simple empathy. He knew the risks they were taking. Joe Palacio had a chance to make a new career in his adopted land. Bobby Guthrie had a wife and five kids to worry about. The three of them had periods of contagious enthusiasm, and then they would get the doubts and the glooms and the hollow laughter. If it worked on a very small scale in the scavenged bathtub, that didn't mean it was going to work out in Hawk Channel, in the Straits of Florida, in seventy-five feet of ocean.

In the morning we went south down Big Spanish, past No Name Key, and under the fixed bridge between Bahia

Honda Key and Spanish Harbor Key. Then the overladen *Flush* was out in the deeps, and we had a nine-mile run at about 220 degrees to lonely little Looe Key, across a slow heave of greasy swell. Soon I was able to pick up the red marker on Looe with the glasses. On the way, while on automatic pilot, I had figured out the quickest and best way to run if things blew up too suddenly. I would pour on all the coal and run just a shade east of magnetic north, perhaps 8 degrees, and if I could manage to make eight knots, I could tuck the *Flush* into Newfound Harbor Channel in maybe forty minutes, and find a protected pocket depending on the wind, maybe in Coupon Bight or close offshore by Little Torch Key.

Bobby Guthrie had the coordinates on the sunken pleasure boat. She lay a half mile southwest of Looe Key. She'd been down there for two months. She was the *'Bama Gal,* owned by a Tampa hotelman, about ninety thousand dollars' worth of cabin cruiser, only six months old. Forty-six feet, fiber glass hull, twin diesels. The hotelman and his wife and another couple had been out fishing and the hotelman had keeled over with a heart attack while fighting a billfish. Nobody else aboard knew how to run the ship-to-shore radio. They barely knew how to run the boat. There was a tug with a tow of three barges about a half mile farther out, so they figured that the tug would have a radio they could use to call a Coast Guard helicopter and get the man to a hospital. The guest ran the boat over toward the tug and cut the engines and they all started waving their arms. Maybe they thought that tugs and barges have some kind of braking system. The tug captain tried evasive tactics, but mass and momentum were too much. The forward port corner of the lead barge put a big ugly hole in the cruiser, but the crew launched a skiff and got the people off in good order before she went down. By the time the Coast Guard arrived, the owner was as dead as the other fish they had caught, which had gone down with the cruiser.

The insurance company had paid off on the cruiser, and Meyer had gotten a release from them, so any recovery was going to be profit—if we could bring it up, tow it in, and find something worth money.

So on that Sunday I worked the *Flush* into the most protected water that Looe provides. It is shaped like a backward "J" that has fallen onto its back, and I put the hooks out in shoal water, as close as I could get without risking being hard aground at low tide. We took the *Muñequita* out and located the *'Bama Gal* after about forty minutes of skin diving and looking. We made a bright red buoy fast to her, and then I ran the *Muñequita* up-current, put the anchor down in about seventy feet, and let her come back to the buoy before snubbing her down, almost at the end of my four hundred feet of anchor line. Not enough scope to be sure of holding.

We had just the two sets of tanks aboard the *Muñequita,* so I went down with Joe Palacio to get a good look at what condition she was in. She lay on a little slope, bow higher than the stern, and she was on about a fifteen-degree list to port, making the hole in the starboard side, a little aft of amidships, easy to see. She was picking up new grass and weed and green slime, but it wasn't too bad yet. We had expected to find her picked clean of everything the skin-diver kids could lift, but by some freak of chance they hadn't found her. The big rods with their Finor reels were still in the rod holders. Binoculars, booze, cameras, tackle boxes, rifle, sunglasses—all the toys and gear and gadgets that people take to sea were either stowed or lay on the cockpit, cabin, or flybridge decking. While Joe busied himself with studying the hatches and the interior layout, and measuring interior spaces, I kept assembling bundles of goodies and, with a couple of pulls on the dangling line, sending them up into the sunlight.

When we went up, I found that all the stuff had looked better down in the depths, green and shadowy, than up on the deck of my runabout, all sodden, leaking, and corroded.

Monday we took the *Flush* out and anchored her over the wreck and worked all day, in shifts, beefing up those places where Palacio thought the floatation might come busting out, and also cutting through some interior bulkheads to make a free flow of water through all the belowdecks areas, and fastening some plywood against the inside of the hull where the big hole was. Whenever we came across anything we could tie a line to and lift to the surface, we did so.

The weather held on Tuesday and by noon Joe was satisfied that we were ready to try. We took the reinforced hose down and clamped it securely in place, leading it through the hole we'd cut into the damaged side above the waterline. We had made no attempt to make her watertight. That was the last thing Palacio wanted.

Bobby Guthrie got his funny-looking pump going. It throbbed, smoked, and stank, but it pulled water up through the intake hose dangling over the side and pumped it down and into the wreck and out through dozens of small openings here and there. Palacio was very nervous. His hands shook as he clamped the small hoses that led from three drums of separate kinds of gunk to the brass nipples on a fitting on the big hose that led down to the wreck. He had flow guages and hand pumps on each drum. As Meyer had explained it to me, Gunk One reacted with the water, raising its temperature. Then Gunk Two and Gunk Three interacted with the heated water as they went swirling down, and when they were released inside the hull down below, they separated into big blobs and, in the cooler water, solidified into a very lightweight plastic full of millions of little bubbles full of the gases released through their interaction on each other and the heated water. Palacio had the three of us manning the hand pumps and he hopped back and forth from one flow gauge to the other, speeding one man up, slowing another down. There was, after about ten minutes, a sudden eruption about forty feet down-current, and a batch of irregular yellow-white chunks the size of cantaloupe appeared and, floating very high on the water, went moving swiftly away in the slight breeze.

Palacio stopped us and cut the flow. Guthrie turned off the big pump. We went down and found that the ventilator on the forward deck had blown out. By the time it was secure, it was time to quit. All day Wednesday there was pump trouble of one kind or another. We thought Palacio would break down and start sobbing.

By midday Thursday everything seemed to be working well for about forty minutes. My arm began to feel leaden. Palacio was gnawing his knuckles. Suddenly Guthrie gave a roar of surprise. The hose began to stand up out of the water like a snake and a moment later the big cruiser came porpoising up, so fast and so close that it threw a big wave aboard, drenching us and killing the pump. She rocked back and forth, streaming water, riding high and handsome. We stomped and yelled and laughed like idiots. She was packed full of those lightweight brittle blobs of foam, and I tried not to think of how damn foolish I had been to never even think of what could have happened if she had come up that fast and directly under the *Flush*.

We wasted no time rigging for towing. We were getting more swell and I did not like the feel of the wind. Between periods of dead calm there would come a hot, moist huff, like a gigantic exhalation. I set it up with short towlines, the *Flush* in the lead, of course, the salvaged *'Bama Gal* in the middle, and Bobby Guthrie aboard the *Muñequita* in the rear. I broke out the pair of walkie-talkies because the bulk of the *'Bama Gal* made hand signals to Bobby back there impossible. The system was for him to keep the *Muñequita*'s pair of OMC 120's idling in neutral, and if our tow started to swing, he could give the engines a little touch of reverse and pull it back into line. I knew the inboard-outboards could idle all day without overheating. Also, when I had to stop the *Flush* down for traffic, Bobby could keep it from riding up on our stern.

It was early Saturday afternoon before we got her to Merrill-Stevens at Dinner Key, and we had to work her in during a flat squall, in a hard gray driving rain, the wind gusting and whistling. I'd phoned a friend via the Miami marine operator earlier in the day, so they were waiting for us. We shoved the *'Bama Gal* into the slings and they picked her out of the water and put her on a cradle and ran her along the rails and into one of the big sheds. Palacio wore a permanent, broad, dreaming grin.

The dockmaster assigned me a slip for the *Flush* and space in the small boat area for the *Muñequita*. By the time we were properly moored, hooked into shoreside power, and had showered and shaved and changed, heavy rain was drumming down, and it was very snug in the lounge aboard *The Busted Flush*, lights on, music on, ice in the glasses, Meyer threatening to make his famous beef stew with chili, beans, and eggs, never the same way twice running. Guthrie had phoned his wife and she was going to drive down from Lauderdale to pick him up Sunday morning. They were tapping the Wild Turkey bourbon we'd found aboard the *Gal,* and I was sticking to Plymouth on ice. Meyer kept everybody from going too far overboard in estimating profit. He kept demanding we come up with "the minimum expectation, gentlemen."

So we kept going over what would probably have to be done and came up with a maximum fifteen thousand to put her in shape, and a minimum forty-five thousand return after brokerage commission.

That is the best kind of argument, trying to figure out how much you've made. It is good to hear the thunder of tropic rain, to feel the muscle soreness of hard manual labor when you move, to have a chill glass in your hand, know the beginnings of ravenous hunger, realize that in a few hours even a bunk made of cobblestones would feel deep and soft and inviting.

They wanted me to come into the fledgling partnership, with twenty-five percent of the action. But struggling ventures should not be cut too many ways. Nor did I want the responsibility, that ever-present awareness of people depending on me permanently to make something work. They were too proud—Guthrie and Palacio—to accept my efforts as a straight donation, so after some inverted haggling we agreed that I would take two thousand in the form of a note at six percent, payable in six months. They wanted to put their take back into improved equipment and go after a steel barge sunk in about fifty feet of water just outside Boca Grande Pass.

I was sprawled and daydreaming, no longer hearing their words as they talked excitedly of plans and projects, hearing only the blur of their voices through the music.

"Didn't we make it that time in an hour and a half? Hey! Trav!"

Meyer was snapping his fingers at me. "Make what?" I asked.

"That run from Lauderdale to Bimini."

They had stopped talking business. I could remember that ride all too well. "Just under an hour and a half from the sea buoy at Lauderdale to the first channel marker at Bimini."

"In what?" Guthrie asked.

I told him what it had been, a Bertram 25 rigged for ocean racing with a pair of big hairy three hundreds in it, and enough chop in the Stream so that I had to work the throttles and the wheel every moment, so that when she went off a crest and was airborne, she would come down flat. Time it wrong and hit wrong, and you can trip them over.

"What was the rush?" Bobby asked.

"We were meeting a plane," Meyer said.

And I knew at that moment he too was thinking of Helena Pearson and a very quick and dirty salvage job of several years back. We were both thinking of her, with no way of knowing she had been dead two days, no way of knowing her letter was at Bahia Mar waiting for me.

Even without the knowledge of her death, Helena was a disturbing memory . . .

2 *FIVE YEARS* ago? Yes. In a winter month, in a cold winter for Florida, Mick Pearson, with his wife Helena and his two daughters, aged twenty and seventeen, crewing for him, had brought his handsome Dutch motor sailer into Bahia Mar, all the way from Bordeaux. The *Likely Lady*. A wiry, seamed, sun-freckled, talkative man in his fifties, visibly older than his slender gray-blond wife.

He gave the impression of somebody who had made it early, had retired, and was having the sweet life. He circulated quickly and readily and got to know all the regulars. He gave the impression of talking a lot about himself, not in any bragging or self-important way, but by amusing incident. People found it easy to talk to him.

Finally I began to get the impression that he was focusing on me, as if he had been engaged in some process of selection and I was his best candidate. I realized how very little I knew about him, how little he had actually said. Once we began prying away at each other, showdown was inevitable. I remember how cold his eyes were when he stopped being friendly sociable harmless Mick Pearson.

He wanted a confidential errand done, for a fat fee. He said he had been involved in a little deal abroad. He said it involved options on some old oil tankers, and some surplus, obsolete Turkish military vehicles, and all I needed to know about it was that it was legal, and he wasn't wanted, at least officially, by any government anywhere.

Some other sharpshooters had been trying to make the same deal, he said. They refused to make it a joint effort,

13

as he had suggested, and tried to swing it alone. But Pearson beat them to it and they were very annoyed at his methods. "So they know I've got this bank draft payable to the bearer, for two hundred thirty thousand English pounds, payable *only* at the main branch of the Bank of Nova Scotia in the Bahamas, at Nassau, which is the way I wanted it because I've got a protected account there. I didn't want them to find out how I was going to handle it, but they did. It's enough money so they can put some very professional people to work to take it away from me. Long, long ago I might have taken a shot at slipping by them. But now I've got my three gals to think of, and how thin their future would be if I didn't make it. So I have to have somebody they don't know take it to the bank with my letter of instructions. Then they'll give up."

I asked him what made him so sure I wouldn't just set up my own account and stuff the six hundred and forty thousand into it.

His was a very tough grin. "Because it would screw you all up, McGee. It would bitch your big romance with your own image of yourself. I couldn't do that to anybody. Neither could you. That's what makes us incurably small-time."

"That kind of money isn't exactly small-time."

"Compared to what it could have been by now, it is small, believe me." So he offered me five thousand to be errand boy, and I agreed. Payable in advance, he said. And after he had given me the documents, he would take off in the *Likely Lady* as a kind of decoy, and I was to start the day after he did. He said he would head for the Bahamas but then swing south and go down around the Keys and up the west coast of Florida to the home he and his gals hadn't seen for over a year and missed so badly, a raunchy sun-weathered old cypress house on pilings on the north end of Casey Key.

That was on a Friday. He was going to give me the documents on Sunday and take the *Likely Lady* out to sea on Monday. At about noon on Saturday, while Helena and her daughters were over on the beach, they came aboard and cracked his skull and peeled the stateroom safe open. It would have been perfect had not Mick Pearson wired his air horns in relay with a contact on the safe door, activated by a concealed switch he could turn off when he wanted to open it himself. So too many people saw the pair leaving the *Likely Lady* too hastily. It took me almost two hours to get a line on them, to make certain they hadn't left by air. They had left their rental car over at Pier 66 and had gone off at one o'clock on a charter boat for some Bahamas fishing. I knew the boat, the *Betty Bee,* a 38-foot Merritt, well-kept, Captain Roxy Howard and usually one or the other of his skinny nephews crewing for him.

I phoned Roxy's wife and she said they were going to Bimini and work out from there, trolling the far side of the Stream, starting Sunday. At that time, as I later learned, the neurosurgeons were plucking bone splinters out of Mick Pearson's brain.

I knew that the *Betty Bee* would take four hours to get across, so that would put her in Bimini at five o'clock or later. There was a feeder flight from there to Nassau leaving at seven fifteen. A boat is a very inconspicuous way to leave the country. Both Florida and the Bahamas have such a case of hots for the tourist dollar that petty officialdom must cry themselves to sleep thinking about all the missing red tape.

It was two thirty before, in consultation with Meyer, I figured out how to handle it. If I chartered a flight over, it was going to be a sticky problem coping with the pair on Bahama soil. Meyer remembered that Hollis Gandy's muscular Bertram, the *Baby Beef,* was in racing trim, and that Hollis, as usual, had a bad case of the shorts, brought on by having too many ex-wives with good lawyers.

So it was three when we banged past the sea buoy outside Lauderdale, Bimini-bound. Meyer could not hold the glasses on anything of promising size we spotted, any more than a rodeo contestant could thread a needle while riding a steer. And if I altered course to take closer looks,

I stood the risk of wasting too much time or alerting a couple of nervous people.

We got to the marker west of the Bimini bar at four thirty, and after a quick check inside to make certain the *Betty Bee* hadn't made better than estimated time, we went out and lay in wait five miles offshore. I faked dead engines, got aboard, alerted Roxy Howard, and we took them very quickly. Roxy was easily alerted as he had become increasingly suspicious of the pair. An Englishman and a Greek. It was useful to do it quickly, as the Greek was snake-fast and armed. We trussed them up and I told Roxy what they'd been up to as I went through their luggage and searched their persons. The envelope with the bearer bank draft was in the Greek's suitcase and with it was the signed letter to the bank identifying me, authorizing me to act for Mick Pearson, with a space for my signature, and another space for me to sign again, probably in the presence of a bank officer. The Greek had two thousand dollars in his wallet, and the Englishman about five hundred. The Englishman had an additional eleven thousand plus in a sweaty money belt. It seemed reasonable to assume that that money had come out of Mick's stateroom safe. As far as I knew, Mick had taken a good thump on his hard skull and certainly had no interest in bringing in any kind of law. Roxy was not interested in tangling with the Bahamian police authorities. And I did not think the Englishman or the Greek would lodge any complaints. And it was obvious that trying to get word out of either of them would call for some very messy encouragement, something I have no stomach for. Theirs was a hard, competent, professional silence.

So I gave five hundred to Roxy. He said it was too much, but he didn't argue the point. We off-loaded them into the *Baby Beef*, and Roxy turned the *Betty Bee* and headed for home port. I ran on down to Barnett Harbour, about halfway between South Bimini and Cat Cay, and put them aboard the old concrete ship that has been sitting awash there since 1926, the old *Sapona* that used to be a floating liquor warehouse during prohibition. I knew they'd have a rough night of it, but they would be picked off the next day by the inevitable fishermen or skin divers. They had their gear, their identification papers, and over twenty-five hundred dollars. And they would think of some explanation that wouldn't draw attention to themselves. They had that look.

I ran back outside and into Bimini Harbor and found a place to tie up, where the boat would be safe. We caught the feeder flight to Nassau, and I called old friends at Lyford Cay. They refused to let us go into the city, and as they had what they called a "medium bash" going, they sent one of their cars to bring us over from the airport. We spent most of Sunday sprawling around the pool and telling lies.

Monday morning I borrowed a car and went into the city to the main offices at Bay Street at Rawson Square. The size of the transaction made it something to be handled in a paneled office in the rear. I was given a receipt that gave the date and hour and minute of the deposit, gave the identification number of the bearer draft rather than the amount, and gave the number of the account maintained by Pearson rather than his name. The receipt was embossed with a heavy and ornate seal, and the bank officer scrawled indecipherable initials across it. I did not know then how good my timing had been.

Meyer and I caught a feeder flight back to Bimini in the early afternoon. The day was clear, bright, and cool. The Stream had flattened out, but even so, a two-and-a-half-hour trip was more comfortable than trying to match our time heading over.

The *Likely Lady* was all buttoned up when I walked around to D-109 to give Mick the receipt. The young couple aboard the big ketch parked next door said they had talked to Maureen, the elder daughter, at noon, and she had said that her father's condition was critical.

I told Meyer and went over to the hospital. When finally I had a chance to talk to Helena, I could see that there was no point in trying to give her the bank receipt or talking about the money. The receipt would have meant as much to her at that moment as an old laundry

17

list. She said with a white-lipped, trembling, ghastly smile that Mick was "holding his own."

I remember that I found a nurse I knew and I remember waiting while she went and checked his condition out with the floor nurses and the specials. I remember her little shrug and the way she said, "He's breathing, but he's dead, Trav. I found out they've got the room assigned already to somebody coming in tomorrow for a spinal fusion."

I remember helping Helena with the deadly details, so cumbersome at best, but complicated by dying in an alien place. He died at five minutes past one on Tuesday morning. Had he died, officially, seventy minutes sooner, the whole bank thing would have been almost impossible to ever get straightened out. I remember the gentle persistence of the city police. But she told them repeatedly that the safe had been empty, that she could not imagine who had come aboard and given her husband the fatal blow on the head.

She and the girls packed their belongings, and I assured Helena that I would see to the boat, get the perishables off her, keep an eye on her. I offered to drive them across the state, but she said she could manage. She was keeping herself under rigid and obvious control. When I gave her the cash and the bank receipt, she thanked me politely. They left to go to the funeral home and, from there, follow the hearse across to Sarasota County. A very small caravan. Prim, forlorn, and quite brave.

Yes, I knew that Meyer was remembering her too. I knew he had probably guessed the rest of it, perhaps wondered about it, but would never ask.

The rain came down and Meyer cooked his famous specialty, never-twice-alike. We ate like weary contented wolves, and the yawning began early. Yet once I was in the big bed in the master stateroom, the other memories of Helena became so vivid they held me for a long time at the edge of sleep, unable to let go . . .

3 . . . *THERE HAD* been heavy rains drumming on the overhead deck of the *Likely Lady* in August of that year in that lonely and protected anchorage we found at Shroud Cay in the Exumas, and under the sound of the rain I had made love to the Widow Pearson in that broad, deep bunk she had shared with the man who, by that August, had been almost six months at rest in Florida soil.

She had come back to Lauderdale in July. She had dropped me a note in June asking me to have someone put the *Likely Lady* in shape. I'd had her hauled, bottom scraped and repainted, all lines and rigging checked, power winches greased, blocks freed, both suits of sail checked, auxiliary generator and twin Swedish diesels tuned. She was less a motor sailer in the classic sense than she was a roomy, beamy powerboat rigged to carry a large sail area, so large in fact that she had a drop centerboard operated by a toggle switch on the control panel, and a husky electric motor geared way, way down. There was maybe two tons of lead on that centerboard, so shaped that when, according to the dial next to the toggle switch, the centerboard was all the way up, sliding up into the divider partition in the belowdecks area, the lead fitted snugly into the hull shape. Mick had showed me all her gadgetry one day, from the automatic winching that made sail handling painless, to the surprising capacity of the fuel and water tanks, to the capacity of the air-conditioning system.

I wonder who has her now. I wonder what she's called. Helena came over on a hot July day. She was of that particular breed which has always made me feel inadequate. Tallish, so slender as to be almost, but not quite, gaunt. The bones that happen after a few centuries of careful breeding. Blond-gray hair, sun-streaked, casual, dry-textured, like the face, throat, backs of the hands, by the sun and wind of the games they play. Theirs is not the kind of cool that is an artifice, designed as a challenge. It is natural, impenetrable, and terribly polite. They move well in their simple, unassuming little two-hundred-dollar cotton dresses, because long ago at Miss Somebody's Country Day School they were so thoroughly taught that their grace is automatic and ineradicable. There are no girl-tricks with eyes and mouth. They are merely there, looking out at you, totally composed, in almost exactly the way they look out of the newspaper pictures of social events.

I asked about her daughters, and she told me that they had gone off on a two-month student tour of Italy, Greece and the Greek Islands, conducted by old friends on the faculty of Wellesley.

"Travis, I never thanked you properly for all the help you gave us. It was . . . a most difficult time."

"I'm glad I could help."

"It was more than just . . . helping with the details. Mick told me he had asked you to . . . do a special favor. He told me he thought you had a talent for discretion. I wanted those people . . . caught and punished. But I kept remembering that Mick would not have wanted that kind of international incident and notoriety. To him it was all some kind of . . . gigantic casino. When you won or you lost, it wasn't . . . a personal thing. So I am grateful that you didn't . . . that you had the instinct to keep from . . . making yourself important by giving out any statements about what happened."

"I had to tell you I'd caught up with them, Helena. I was afraid you'd want me to blow the whistle. If you had, I was going to try to talk you out of it. The day I get my name and face all over the newspapers and newscasts, I'd better look for some other line of work."

She made a sour mouth and said, "My people were so

certain that Michael Pearson was some kind of romantic infatuation, we had to go away together to be married. He was too old for me, they said. He was an adventurer. He had no roots. I was too young to know my own mind. The usual thing. They wanted to save me for some nice earnest young man in investment banking." She looked more directly at me, her eyes narrow and bright with anger. "And one of them, after Mick was dead, had the damned blind arrogant gall to try to say: I told you so! After twenty-one years and a bit with Mick! After having our two girls, who loved him so. After sharing a life that . . ."

She stopped herself and said, with a wan smile, "Sorry. I got off the track. I wanted to say thank you and I want to apologize for being stupid about something, Travis. I never asked, before I left, what sort of . . . arrangement you had with Mick. I know he had the habit of paying well for special favors. Had he paid you?"

"No."

"Was an amount agreed upon?"

"For what I had thought I was going to do. Yes."

"Then did you take it out of the cash before you gave me the rest of it, the cash that had been in the safe?"

"No. I took out five hundred for a special expense and two hundred and fifty for a rental of a boat and some incidental expenses."

"What was the agreed amount?"

"Five thousand."

"But you did much much more than what he . . . asked you to do. I am going to give you twenty thousand, and tell you that it isn't as much as it should be."

"No. I did what I did because I wanted to do it. I won't even take the five."

She studied me in silence and finally said, "We are *not* going to have one of those silly squabbles, like over a restaurant check. You *will* take the five because it is a matter of personal honor to me to take on any obligation Mick made to anyone. I do not think that your appreciation of yourself as terribly sentimental and generous about widows and orphans should take priority over my sense of obligation."

"When you put it that way——"

"You will take the five thousand."

"And close the account without any . . . squabbling."

She smiled. "And I planned it so carefully."

"Planned what?"

"You would take the twenty thousand and then I would feel perfectly free to ask you a favor. You see, I have to go to that bank in Nassau. On the transfer of those special accounts there has to be an actual appearance in person, with special identification, as prearranged by the owner of the account. I was going to fly over and see them and fly back, and find someone to help me take the *Likely Lady* around to Naples, Florida. A man wants her, and the price is right, and he would pick her up here, but . . . I can't bear to part with her without . . . some kind of a sentimental journey. So I thought after you took the money, I could ask you, as a favor, to crew for me while we take her over to the Bahamas. Mick and I planned every inch of her. We watched her take shape. She . . . seems to know. And she wouldn't understand if I just turned my back on her. Do you find that grotesque?"

"Not at all."

"Would——?"

"Of course."

So we provisioned the *Likely Lady* and took off in the heat of early July. I had the stateroom Maureen and Bridgit had used. We fell into an equitable division of the chores without having to make lists. I made the navigation checks, kept the charts and the log, took responsibility for fuel, engines, radio and electronic gear, minor repairs and maintenance, topside cleaning, booze, anchoring. She took care of the proper set of the sails, meals, laundry, belowdecks housekeeping, ice, water supply, and we shared the helmsman chore equally.

There was enough room aboard to make personal privacy easy to sustain. We decided that because we were on no schedule and had no deadlines, the most agreeable procedure was to move during the daylight hours and lie at anchor at night. If it was going to take too long to find the next decent anchorage, we would settle for an early stop and then take off at first light.

There were several kinds of silence between us. Sometimes it was the comfortable silence of starlight, a night breeze, swinging slowly at anchor, a mutual tasting of a summer night. Sometimes it was that kind of an awkward silence when I knew she was quite bitterly alone, and saying good-bye to the boat and to the husband and to the plans and promises that would not be filled.

We were a man and a woman alone among the sea and the islands, interdependent, sharing the homely chores of cruising and living, and on that basis there had to be a physical awareness of each other, of maleness and femaleness. But there was a gratuitous triteness about the unconventional association that easily stifled any intensification of awareness.

It was five years back, and she was that inevitable cliché, an older woman, a widow, who had invited the husky younger male to voyage alone with her. I knew she had married young, but I did not know how young. I could guess that she was eleven years older than I, give or take two years. At the start her body was pale, too gaunted, and softened by the lethargy of months of mourning. But as the days passed, the sun darkened her, the exertion firmed the slackened muscles, and as she ate with increasing hunger, she began to gain weight. And, as a result of her increasing feeling of physical well-being, I began to hear her humming to herself as she did her chores.

I suspect that it was precisely because any outsider, given the situation and the two actors on the stage, would have assumed that McGee was dutifully and diligently servicing the widow's physical hungers during the anchored nights that any such relationship became impossible. Not once, by word, gesture, or expression, did she even indicate that she had expected to have to fend me off. She moved youthfully, kept herself tidy and attractive, spent just enough time on her hair so that I knew she was perfectly aware of being a handsome woman and did certainly not require any hard breathing on my part to confirm her opinion. Nor did she play any of those half-innocent, half-contrived games of flirtation that invite misinterpretation.

We had a lot of silences, but we did a lot of talking too. General talk, spiced with old incident, about the shape of the world, the shape of the human heart, good places we had been, good and bad things we had done or had not quite done. We went up around Grand Bahama, down the eastern shore of Abaco, over to the Berry Islands, down to Andros, and at last, after fourteen days, over to New Providence, where we tied up at the Nassau Harbour Club.

She went alone to the bank and when she came back, she was very subdued and thoughtful. When I asked her if anything had gone wrong, she said that it had been quite a good deal more money than she had expected. She said that changed a few things and she would have to think about the future in a different way. We went out to dinner and when I got up the next morning, she was already up, drinking coffee and looking at the *Yachtsman's Guide to the Bahamas*.

She closed the book. "I suppose we should think about heading back," she said. "I hate to."

"Do you have a date to keep?"

"Not really. Somebody I have to see, eventually. A decision to make."

"I'm in no hurry. Let's look at some more places. Exumas. Ragged Islands too, maybe." I explained to her how I take my retirement in small installments, whenever I can afford it, and if it was late August or early September when we got back, I wouldn't mind at all. She was overjoyed.

So we sailed to Spanish Wells, then down the western shore of Eleuthera, and then began to work our way very slowly down the lovely empty chain of the Exumas, staying over wherever we wanted to explore the beaches and the technicolor reefs. We did a lot of swimming and walking. I was suddenly aware that her mood was changing. She seemed remote for a few days, lost in thought, almost morose.

The day she suddenly cheered up I realized that she had begun to deliberately heighten my awareness of her. I had the feeling that it was a very conscious decision, something that she had made up her mind to during those days when she seemed lost in her own thoughts and memories. As she was a tasteful, mature, elegant, and sensitive woman, she was not obvious about it. She merely seemed to focus her physical self at me, enhancing my awareness through her increased awareness of me. Inevitably it would be the male who would make the overt pass. It baffled me. I could not believe she was childish enough or shallow enough to set about enticing a younger man merely to prove that she could. There was more substance to her than that. She had begun something that would have to be finished in bed, because I did not think she would begin it without having recognized its inevitable destination. It was all so unlikely and so deliberate that I had to assume she had some compulsion to prove something or to disprove something. Or maybe it was merely a hunger that came from deprivation. So I stopped worrying myself with wondering about her. She was a desirable and exciting woman.

So when she provided the opportunity, I made the expected pass. Her mouth was eager. When she murmured, "We shouldn't," it meant, "We shall." Her trembling was not faked. She was overly nervous about it, for reasons I could not know until later.

The first time was just at dusk in her big wide double bunk in the master stateroom. Her body was lovely in the fading light, her eyes huge, her flesh still hot with the sun-heat of the long beach day, her shoulder tasting of the salt of the sea and the salt of perspiration. Because she was tense and anxious, I took a long gentling time with her, and then when finally, in full darkness, she was readied, I took her, in that ever-new, ever-the-same, long, sliding, startling moment of penetration and joining, which changes, at once and forever, the relationship of two people. Just as it was happening she pushed with all her might at my chest and tried to writhe away from me, calling out, "No! Oh, please! No!" in a harsh, ugly, gasping voice. But she had been a moment late and it was done. She wrenched her head to the side and lay under me, slack and lifeless.

I could guess what had happened to her. She had arrived at her decision to bring this all about through some purely intellectual exercise, some kind of rationalization that had seemed to her to be perfectly sane and sound. But a coupling cannot be carried out in some kind of abstract form. I could guess from knowing her that she had never been unfaithful to Mick Pearson. All pretty little rationalizations and games of conjecture can be wiped out in an instant by the total and immediate and irrevocable fleshy reality. The ultimate intimacy exists on a different plane than do little testings and tryings. When she made a small whimpering sigh, I began to move apart from her, but she quickly caught at me and kept me with her.

Five years ago, but I had the memories in full textural detail of how often and how desperately Helena struggled to achieve climax. She wore herself into exhaustion. It was ritualistic and ridiculous. It was like some kind of idiotic health club: Orgasm is *good* for you. It was like some dogged kind of therapy. It was completely obvious that she was a healthy, sexually accomplished, passionate woman. But she was so concentrated on what she thought was some sort of severe necessity that she choked up. She would manage to get herself right out to the last grinding panting edge of it and get hung up there and then slowly, slowly fade back and away. And apologize, hopelessly, and plead with me to please be patient with her.

Four or five days later, wooden with fatigue, she confessed what had led her into this grotesque dilemma. Her voice was drab, her sentences short and without color. A man wanted to marry her. A very dear man, she said. The sex part of her marriage to Mick had been very very wonderful, always. During the months since his death, she had felt as if that part of her had died along with him. She did not want to cheat the man who wanted to marry her. She liked him very much. She liked me

26

equally well. So it had seemed reasonable to assume that if she found she could enjoy sex with me, then she could enjoy it with him. Sorry she had used me in such a cynical way. But she had to make up her mind whether or not to marry him. That was one of the factors. Sorry it had turned into such a dismal trying thing. Sorry to be such a dull mess. Sorry. Sorry.

It is no good telling somebody they're trying too hard. It is very much like ordering a child to go stand in a corner for a half hour and never once think about elephants.

So when she said there was no point in going on with such a stupid performance, I agreed. I let one day, one night, and one day pass. She was embarrassed and depressed. That night I began howling and roaring and thrashing at about one in the morning. She came hurrying in and I made it quite an effort for her to shake me awake. I had made certain that it had been such a physical day that she would be weary.

Woke up. Sagged back, deliberately trembling. Said it was an old nightmare that happened once or twice a year, based upon an exceptionally ugly event I could not ever tell anyone, not ever.

Up until then I had been all too competent. Big, knuckly, pale-eyed, trustworthy McGee, who had taken care of things, first for Mick and then for her. Could handle boats, navigation, emergencies. So I had presented her with a flaw. And a built-in way to help. She told me I had to tell someone and then it would stop haunting me. In a tragic tone I said I couldn't. She came into my narrower bunk, all sympathy and gentle comfort, motherly arms to cradle the trembling sufferer. "There is nothing you can't tell me. Please let me help. You've been so good to me, so understanding and patient. Please let me help you."

Five years ago, and back then the scar tissue was still thin and tender over the memories of the lady named Lois. There was enough ugliness in what had happened to her to be suitably persuasive. The world had dimmed a little when she was gone, as if there were a rheostat on the sun and somebody had turned it down, just one notch.

I pretended reluctance and then, with a cynical emotionalism, told her about Lois. It was a cheap way to use an old and lasting grief. I was not very pleased with myself for selecting Lois. It seemed a kind of betrayal. And with one of those ironic and unexpected quirks of the emotions, I suddenly realized that I did not have to pretend to be moved by the telling of it. My voice husked and my eyes burned, and though I tried to control myself, my voice broke. I never *had* told anyone about it. But where does contrivance end and reality begin? I knew she was greatly moved by the story. And out of her full heart and her concern, and her woman's need to hold and to mend, she fumbled with her short robe and laid it open and with gentle kisses and little tugs, with caresses and murmurings, brought us sweetly together and began a slow, long, deep surging, earth-warm and simple, then murmured, "Just for you, darling. Don't think about me. Don't think about anything. Just let me make it good for you."

And it happened, because she was taking a warm, dreamy, pleasurable satisfaction in soothing my nightmared nerves, salving the wound of loss, focusing her woman-self, her softnesses and pungencies and opened-taking on me, believing that she had been too wearied by the energies of the day to even think of her own gratification but unaware of the extent to which she had been sexually stimulated by all the times when she had tried so doggedly and failed. So in her deep sleepy hypnotic giving it built without her being especially aware of herself, built until suddenly she groaned, tautened, became swollen, and then came across the edge and into the great blind and lasting part of it, building and bursting, building and bursting, peak and then diminuendo until it had all been spent and she lay slack as butter, breath whistling, heart cantering, secretions a bitter fragrance in the new stillness of the bed.

I remember how she became, for the whole ten days we remained at anchor in the cove at Shroud Cay, like a kid beginning vacation. A drifting guilt, a sadness about Mick—these made her pleasure the sweeter. There was no cloying kittenishness about her, as that was a style that would not have suited her—or me. She was proud of herself and as bold, jaunty, direct, and demanding as a bawdy young boy, chuckling her pleasures, full of a sweet wildness in the afternoon bunk with the heavy rain roaring on the decks over us, so totally unselfconscious about trying this and that and the other, first this way and that way and the other way, so frankly and uncomplicatedly greedy for joy that in arrangements that could easily have made another woman look vulgarly grotesque she never lost her flavor of grace and elegance.

For that brief time we were totally, compulsively involved with the flesh, pagans whose only clock was that of our revived desires, learning each other so completely that, in consort, we could direct ourselves, joined or unjoined, as though we were a single octopoidal creature with four eyes, twenty fingers, and three famished mouths. When we raised anchor and moved on, the tempo diminished, and the affair became a more sedate and comfortable and cozy arrangement, with ritual supplanting invention, with morning kisses that could be affection without any overtone of demand, with waking in the broad bunk to feel the heated length of her asleep, spoon style, against my back, and be content she was there, and be content to drowse off again.

The last day of August was our last day in the islands and we spent the night anchored wide of the Cat Cay channel, and would cross the Stream the next day. She was solemn and thoughtful at dinner. We made love most gently and tenderly, and afterward when I held her in my arms, both of us on the edge of sleep, she said, "You understood that it was our last time, dear?"

"A way to say good-bye. A good way."

She sighed. "I had twenty-one years with Mick. I'll never be . . . a whole person without him. But you did some mending, Travis. I know that . . . I can stumble through the rest of my life and accept what I've got left, live with less. Make do. I wish I could be in love with you. I would never let you go. I would be your old, old wife. I think I would dye your hair gray and have my face lifted and lie about my age. I'd never let you get away, you know."

I began to tell her a lot of things, very significant and important and memorable things, and when I stopped, waiting for applause, I discovered she was asleep.

When the *Likely Lady* was back in a slip at Bahia Mar, she took one wistful walk around the deck and made a sour little smile and said, "Good-bye to this too. I'll let the man who wants her pick her up here. Will you show him through her and explain everything?"

"Sure. Send him to me."

When I had put her luggage in the trunk of the rental car, and kissed her good-bye, and she had gotten behind the wheel, she looked out at me, frowning, and said, "If you *ever* need *anything,* darling, anything I can give you, even if I have to steal to get it . . ."

"And if you start coming unglued, lady . . ."

"Let's keep in touch," she said, blinked her eyes very rapidly, grinned, gunned the engine, and scratched off with a reckless shriek of rubber, lady in total command of the car, hands high on the wheel, chin up, and I never saw her again.

4 FORGET THE Lady Helena and get some sleep. Stop damning Meyer for bringing up that trip to Bimini and thus opening up that particular little corner of the attic in the back of my head.

She had married the sweet guy, had invited me, but I had been away when the invitation came. Then postcards from the Greek Islands, or Spain, or some such honeymoon place. Then nothing until a letter three years ago, a dozen pages at least, apologizing for using me once again as a foil, clarifying her own thoughts by writing to me.

She was divorcing Teddy. He was a sweet, nice, thoughtful man who, quite weak to begin with, had been literally overwhelmed and devoured by her strength. He had diminished, she said, almost to the point of invisibility. All you could see was his pleasant uncertain smile. She admitted that she kept prodding him, pushing at him, hoping for that ultimate masculine reaction that would suddenly fight back and take over the chore of running a marriage. Maybe, she wrote, living with a dutiful creature on an invisible leash was preferable to being alone but not for her. Not when she could see herself becoming more domineering, unpleasant, and more shrill—week by week, month by month. So she was cutting him loose while he could still feed and bathe himself. She was getting the divorce in Nevada. When she had married, she had closed the house on Casey Key, had considered selling it many times, but something had kept her from making a final decision. Now she was glad. She would go back there and see if she could recover what some people had once thought a pleasant disposition.

She said that her elder daughter, Maurie, had been married for six months to a very bright and personable young man in the brokerage business, and seemed deliciously happy. She said they were living in the city of Fort Courtney, Florida, about a hundred miles northeast of Casey Key, and it seemed a workable distance for a mother-in-law to be. She reported that Bridget, known as Biddy—and nineteen at the time she wrote to me three years ago—had transferred from Bryn Mawr to the University of Iowa so she could study with a painter she admired extravagantly, and had changed her major to Fine Arts.

Though it had dealt with personal, family matters, it had not been a particularly intimate letter. No one reading it could have ever guessed at the relationship we'd had on that lazy long cruise of the *Likely Lady* through the Bahamas.

She asked me to stop and see her the next time I was over in the Sarasota area. I never did.

I had thought of her a few times. Something would remind me of her, the look of a boat under sail, or the sound of hard rain, or a scent like that of the small pink flowers that grew out of the stony soil of the Exumas, and she would be in and out of my thoughts for a week or so. Now it had happened again, thanks to Meyer, and I would be remembering Helena Pearson for a few days or a few weeks. It had been one of those relationships you cannot really pin down. To the average outsider it would have been something to smirk about. The older woman, half a year widowed, who sends her daughters away so that she can go cruising with a man young enough to be the son of her dead husband, a new consort of considerable size, obviously fit and durable and competent and discreet, and obviously uninterested in any kind of permanent relationship.

Yet I was quite certain that it had not been a situation she had planned. It had arisen through two sets of rationalizations, hers and mine, and the truth of it was perhaps something quite different from what we suspected. For her perhaps it was the affirmation of being still alive after the intense emotional focus of her life was gone forever. Maybe it had been something the body had created in the mind, just for its own survival, because with her perhaps a sexual continence would have been a progressive thing, parching and drying her, month by month, until all need would have been prematurely ended. My own supercilious little rationalization had been, in the beginning of it, that it would have been both cruel and stuffy to have failed to respond when she began her tentative invitations, to have let her know through my lack of response that the age differential did indeed put me off, and that I felt both clumsy and self-conscious in the role of the available younger man in a kind of floating bedroom farce. The least I could do would be to respond with as much forced enthusiasm as I could manage. But a sweet and immediate reality of the flesh had erased the reasons and the rationalizations. She was all limber girl in the

32

half-light, slenderly, elegantly voluptuous, so consistently determined to never take more pleasure than she was able to give that she made a few intervening women seem dreary indeed.

At last I was able to dim the vivid qualities of the memory and slide away into the earned sleep . . .

Sunday, October sixth, was still and gray and breathlessly muggy. Bobby Guthrie's wife came for him at ten in the morning and they gave Joe Palacio a ride back into Miami. Monday they would get the Merrill-Stevens appraisals and estimates, based on detailed inspections. Meyer and I got the *Flush* out into the channel and headed north for Lauderdale at about eleven, with the *Muñequita* in tow and a pale sun beginning to burn through the overcast. *The Busted Flush* was still burdened with the gear and goop of Floatation Associates. Meyer assured me that as soon as the partnership had turned the *'Bama Gal* into money, they would move their stuff over onto the work boat Bobby had located, which they could buy at the right price.

"Bobby will build special chemical tanks right into the work boat and rig up some automatic pumps with flowmeters so that one man can handle the flow of the stuff down to the job."

"That's nice."

"After another good piece of salvage, we're going to install the same kind of a setup, but smaller, on a truck, and put a good winch on it. It will make it easy to pick automobiles out of the canals."

"That's nice."

"Am I boring you or something, McGee?"

"If I was all hot to get tangled up in a nice profitable little business with three nice people, I'd probably be chuckling and dancing and singing. Lots of luck, Meyer."

He stared at me, shrugged, and went below to start taking the cameras and reels apart to see if the rinsing in fresh water had made them salvageable. He was in one of his mother-hen periods, but this time he was taking care of Guthrie and Palacio instead of McGee. They were in good hands. But Meyer was going to be a bore until the little business was safely launched.

I had no plans. I felt mildly restless. I decided I would help the trio get their work boat set up and then maybe I would round up a batch of amiable folk and cruise on up the waterway, maybe as far as Jax. In another month or so I would have to start looking for a client so whipped-down he would snap at my kind of salvage, at my fifty-percent fee. Meanwhile, some fun and games, a little action, some laughs.

There was a note in my post office box about something I had to sign for, so I didn't get Helena's letter until Monday, a little before noon.

First there was a crisp white envelope with the return address in raised black letters: FOLMER, HARDAHEE, AND KRANZ, ATTORNEYS AT LAW. There was a cashier's check for $25,000 paperclipped to the letter signed by one D. Wintin Hardahee in tiny little purple script. The letter was dated Sept 28th, and the check was dated Sept 27th.

My dear Mr. McGee:

Pursuant to the wishes of Mrs. Helena Trescott . . .

[The Trescot put me off the track for a moment, and then I remembered the wedding I had missed, when she had married a Theodore Trescott.]

I am herewith enclosing a cashier's check in the amount of twenty-five thousand dollars ($25,000.00) along with a letter which Mrs. Trescott asked me to mail with the cashier's check.

She has explained to me that this sum is in payment of an obligation of several years' standing, and because it does not seem probable that she will survive her present critical illness, she wished to save you the trouble of presenting a claim against her estate.

If you have any questions about this matter, you can reach me at the address and telephone number given above.

Yours very truly,

The law firm was in Fort Courtney, Florida. Her letter was thick, sealed in a separate envelope, and addressed to me. I walked back to the *Flush* and put it, unopened, on the desk in the lounge. I took one of the big glasses and laid an impressive belt of Plymouth atop the cubes, and then roamed about, sipping at it, continually catching a glimpse of the letter out of the corner of my eye. The eerie coincidence of not having thought of her for maybe almost a year, then having such vivid memories just one week after the letter had been mailed, gave me a hollow feeling in the middle.

But it had to be read and the gin wasn't going to make it any easier.

Travis, my darling,

I won't bore you with clinical details—but oh I am so sick of being sick it is almost a relief to be able to see in their eyes that they do not expect me to make it . . . sick unto death of being sick—a bad joke I guess. Remember the day at Darby Island when we had a contest to see who could invent the worst joke? And finally declared it a draw? I'm not very brave. I'm scared witless. Dying is so damned absolute—and today I hurt like hell because I made them cut way down on the junk they are giving me so I could have a clear head to write to you . . . Forgive lousy handwriting, dear. Scared, yes, and also quite vain, so vain I would not look forward to walking out of this place—tottering out, a gray little old lady, all bones and parchment.

Up until a year ago, dear, I looked very much as I looked that marvelous summer we had together, and might look almost as well this year too, except for a little problem known familiarly as Big C. A year ago they thought they took it all out, but then they used cobalt, and then they went in again, and everything was supposed to be fine, but it popped up in two more places, and Thursday they are going to do another radical, which they are now building me up for, and I think Dr. Bill Dyckes is actually, though maybe he wouldn't even admit it to him-

*self, letting me leave this way instead of the long lousy
way that I can expect if they don't operate.*

*I said I wasn't going to bore you! I'm tempted to tear
this up and start again, but I think that one letter is about
all I can manage. About the check Mr. Hardahee arranged for, and which you will get with this letter, please
don't get stuffy about it. Actually, practically by accident,
I became medium rich—an old friend of Mick's took over
the investment thing shortly after Mick died. He is very
clever and in the business of managing money for people.
For the last five and a half years he has been buying
funny little stocks for my account, things I never heard of
before, and some of them are never heard of again, but a
lot of them go up and up and up, and he smiles and smiles
and smiles. But lately, of course, he has been changing everything around so that it will all be neat for the estate
taxes. Don't have strange ideas about you getting money
that should go to my girls, because they will be getting
enough. Anyway, the money is sort of a fee . . .*

*It's about my big daughter, Travis. Maureen. She's
practically twenty-six. She's been married to Tom Pike for
three and a half years now. They have no children. She's
had two miscarriages. Maurie is a stunning-looking young
woman. When she had her second miscarriage, a year ago,
she was quite sick. I would have been able to take care of
her, but at about that time I was in the hospital for my
first operation—Gad, talk about soap operas! . . . Bridget
had come down to help out, and Biddy is still here, because things are a Godawful mess. You see, I always
thought that Maurie was the solid-as-a-rock one, and Biddy—she's twenty-three now—would be the one who'd
manage to mess herself up because she is sort of dreamy
and unreal and not in touch. But Biddy has had to hang
around not only on account of me but because Maurie has
tried three times to kill herself. It seems even more unreal
to me when I see my hand write the words on this paper
—kill herself—such a stupid and frightening waste. Tom
Pike is a darling. He could not be nicer. He and Biddy are
trying as hard as they can to bring Maurie out of it, but
she just doesn't seem right to me. As if she can't really be*

reached. Tom has tried all kinds of professional care and advice, and they have been trying to make me believe that her troubles are over now. But I can't believe it. And I certainly can't get up out of this damned bed and take charge. Let us just say I am not likely to ever get up out of this damned bed.

Remember on our cruise when you told me how you live, what you do? Maybe I am stretching the definition, but in this situation my elder is trying to steal her own life. Do you ever operate on a preventative basis? I want you to try to keep her from stealing her life away. I don't have any idea how you would go about it, or whether anything you could do would be of any use at all. Certainly fifty percent of Maurie's life would be worth far more than twenty-five thousand.

I have been thinking of you these past days, finally deciding there is no one else I could ask this of, and no one else I would trust to be able to do anything to help. You are so darn shrewd and knowing about people, Travis. I know that you put a raggedy widow-lady back together again with great skill and taste and loving kindness. In my memories of that summer you are two people, you know. One was a young man so much younger than I that at times, when we were having fun and you seemed particularly boyish, you made me feel like a depraved and evil old hag. At other times there was something so . . . kind of ancient and knowledgeable about you, you made me feel like a dumb young girl. Had it not been for the time we had together, I might have been able to adjust to spending the rest of my life with Teddy Trescot . . . Anyway, my lasting impression was that there cannot be too many things in this world you would not be able to cope with. And I don't mean just muscle and reflex . . . I mean in the gentle art of maneuvering people, as I think Maurie needs to be maneuvered. Can't she comprehend how valuable life is? I certainly can, right now more than ever.

Believe me, darling, I am very tempted to drop one of those horrid death-bed demands upon you—Save my daughter's life! But I cannot bring myself to the point of such dra-

matic corn. You will if you want to and you won't if you don't. It is that simple.

I just had a couple of bad ones and couldn't keep my jaw shut tight enough and so I humiliated myself by squealing loud enough to bring the nurse scuttling in, and so they gave me a shot and things are beginning to get a little vague and swimmy. I will hang on long enough to sign this and seal it, but it might get to sounding a little drunky before I do . . . I wrote about you being two people to me . . . I am two people to myself . . . Do you know how strangely young the heart stays, no matter what? One of me is this wretched husk here in the electric bed, all tubes and bad smells and hurt and the scars that didn't do much good, except for a little while . . . the other me is caught back there aboard the Lady *in Shroud Cay, and the other me is being your bounding, greedy hoyden, romping and teasing in the nakedy bed, such a shameless widow-wench indeed, totally preoccupied with our finding, over and over, that endless endless little time when it was all like deep hot engines running together . . . the heart stays young . . . so damnably yearningly unforgivably young . . . and O my darling hold that other me back there long ago far away hold her tightly and do not let her fade away, because . . .*

Signed with a scrawled "H." They keep emptying out the world. The good ones stand on trap doors so perfectly fitted into the floor you can't see the carpentry. And they keep pulling those lousy trip cords.

So do your blinking, swallowing, sickening, ol' Trav, and phone the place. The girl said that Mr. Hardahee had left for lunch, and then she said he hadn't quite, and maybe she could catch him, and she asked was it important, and I said with a terrible accuracy that it was a matter of life and death. D. Wintin Hardahee had a purry little voice, useful for imparting top-secret information. "Ah, yes. Yes, of course. Ah . . . Mrs. Trescott passed away last Thursday evening . . . ah . . . after the operation . . . in the recovery room. A very gallant woman. Ah . . . I count it a privilege to have made her acquaintance, Mr. McGee."

38

He said there had been a brief memorial service yesterday, Sunday.

There have been worse Mondays, I am sure.

Name three.

Helena, dammit, this is not one of your better ideas. This Maureen of yours is getting devoted attention from people who love her. Maybe she just doesn't like it here. And anybody could make out a pretty long list of contemporary defects. Am I supposed to be the kindly old philosopher, woman, and go set on her porch, and spit and whittle and pat her on the hand and tell her life can be beautiful? Hang around, kid. See what's going to happen next.

I remember your daughters, but not too distinctly, because it was five years ago. Tallish, both slender-lithe blondes with the long smooth hanging sheath of hair, blunt-featured, a bit impassive with all that necessity for total cool that makes them look and act like aliens observing the quaint rites of earthlings. The infrequent blink is when the gray-blue eyes take pictures with hidden cameras. A considerable length of sea-brown legs and arms protruding from the boat clothes, resort clothes. Reservedly polite, quick-moving to go perform the requested errand or favor, a habit of standing close together and murmuring comments to each other, barely moving the shape of the unmadeup girl mouths.

What the hell makes you think—*made* you think—I could communicate with either of them on any level, Helena Pearson Trescot? I am not as much older than your elder daughter than you were older than I, but it is a large gap. Don't trust anybody over thirty? Hell, I don't trust anybody under thirty or over thirty until events prove otherwise, and some of my best friends are white Anglo-Saxon Protestant beach girls.

Helena, I think slaying oneself is a nasty little private, self-involved habit and, when successful, the residual flavor is a kind of sickly embarrassment rather than a sense of high tragedy. What is it you want of me? I am not suited to the role of going around selling the life-can-be-beautiful idea. It can be, indeed. But you don't buy the concept from your friendly door-to-door lecture salesman.

No thanks. Husband Tommy and sister Biddy can cope. Besides, what in the world would I say to the three of them? Helena sent me?

Besides, dear lady, you left me the out. "You will if you want to and you won't if you don't. It is that simple."

I don't.

Tell you what I *will* do, though. Just to play fair. I'll take a little run up there, for some reason or other I'll dream up, and prove to both of us just how bad your suggestion is. Let's say we'll both sleep better. Okay? Fair to all?

5 *COURTNEY COUNTY:* Pop. 91,312.

County Seat: Incorporated municipality of Fort Courtney. Pop. 24,808. Gently rolling country. Acres and acres of citrus groves, so lushly productive the green leaves on the citrus trees look like dark green plastic, the profusion of fruit like decorative wax. Ranchland in the southern part of the county. Black angus. White fences. Horse breeding as a sideline. An industrial park, a couple of nice clean operations making fragments of the computer technology, one a branch of Litton Industries, one spawned by Westinghouse, and one called Bruxtyn Devices, Inc., which had not yet been gobbled up by anybody.

Lakes amid the rolling land, some natural and some created by the horrendous mating dance of bulldozer and land developer. Golf clubs, retirement communities, Mid-Florida Junior College.

No boomland this. No pageants, gator farms, Africalands, shell factories, orchid jungles. Solid, cautious growth, based on third- and fourth-generation money and control—which in Florida is akin to a heritage going back to the fourteenth century.

My afternoon flight on that Thursday a week after Helena's death, wing-dipped into the final leg of the landing pattern, giving me a sweeping look at downtown, half shielded by more trees than usual, at peripheral shopping plazas, at a leafy residential area with curving roads, with the multiple geometry of private swimming pools, and then a hot shimmering winking of acres of cars in a parking area by one of the industrial plants, and then we came down, squeak-bounce-squeak-bounce, and the reverse roar of slowing to taxi speed.

I had decided against arriving in my vivid blue Rolls pickup of ancient vintage. *Miss Agnes* makes one both conspicuous and memorable. I certainly was not on any secret mission, but I did not want to be labeled eccentric. I had a mild and plausible cover story and I was going to be very straight-arrow about the whole thing. I just couldn't barge in and say, "Your mother asked me to see if I could get you to stop killing yourself, kid."

The girls were going to remember me not only because I had been a small part of their lives back when Mick had been killed but also because there are not too many people my size wandering around, particularly ones that have a saltwater tan baked so deeply that it helps, to a certain extent, in concealing visible evidence of many varieties of random damage and ones who tend to move about in a loose and rather sleepy shamble, amiable, undemanding, and apparently ready to believe anything.

Because the girls would remember me, I had to have a simple and believable story. The simple ones are the best anyway. And it is always best to set them up so that they will check out, if anybody wants to take the trouble. The fancy yarns leave you with too much to keep track of.

I walked across the truly staggering heat of the hardpan and into the icy chill of the terminal building. A crisp computerized girl in a company uniform leased me an air-conditioned Chev with impersonal efficiency, then turned from robot into girl when I sought her advice on the most pleasant place to stay for a few days. She arched a brow, bit her lip, and when I said I never had any trouble with my expense accounts, she suggested the Wahini Lodge on Route 30 near the Interchange, go out to the highway and turn left and go about a mile and it would be on my right. It was new, she said, and very nice.

It was of the same Hawaiian fake-up as most of Honolulu, but the unit was spacious and full of gadgetry and smelled clean and fresh. I was able to put the car in shade under a thatched canopy. Out the other side of the unit I could see green lawn, flowering shrubs partially blocking the view of a big swimming pool in the middle of the motel quadrangle. It was about three thirty in the afternoon when I dialed for an outside line and dialed the number for Thomas Pike. The address was 28 Haze Lake Drive.

A female voice answered, hushed and expressionless.

"Mrs. Pike?"

"Who is calling please?"

"Are you Maureen?"

"Please tell me who is calling."

"The name might not mean anything."

"Mrs. Pike is resting. Perhaps I could give her a message."

"Bridget? Biddy?"

"Who is calling, please."

"My name is Travis McGee. We met over five years ago. At Fort Lauderdale. Do you remember me, Biddy?"

". . . Yes, of course. What is it you want?"

"What I want is a chance to talk to you or Maurie, or both of you."

"What about?"

"Look, I'm not selling anything! And I happened to do some small favors for the Pearson women when Mick died. And I heard about Helena last Monday and I'm very sorry. If I've hit you at the wrong time, just say so."

"I . . . I know how I must have sounded. Mr. McGee, this wouldn't be a very good time for you to come here. Maybe I could come and. . . . Are you in town?"

"Yes. I'm at the Wahini Lodge. Room One-0-nine."

"Would it be convenient if I came there at about six o'clock? I have to stay here until Tom gets home from work."

"Thanks. That will be just fine."

I used the free time to brief myself on the geography. The rental had a city-county map in the glove compartment. I never feel comfortable in any strange setting until I know the ways in and the ways out, and where they lead to, and how to find them. I learned it was remarkably easy to get lost in the Haze Lake Drive area. The residential roads wound around the little lakes. There was a big dark blue rural mailbox at the entrance to the pebbled driveway of number 28, with aluminum cutout letters in a top slot spelling T. PIKE. Beyond the plantings I saw a slope of cedar-shake roof and a couple of glimpses of sun-bright lake. The house was in one of the better areas but not in one of the best. It was perhaps a mile from the Haze Lake Golf and Tennis Club and about, I would guess, $50,000 less than the homes nearer the club.

On my way back from there toward the city I found a precious, elfin little circle of expensive shops. One of them was a booze shoppe, with enough taste to stock Plymouth, so I acquired a small survival kit for local conditions.

Biddy-Bridget called on the house phone at five after six, and I walked through to the lobby and took her around to the cocktail lounge close to the pool area, separated from the hot outdoors by a thermopane window wall tinted an unpleasant green-blue. She walked nicely in her little white skirt and her little blue blouse, shoulders back and head high. Her greetings had been reserved, proper, subdued.

Sitting across from her at a corner table, I could see both portions of the Helena-Mick heritage. She had Helena's good bones and slenderness, but her face was wide through the cheekbones and asymmetrical, one eye set higher, the smile crooked, as Mick's had been. And she had his clear pale blue eyes.

The years from seventeen to twenty-three cover a long, long time of change and learning. She had crossed that boundary that separates children from people. Her eyes no longer dismissed me with the same glassy and patronizing indifference with which she might stare at a statue in a park. We were now both people, aware of the size of many traps, aware of the narrowing dimensions of choice.

"I remembered you as older, Mr. McGee."

"I remember you as younger, Miss Pearson."

"Terribly young. And I thought I was so grown up about everything. We'd been moved about so much . . . Maurie and me . . . I thought we were terribly competent and Continental and sophisticated. I guess . . . I know a lot less than I thought I knew back then."

After our order was taken, she said, "Sorry I wasn't very cordial on the phone. Maurie gets . . . nuisance calls sometimes. I've gotten pretty good at cooling them."

"Nuisance calls?"

"How did you know where to find us, Mr. McGee?"

"Travis, or Trav, Biddy. Otherwise you make me feel as old as you thought I was going to be. How did I find you? Your mother and I kept in touch. A letter now and then. Family news."

"So you had to hear from her during . . . this past year, or you wouldn't have asked if you were talking to me."

"I got her last letter Monday."

It startled her. "But she'd——"

"I was away when it arrived. It had been mailed back in September."

"Family news?" she said cautiously.

I shrugged. "With her apologies for being so depressing. She knew she'd had it. She said you'd been here ever since Maurie was in bad shape after her second miscarriage."

Her mouth tightened with disapproval. "Why would she write such . . . personal family things to somebody we hardly knew?"

"So I could have them published in the paper, maybe."

"I didn't mean it to sound rude. I just didn't know you were such a close friend."

"I wasn't. Mick trusted me. She knew that. Maybe people have to have somebody to talk to or write to. A sounding board. I didn't hear from her at all while she was married to Trescott."

"Poor Teddy," she said. I could see her thinking it over. She nodded to herself. "Yes, I guess it would be nice to be able to just spill everything to somebody who . . . wouldn't talk about it and who'd . . . maybe write back and say everything would be all right." She tilted her head and looked at me with narrowed eyes. "You see, she wasn't ever really a whole person again after Daddy died. They were so very close, in everything, sometimes it would make Maurie and me feel left out. They had so many little jokes we didn't understand. And they could practically talk to each other without saying a word. Alone she was . . . a displaced person. Married to Teddy, she was still alone, really. If being able to write to you made her feel . . . a little less alone . . . then I'm sorry I acted so stupid about it." Her eyes were shiny with tears and she blinked them away and looked down into her glass as she sipped her drink.

"I don't blame you. It's upsetting to have a stranger know the family problems. But I don't exactly go around spreading the word."

"I know you wouldn't. I just can't understand why . . . she had to have such a hellish year. Maybe life evens things up. If you've been happier than most, then . . ." She stopped and widened her eyes as she looked at me with a kind of direct suspicion. "Problems. About Maurie too?"

"Trying to kill herself? Not the details. Just that she was very upset about it and couldn't understand it."

"*Nobody* can understand it!" She spoke too loudly and then she tried to smile. "Honestly, Mr. . . . Travis, this has been such a . . . such a terrible . . ."

I saw that she was beginning to break, so I dropped a bill on the table and took her just above the elbow and walked her out. She walked fragile and I took a short cut across the greenery and through a walkway to 109. I unlocked it and by the time I pulled the door shut behind us, she had located the bath, and went in a blundering half-trot toward it, making big gluey throat-aching sobbing sounds, *"Yah-awr, Yah-awr!"* slammed the door behind her. I could hear the muffled sounds for just a moment and then they ended, and I heard water running.

I went down to the service alcove and scooped the bucket full of miniature cubes and bought three kinds of mix out of the machine. I put some Plymouth on ice for myself, drew the thinner, semiopaque draperie across the big windows, and found Walter Cronkite on a colorcast speaking evenly, steadily, reservedly of unspeakable international disasters. I sat in a chair-thing made of black plastic, walnut, and aluminum, slipped my shoes off, rested crossed ankles on the corner of the bed, and sipped as I watched Walter and listened to doom.

When she came shyly out, I gave her a very brief and indifferent glance and gestured toward the countertop and said, "Help yourself."

She made herself a drink and went over to a straight chair and turned it toward the set. She sat, long legs crossed, holding her glass in both hands, taking small sips and watching Walter.

When he finished, I went over and punched the set off, went back and sat this time on the bed, half-facing her.

"Getting any painting done?"

She shrugged. "I try. I fixed it up over the boathouse into sort of a studio." She made a snuffling hiccupy sound. The flesh around her eyes was pink, a little bit puffed. "Thanks for the rescue job, Trav. Very efficient." Her smile was wan. "So you know about the painting too."

"Just that it was your thing a couple of years ago. I didn't know if you still kept at it."

"From what I'm getting lately, I should give up. I can't really spend as much time on it as I want to. But . . . first things first. By the way, what *did* you want to talk to Maurie about?"

"Well, I hated to bother you gals so soon after Helena's death. Especially about something pretty trivial. A friend of mine—his name is Meyer—can't seem to get that custom motor sailer you people used to have out of his mind. The *Likely Lady*. She must be six years old now or a little more. He's been haunting the shipyards and yacht brokers for a long time, looking for something like her, but he can't turn anything up. He wants to try to track her down and see if whoever owns her now will sell. As a matter of fact, I'd already promised him I'd write to Helena when . . . her letter came. I made a phone call and found out she had . . . was gone. I told Meyer this was no time to bother you or Maureen. But then I wondered if . . . well, there was anything at all I could do. I guess that because I was on the scene the last time, I'm kind of a self-appointed uncle."

Her smile was strained. "Don't get me started again. Lately I just can't stand people being nice to me." She put her glass down and went over and stared at herself in the mirrored door of the bathroom, at close range. After a few moments she turned away. "It works. It always has worked. When we were little and couldn't stop crying, Mom would make us go and stand and try to watch ourselves cry. You end up making faces at yourself and laughing . . . if you're a little kid." She was frowning as she came back to her chair and her drink. "You know, I just can't remember the name of the man who bought the *Lady*. I think he was from Punta Gorda, or maybe Naples. But I know how I could find out."

"How?"

"Go down and open up the house at Casey Key and look in Mom's desk. I have to do that anyway, the lawyers say. She was very tidy about business things. File folders and carbon copies and all that kind of thing. It will all be in the folder for that year, the year she sold it. It was such a great boat. I hope your friend finds her and can buy her. Daddy said she was forgiving. He said you could do some absolutely damfool thing and the *Lady* would forgive you and take care of you. If you could give

47

me your address, I could mail you the name and address of the man who bought her."

"Do you plan to go down there soon?"

"We talked about going down Saturday morning and driving back Sunday afternoon. It ought to give us enough time. But it depends on . . . how Maurie is."

"Is she physically ill?"

"In addition to being mentally ill? Is that what you mean?"

"Why the indignation? Trying to knock yourself off isn't exactly normal behavior."

"I get . . . too defensive about her, maybe."

"Just what *is* wrong with her?"

"It depends on who you ask. We've gotten more answers than we can use. And more solutions. Manic depressive. Schizophrenia. Korsakov's Syndrome. Virus infection of a part of the brain. Alcoholism. Name it, and somebody has said she has it."

"Korsa-who?"

"Korsakov. Her memory gets all screwed up. She can remember everything prior to this past year, but the past year is a jumble, with parts missing. I think sometimes she uses it as a . . . convenience. She can really be terribly sly. As if we were against her or something. And she does manage to get terribly stinking drunk, and she does manage to sneak away from us, no matter how careful we both are. We put her in a rest home for two weeks, but she was so upset by it, so confused and baffled by it all, we just couldn't stand it. We had to bring her home. She was like a little kid, she was so pleased to be home. Oh, she's not buggy-acting at all. She's sweet and dear and a lovely person, really. But something has just . . . broken, and nobody knows what it is yet. If I hadn't told you all this, you could come to the house and never know anything was wrong, really."

"But she has tried to kill herself?"

"Three times. And two of them were very close calls. We found her in time the time she took the sleeping pills. And Tom found her in the tub after she cut her wrist. The other time it was just something she'd prepared, a noose thing out of quarter-inch nylon, over a beam in the boathouse. All clumsy knots, but it would have worked."

"Does she say why she keeps trying?"

"She doesn't remember why. She can sort of remember doing it, in a very vague way, but not why. She gets very frightened about it, very weepy and nervous."

"Who's taking care of her now?"

"Tom is home with her. Oh, you mean what doctor? Nobody, actually. You could say we've run out of doctors. There are things Tom and I can do for her. She was doing pretty well until Mom died. Then she had . . . some bad days."

"Would she remember me?"

"Of course! She hasn't turned into some kind of a moron, for heaven's sake!"

"What about those nuisance phone calls you mentioned?"

Her expression was guarded. "Oh, just from people she gets involved with when she . . . manages to sneak out."

"She gets involved with men?"

"She goes out alone. She gets tight. She's very lovely. It's hell on Tom and it isn't any of your business."

"That's no way to speak to your kindly old uncle."

A wan smile. "My nerves are ragged. And that part of it just . . . makes me want to resign from the human race. Those damned oily voices on the phone, like filthy children wondering if Maurie can come out and play. Or like the way you see packs of dogs, following. They don't know she's sick. They don't even give a damn."

"How often does she sneak off?"

"Not often. Maybe three times in the last four months. But that's three times too many. And she never remembers much about it."

I took her empty glass and built her a fresh drink and took it to her, saying, "You must have some kind of a theory. You probably know her as well as anyone in the world. What started all this?"

"When she had the second miscarriage, it was because of some kind of kidney failure. She had convulsions. I thought that could have done something to her brain. But

49

the doctors say no. Then I thought she might have a tumor of the brain, but they did all kinds of tests and there's nothing like that at all. I don't know, Travis. I just don't know. She's the same Maurie, but yet she's not. She's more . . . childlike. She breaks my heart."

"Care if I stop by and say hello?"

"What good would it do?"

"And what harm could it do?"

"Is it just kind of a sick curiosity?"

"I guess that's my bag, going around staring at crazies."

"*Damn* you! I just meant that——"

"She's not on display? Right? Okay. She was twenty. She took that ugly business about Mick with a great deal of class and control. I knew how much she adored her father. Look, I didn't ask to be let in on all the family secrets. But I was. I'd like to see what she's like. Maybe you're too close to it. Maybe she's better than you think she is. Or worse. Can you think of anybody else who hasn't seen her since she was twenty?"

"N-No. Suppose I ask Tom what he thinks. And phone you here either later this evening or in the morning."

When she finished her drink, I walked her out to her little red Falcon wagon. She thanked me for the drinks and apologized for being so tired and cross and edgy, and drove off.

She phoned in the morning and invited me to lunch at the house. She said Maurie was looking forward to seeing me again, and that Tom would join us for lunch if he could get away.

6 *BRIDGET PEARSON* apparently heard the sound of tires on the driveway pebbles and appeared from behind the house, on the lake side. She wore yellow shorts and a white sleeveless top and had her hair tied back with yellow yarn. Her sunglasses were huge and very black.

"So glad you could make it! We're out back. Come along. Tommy fogged the yard before he went to work, and there's hardly a bug. He should be along any minute."

She kept chattering away, slightly nervous, as I followed her out to the slope of lawn overlooking the lakeshore. Tall hedges of closely planted punk trees shielded the area from the neighboring houses. There was a redwood table and benches under a shade tree, a flourishing banyan. The two-story boathouse was an attractive piece of architecture, in keeping with the house. There was a T-shaped dock, iron lawn furniture painted white, a sunfish hauled up onto the grass, a little runabout tethered at the dock. The makings of the picnic lunch were stacked on one end of the redwood table. A charcoal fire was smoking in a hibachi. She pointed out the pitcher of fresh orange juice, the ice bucket, the glasses, the vodka bottle, and told me to make myself a drink while she went to tell Maurie I'd arrived.

In a few moments Maureen came out through the screened door of the patio, moving down across the yard toward me, smiling. Her dead mother had written me that she was stunning. In truth she was magnificent. Her presence dimmed the look of Biddy, as if the younger sister were a poor color print, overexposed and hastily developed. Maurie's blond hair was longer and richer and paler. Her eyes were a deeper, more intense blue. Her skin was flawlessly tanned, an even gold that looked theatrical and implausible. Her figure was far more rich and abundant and had she not stood so tall, she would have seemed overweight. She wore a short open beach robe in broad orange and white stripes over a snug blue swimsuit. She moved toward me without haste, and reached and took my hands. Her grasp was solid and dry and warm.

"Travis McGee. I've thought of you a thousand times." Her voice was slow, like her smile and her walk. "Thank you for coming to see us. You were *so* good to us a long time ago." She turned and looked over her shoulder toward Biddy and said, "You're right. He isn't as old as I thought he'd be either." She stretched up and kissed me lightly on the corner of the mouth and squeezed my hands hard and released them. "Excuse me, Travis dear, while I go do my laps. I've missed them for a few days, and if I stop for any length of time, I get all saggy and soft and nasty."

She walked out to the crossbar of the T and tugged a swimcap on, dropped the robe on the boards and dived in with the abrupt efficiency of the expert. She began to swim back and forth, the length of the crossbar, so concealed by the dock that all we could see were the slow and graceful lift and reach of her tanned arms.

"Well?" Biddy asked, standing at my elbow.

"Pretty overwhelming."

"But different?"

"Yes."

"How? Can you put your finger on it?"

"Maybe she seems as if she's dreaming the whole scene. She sort of . . . floats. Is she on anything?"

"Like drugs? Oh, no. Well, when she gets jumpy, we give her a shot. It's sort of a long-lasting tranquilizer. Tom learned from one of the doctors and taught me how."

I watched the slow and apparently tireless swimming

and moved to the table to finish making my drink. "There's nothing vague or dazed about her eyes. But she gives me a funny kind of feeling, Biddy. A kind of caution. As if there's no possible way of guessing just what she might do next."

"Whatever comes into her head. Nothing violent. But she is just . . . as primitive and natural as a small child. Wherever she itches, she'll scratch, no matter where she is. Her table manners are . . . pretty damned direct. They get the job done and in a hurry. And she says whatever she happens to be thinking, and it can get pretty . . . personal. Then if Tom or I jump on her about it, she gets confused and upset. Her face screws up and her hands start shaking and she goes running off to her bedroom usually. But she can talk painting or politics or books . . . just so long as it's things she learned over a year ago. She hasn't added anything new this year."

We heard another car on the pebbles and she went hurrying off around the corner of the house. She reappeared, talking rapidly and earnestly to the man walking slowly beside her. A certain tension seemed to be going out of his posture and expression, and he began to smile. She brought him over and introduced him.

He was tall and wiry, dark hair, dark eyes, a face that had mobility and sensitivity, and might have been too handsome without a certain irregularity about his features, a suggestion of a cowlicky, lumpy, aw shucks, early-jimmy-stewart flavor. His voice did not have the thin country whine of Mr. Stewart, however. It was surprisingly deep, rich, resonant, a *basso* semi-*profundo*. Mr. Tom Pike had exceptional presence. It is a rare attribute. It is not so much the product of strength and drive as it is a kind of quality of attention and awareness. It has always puzzled and intrigued me. People who without any self-conscious posturing, any training in those Be Likable and Make Friends courses, are immediately aware of you, and curious about you, and genuinely anxious to learn your opinions have this special quality of being able to somehow dominate a room, a dinner table, or a backyard. Meyer has it.

He shed his lightweight sports jacket and pulled his tie off, and Biddy took them from him and carried them into the house. With a tired smile he said, "I've been worrying all morning about how Maureen would react to you. It can be very good or very bad, and no way to tell in advance. Biddy says it's been fine so far."

"She looks great."

"Sure. I know. Dammit, it makes me feel . . . so disloyal to have to act as if Biddy and I were keeping some kind of defective chained up in the cellar. But too much exposure to outsiders shakes her up." His quick smile was bitter and inverted. "And when she gets upset, you can be very very sure she's going to upset the outsider, one way or another. She's going to find her way out of the thicket. Someday. Somehow."

"It must be pretty rough in the meanwhile, Tom."

"And there's another reason I feel guilty. Because most of it lands right on Biddy. I'm out of here all day working. We've tried and tried to find somebody to come in and help out, somebody kind and patient and well-trained. We've interviewed dozens. But when they find out the trouble is maybe in some psychiatric area, they back away."

Biddy had returned and was busying herself with the food. I asked what luck they were having with the doctors. He shrugged. "They raise your hopes, then say sorry. One recent diagnosis was that a calcium deposit was diminishing the flow of blood to the brain. A series of tests, and then he says sorry, it isn't that at all. The symptoms just don't fit anything in their books. But I have some people who keep checking, writing letters."

"Excuse a painful question, Tom. Is she deteriorating?"

"I keep wondering about that. I just don't know. All we can do is wait and watch. And hope."

Maurie stopped swimming, put her palms flat on the dock, and came vaulting up, turning in the air to sit on the edge, lithe as a seal. She got up and smiled up the slope at us. She used the short robe to pat her legs dry, then put it on, pulled her swimcap off, and shoved it into the robe pocket, shaking her hair out as she walked. As she approached Tom Pike her slow, floating assurance seemed to desert her. She came to him with downcast eyes, shoulders slightly hunched, her welcome smile nervous, her walk constricted. She made me think of a very good dog aware of having disobeyed her master and hoping to be so engaging and obedient that the infraction will be forgiven and forgotten. He kissed her briefly and casually and patted her shoulder and asked her if she had been a good girl. She said shyly that she had been good. It was a most plausible attitude and reaction. She was the wife and no matter how lost she had become, she could not help knowing that she no longer measured up to what they both expected of her. It seemed more an awareness of inadequacy than a conscious guilt.

Mosquitoes were beginning to regroup under the banyan shade. Tom went and got the little electric fogger and plugged it into a socket on one of the flood lamps and killed them off, commenting to me when he was finished that he hated to use it because it was so unselective. "When I was a kid, we'd sit on the screened porch on a summer evening and see clouds of mosquito hawks—dragonflies—darting and swooping, eating their weight. Then the bats would begin when the sun went down. So we've killed off the mosquito hawks with the spray and we've killed the other bugs the bats ate, and now there's nothing left but billions of mosquitoes and gnats, and we have to keep changing the spray as they get immune."

"You grew up around here?"

"In the general area. Here and there. We moved around a lot. Steaks ready, Bid? Time for one more drink, then, Trav. Let me fix it for you. Maurie, darling, you are supposed to be tossing the salad, not sampling it."

She hunched herself. "I didn't mean . . . I wasn't——"

"It's all right, darling."

At one point while we were eating, one scene, like a frozen frame, like a color still, underlined the strange flavor of the relationships, of the ménage. Maurie and I were on the same bench on one side of the picnic table,

Maurie on my left. Biddy was across from me. Maurie was eating very politely and properly, and I glanced over and saw the two of them watching her. Husband and kid sister, looking at the wife with the same intent, nervous approval, as a couple might watch their only child plodding through a simple piano solo for visiting relatives. Then the frozen frame moved once again as Biddy lifted the poised fork to her lips and as Tom Pike began chewing again.

Later, as Biddy was saying something to me, Tom's low voice in a sound of warning, saying merely "Darling!" made Biddy stop abruptly and look quickly at Maureen. I turned and looked at her and saw that she had hunched herself over her plate, head low, had picked up her steak in a greedy fist, and was tearing and gobbling at it. She dropped it back onto her plate and sat, eyes downcast, while under the shelter of the edge of the table she wiped her greasy fingers on the top of her bare thigh, leaving streaks of sheen across the firm brown.

"You forgot again, dear," Tom said in a gentle voice.

Maurie began to tremble visibly.

"Don't get upset, honey," Biddy said.

But suddenly she wrenched herself up and away, striking the edge of the table so solidly with her hip that drinks and coffee slopped out of the glasses and cups. She ran toward the house, sobbing audibly in her blundering, hopeless flight. Tom called sharply to her, but she did not look back or slow down. Biddy got up quickly and hurried after her.

"Sorry," Tom said. "I guess you can see why we don't . . . Biddy will get her settled down and . . ." He pushed his plate away and said, "Ah, the *hell* with it!" and got up and walked down toward the lake shore.

He was still there when Biddy came walking back out. She sat opposite me. "She's resting now. In a little while she won't remember what happened. I want to have Tom look at her and see if he thinks she needs a shot. Is . . . is he all right?"

"He acted upset."

"It's because she was doing so well."

She stared down toward the silent figure by the lake shore. I was at an angle to her that gave me a chance to see more than she would have wanted me to see. Her face had a soft and brooding look, lips parted. It was adoration, worship, hopeless helpless yearning love. I knew why she had started to go to pieces in the cocktail lounge. It was a situation nicely calculated to fray her to the breaking point, to have been for a year in this house with the deteriorating wife, the concerned and suffering husband. Loyalty to the big sister. And a humble self-sacrificing love for the husband.

After a little while we all went inside. Tom went up and looked at her and came back and said she was sleeping. He sat for a moment, glancing at his watch.

"Nice to meet you, Travis. Just . . . sorry that it had to be . . . to be . . ." His voice thickened and his mouth twisted, and he suddenly buried his face in his hands. Biddy hurried to him and shyly, hesitantly, put her hand on his shoulder.

"Tom. Please, Tom. It will work out."

He sighed and straightened up and dug in his pocket for a handkerchief. His eyes still streaming, he said in a husky voice, "Sure, honey. It will all be peachy dandy by and by." He mopped his eyes and blew his nose. "I apologize for myself too. See you around." She followed him out and I heard him saying something about getting home late. The car door slammed. He drove out. She came back into the two-level living room. Her eyes looked moist.

"He's . . . quite a guy, Travis."

"Little tough to go back to the office and sell stocks and bonds, I guess."

"What? Oh, he hasn't done that in a long time now. Over two years. He started his own company."

"Doing what?"

"It's called Development Unlimited. It's sort of a promotion company. They do a lot of land-syndication things. I don't really know how it works, but it's supposed to be a wonderful idea for people in high tax brackets, like doctors and so on. They pay a lot of interest in advance when they buy the land, and then they sell it later for capital gains. Tom is very clever at things like that. And they set up shares in apartment houses and do something very clever about depreciation and losses and cash flow and all that. He tried to explain it to me, but I have no head for that kind of thing. I guess he's doing well because he has to go out of town a lot and arrange deals in other places too. To have Maurie the way she is makes . . . his success so kind of hollow. He is really a marvelous human being."

"He seems to be."

She wanted to show me her studio and her paintings. But she was making too obvious an effort to entertain me. The shine had gone out of her day. I said I should be getting along. I wrote out my address for her and told her to send me the name of the man who had bought the *Likely Lady* when she went through her mother's papers.

We stood out by my car and told each other we hoped we'd see each other again someday. Maybe we *did* hope so. Hard to say.

I got back to the Wahini Lodge at three. I stretched out on the bed and told myself that it had to be the end of the obligation, if there was any. I had taken a good look. It was a sorry little situation. Prognosis bad. When you can't identify the disease, the prognosis is always bad. And two nice people, Tom Pike and Bridget Pearson, were stuck with it. Maybe if Maurie could knock herself off in such a way that Tom wouldn't blame Biddy and she wouldn't blame him or herself, they might be able to make a life. A lot of widowers have married kid sisters and enjoyed it.

The restlessness was back in full force. I didn't want to go home to Lauderdale. I didn't want to stay where I was. And I couldn't think of anywhere to go. I felt like a bored kid on a rainy day. Maurie kept sliding into my mind and I kept pushing her out. Go away, woman. Have a nice sleep.

I went into the bathroom. I glanced at my toilet-article kit atop the pale yellow formica of the countertop, and my random restless thoughts were gone in an instant, and I was totally focused, the back of my neck feeling prickly and cool.

Caution is like the seat belt habit. If you are going to use seat belts, then you'd better make it automatic by latching your belt every single time you get into the car. Then you stop thinking about the seat belt and you do not have to make any decisions about seat belts because you are always strapped in.

I have a lot of little rituals that are completely automatic. They are the habits of caution. A lot of these habits are seemingly casual and accidental arrangements of things. When I leave the toilet kit open, the last thing I usually replace in it is the toothbrush. I am a brush-last type. I lay it, bristles-up, across the other items in such a way that it is fairly stable and is on a perfect diagonal, aimed from corner to corner out of the case. When I reach into the case in the morning to take the stuff out, I am not consciously aware of the precise placement of the toothbrush. I am suddenly very aware, however, if it is not in its proper place and alignment.

I reconstructed the morning. By the time I came back from breakfast, the maid had done the room. I had been in the bathroom, and had the brush been in the wrong place, I would have noticed it. I studied the new position of it. No passing truck, no sonic boom, could have moved it so far from its proper position.

All right. So somebody had been messing with my stuff, poking around. Petty thief with a passkey. Very easy to prove. All I had to do to prove it was lift the soap dish. (Only masochists use those sorry little slivers of lilac that motels call soap.) Two twenties, folded twice. I unfolded them. There were still two. A dumb thief would take them both. A slightly less stupid thief would take one.

If you are in a line of work where people can get very emotional about the fact you are still walking around and breathing, a forty-dollar decoy is a cheap method of identifying the visitor. Had the money been gone, it would not have been absolute assurance that it had been a visit by a sneak thief. A professional of enough experience and as-tuteness would take it anyway, knowing that if I had left any little trap around the place, the missing money would be a false trail.

I went back to the bed, sat on the edge of it and glow-ered at the carpeting. I had brought nothing with me that could possibly clue anybody about anything. My tempo-rary address was known to Biddy, Tom Pike, the car rental girl, and whoever they might have told or who might have questioned them.

Biddy and Tom knew that I would be away from the motel at lunchtime. Tom would have had time to come to the motel before going home. Looking for what? Helena's letter? Work on that assumption and stay with it until it breaks down. But why? What could be in the letter? Un-less Biddy was one hell of an actress, she hadn't known there was a letter until I told her. Seemed doubtful that Helena would mention having written me a letter. It was too highly personal a letter, for one thing. D. Wintin Hardahee had known for sure. And maybe a nurse had known. Forget the why of it, at least for now. Start at a known point or with a known angle, which is the basis of all navigation.

I knew that it could be some foul-up in identification. Maybe I looked like somebody somebody was looking for. Maybe it had been a little once-over by the law. Maybe there was a nut on the loose with a toothbrush fe-tish.

I phoned Mr. D. Wintin Hardahee, of Folmer, Harda-hee, and Krantz, located in the Courtney Bank and Trust Company building on Central Avenue. I got through to his secretary, who said that Mr. Hardahee was in a meet-ing. She did not know when it would be over. Yes, if I wanted to take a chance on coming in and waiting to see him, that was all right, but if the meeting lasted past five, he would not be able to see me until Monday.

I was going to walk very lightly and keep looking and listening for anything off-key in my immediate area.

And I was no longer restless. Not at all.

7 .*AT FOUR THIRTY* Hardahee's matronly secretary came into the paneled waiting room to lead me back to his office. As middle partner in the firm, he had a corner office with big windows. He was round, brown, bald, and looked very fit. He had some tennis trophies atop a bookcase. He spoke in the hushed little voice I remembered from our phone conversation, a voice that did not suit him at all. He leaned across his desk to shake hands and waved me into a deep chair nearby.

"She was a fine woman. Shame to go that way," he said. He seemed to be slightly wary and curious. "Is there any way I can help you, Mr. McGee?"

"I just wanted to ask a couple of questions. If any of them are out of line, just say so."

"I'll tell you what I can. But perhaps you should understand that I was not Mrs. Trescott's personal attorney. Her affairs are handled in New York, legal, tax and estate, and so on. Apparently she telephoned or wrote her people in New York and asked them to recommend someone here to handle a confidential matter for her. A classmate of mine is one of the partners in the firm she had been dealing with up there, so when they gave her my name, she phoned me and I went to see her in the hospital. Perhaps they'll call on me to handle some of the estate details at this end, but I have no way of knowing."

"Then, you didn't tell anyone about the letter and the check?"

"I told you that she wanted it handled as a confidential matter. She wrote a check on her New York account and

61

I deposited it in our escrow account. When it cleared, I had a cashier's check made out to you, as she requested. She gave me a sealed letter to go with it. If you were not the recipient, I would disclaim knowledge of any such transaction."

"Sorry, Mr. Hardahee. I didn't mean to——"

"Perfectly all right. You couldn't have known how it was handled until I told you."

"I told her younger daughter about getting a letter from her. I had lunch there today, with the Pikes and Miss Pearson. I assumed from Helena's letter that she was staying there before she went into the hospital this last time."

"That is correct."

"Can I establish a confidential relationship too? I guess I could as a client, but I don't know what kind of law you work with, Mr. Hardahee."

"Both the other senior partners are specialists. I'm the utility man. Play almost any position."

"Do you represent Tom Pike directly or indirectly in any way? Or either of the daughters?"

"No one in the firm represents them in any way."

"Very quick and very definite."

He shrugged. "I try to be a good and careful attorney, Mr. McGee. When I got a note from Walter Albany in New York saying Mrs. Trescott might contact me, once I established who she was, and her condition, it struck me that because Tom Pike has many contracts in the legal profession here it might develop into some sort of an inheritance problem. So I checked our shop to make certain we wouldn't be in any conflict of interests if the transaction led eventually into a dogfight."

"And you based that guess on her having gone through New York to find a local attorney instead of asking her son-in-law?"

He ignored the question. "A client has to have a legal problem. What's yours?"

"I'm in One-O-nine at the Wahini Lodge. When I returned this afternoon, after being at the Pike home, I discovered by accident that somebody had gone through the stuff in my room. Forty dollars in cash was untouched. No sign of forcible entry. Nothing missing."

"And thus nothing you can report?"

"That's right."

"What is the legal problem?"

"In her letter Helena Trescott asked me to see what I could do to keep Maureen—Mrs. Tom Pike—from killing herself. It was a confidential request. We're old friends. She has confidence in me. So did her first husband, Mick Pearson. A dying woman can ask for a damfool favor, I guess. So I came up and checked. I had a logical reason for getting in touch. Imaginary but logical. So I looked the scene over and Mrs. Pike is in a pretty spooky condition, but there isn't anything I could do that isn't being done. I had to make sure, because Helena *did* ask me. So I was at the point of deciding I should check out and leave town when I found out somebody had gone through the room."

"Looking for the letter? Because they knew there *had* been a letter, and it made somebody uneasy not to know what was in it?"

"That was one of the things that occurred to me."

"As if somebody might be concerned about an inheritance situation?"

"I didn't think about that."

"Walter Albany said her resources were 'substantial.' "

"Meaning how much?"

"Hmmm. To interpret the trust attorney lingo, taking into account the area where Walter practices, I would say that adequate would mean up to a quarter million, comfortable from there up to a million, and substantial could mean anything from there on up to . . . let's say five or six million. Beyond that I think Walter would say 'impressive.' So you thought it over and you came to see me because you want to know how many people knew there *was* such a letter. Me and my secretary and the deceased. And you, and whoever you may have told."

"And a nurse?"

"Possibly. I wouldn't know."

"I told Miss Pearson, the sister, yesterday when she

came over to the motel to have a drink with me. She had no idea her mother and I had stayed in touch the past five years. I had to account for being fairly up to date. But I said nothing about what Helena asked me to do."

"You brought the letter with you? It was in the room?"

"No."

"If somebody were looking for it, would they look elsewhere? At your home in Fort Lauderdale?"

"They might, but they wouldn't find it."

"Would you know someone had looked for it?"

"Definitely."

He looked at his watch. It was after five. He frowned. "What kind of work do you do, Mr. McGee?"

"Salvage consultant."

"So what you want to find out from me is whether you should trust your initial judgment of Mr. and Mrs. Pike and Miss Pearson or whether the incident at your hotel room is sufficient cause for you to look more closely?"

"Mr. Hardahee, it is a pleasure to deal with someone who does not have to have detailed drawings and specifications."

He stood up. "If you can manage it conveniently, you might join me for a drink at the Haze Lake Club at seven fifteen. If I'm not in the men's bar, tell Simon, the bartender, that you are my guest. I have a date to play doubles in . . . just twenty minutes."

When I walked in, I saw that D. Wintin Hardahee had finished. He was at the bar with a group of other players, standing with tall drink in hand in such a way that he could keep an eye on the door. When I appeared, he excused himself and came over to meet me and took me over to a far corner by a window that looked out at the eighteenth green. In the fading light the last foursomes were finishing.

Hardahee was in white shorts and a white knit shirt, with a sweat-damp towel hung around his neck. I was correct about his fit look. His legs were brown, solid, muscular, and fuzzed with sun-bleached hair. The waiter came over and Hardahee said the planter's punch was exceptional, so I ordered one without sugar and he asked for a refill.

"Win your match?"

"The secret of winning in doubles is to carefully select and train your partner. That blond boy over there is mine. He is constructed of rawhide, steel wire, and apparently has concealed oxygen tanks. He's keeping my name fresh and new on the old trophies and making all the other players hate me."

"Everybody hates a winner."

"Mr. McGee, since talking to you, I have been synthesizing all the bits and pieces of information I have concerning Tom Pike. Here is my subjective summary. He is energetic, with considerable fiscal imagination, a great drive. He has personal charm with magnetism. A lot of people are rabidly and warmly loyal to him, people who from time to time have been on his team, or connected with his team in one way or another, and who have made out very well and had some fun doing it. They think he can do no wrong. He has the traits and talents of the born entrepreneur, meaning he is elusive, fast-moving, and very hard-nosed, as well as being something of a born salesman. So there are people who have necessarily been in the way of the deals he has assembled from time to time and they have been bruised and are eager to claim they were tricked, and quite obviously they hate him. I know of no successful legal action brought against him. As you said, everybody hates a winner. It is a mistake to confuse shrewdness, misdirection, and opportunism with illegality. I can think of no one who knows Tom who is indifferent to him. He polarizes emotions. My guess would be this. If he knew you had a letter his mother-in-law wrote before her death and if he thought there was any information in it of any use to him, he would have come to you and sooner or later you would have found yourself telling or showing him the part or parts he wanted to know about."

"How would he manage that?"

"By studying you to find out what you want and then offering it to you in such a way you would feel grateful toward him. Money or excitement or advance knowledge or whatever happens to be your choice of private vices. If he had to have something, I think he would go after it his own way first."

"And if that didn't work?"

"He'd probably turn the problem over to one of the many people aching to do him a favor, no matter what it might be."

"And you don't like him."

He pursed his lips. ". . . No. I think I like Tom. But I would be uneasy about getting into any kind of business association with him. I'm quite sure I'd make out very well, as have many others, but the inner circle seems to become . . . a group of faceless men. In any kind of speculation tight security is imperative. They seem to become very . . . submissive? No. That isn't accurate. Retiring, discreet, and slightly patronizing toward the rest of the working world. I guess I am not a herd animal, Mr. McGee. Even if it would fatten my purse."

"So if it wasn't Pike or one of his admirers, how come I had a visitor, then?"

"My considered opinion is that it beats the hell out of me."

"Well, if somebody was looking for something they think I have, and wants it badly enough to take a chance of getting caught going in or out of a motel room, the next place to look is in my pockets."

"If it's smaller than a bread box."

"I think I'll hang around and do a little trolling."

"Keep in touch."

"I will indeed."

I drove back to the Lodge and ate one of the fake-Hawaiian special dinners, then went from the dining room into the cocktail lounge and stood at the bar. Business was very light. Some young couples were sploshing around outside in the big lighted pool. The bar was a half rectangle and I became aware of a girl alone at an end stool, by the wall, under a display of ancient fake Hawaiian weapons. She wore a weight of red-gold wig that dwindled her quite pretty and rather sharp-featured face. She wore a white dress, which seemed in better taste than the wig and the heavy eye makeup. She had a cluster of gold chain bracelets on one arm, smoked a cigarette in a long gold and white holder, and was drinking something wine-red out of a rocks glass, a measured sip at a time, as self-consciously slow and controlled as her drags at the cigarette.

I became aware of her because she wanted me to be aware of her. It was puzzling because I had appraised the motel as no hangout for hookers. Also, though she was apparently dressed and prepared for the part, her technique was spotty and inept. There are the ones who operate on the mark of their choice with the long, wide-eyed, arrogant-insolent-challenging stare, then properly leave it up to him to make the next move. There is the jolly-girl approach, the ones who say to the barkeep in a voice just loud enough to carry to the ears of the mark, "Geez, Charlie, like I always say, if the guy doesn't show, the hell with him. I'm not going to cry my eyes out, right? Gimme another one of the same, huh." Then there's the fake prim, the sly sidelong half-shy inquisitive glance, and the quick turn of the head, like a timid doe. Or the problem approach, troubled frown, gesture to have the mark come over, and then the dreary little set piece: Excuse me, mister, this may sound like a crazy kind of thing, but a girl friend of mine, she asked me to be here and tell the guy she had a date with she can't make it, and I was wondering if you're George Wilson. Or: Would you mind, mister, doing me a crazy kind of favor? I got to wait here to get a phone call, and there's some nut that was bugging me before and said he was coming back, and if you'd sit next to me, then he won't give me any problems, okay?

But this one didn't have any routine to depend on. Her infrequent glance was one of a puzzled uncertainty. I decided that it was another instance of the courage of The Pill bringing the bored young wife out hunting for some action while hubby was up in Atlanta at another damned sales meeting. I wondered how she'd manage if I gave her no help at all.

What she did was get up and head for the women's room. She had to walk behind me. So she dropped her lighter and it clinked off the tile and slid under my feet. I backed away so I could stoop and pick it up, but my heel came down on her sandaled toes. I recovered in time to keep from coming down with all my weight, but I came down hard enough to make her yelp with anguish. I turned around and she limped around in a little circle, saying, "Oh, dear God!" while I made apologetic sounds. Then we compounded it by both bending at the same instant to pick up the lighter. It was a solid, stinging impact, bone against bone, hard enough to unfocus her eyes and unhinge her knees. I caught her by the arms, moved her gently over, and propped her against the bar.

"Now I will bend over and pick up the lighter."

"Please do," she said in a small voice. She grasped the edge of the bar, head bowed, eyes shut.

I wiped the lighter off with the paper napkin from under my drink and placed it in front of her. "Are you all right?"

"I guess so. For a minute there my toes didn't hurt at all."

She straightened, picked the lighter off the bar, and made a rather wide circle around me and headed for the women's room. I motioned the bartender over and said, "Amateur night?"

"New to me, sir. You got each other's attention anyways."

"House rules?"

"They say to me, they say, Jake, use your judgment."

"So what do you say to me?"

"Well . . . how about bon voyage?"

"How was she doing before I showed, Jake?"

"There were two tried to move in on her, but she laid such a cool on them I cased her for strictly no action, that is, until she began to throw it at you."

"She's in the house?"

"I don't know. I'd guess not, but I don't know."

When I heard the tack-tack of her heels on tile returning, I smiled at her and said, "I have liability coverage. Like for broken toes, concussion, lacerations."

She stopped and looked up at me, head tilted. "I think it was a truck, but I didn't get the license number. I could settle my claim for some medication, maybe. On the rocks."

So I followed her and took the bar stool beside her and asked Jake for more of the same for two, and winked at him with the eye farther from her. Ritual of introduction, first names only. Trav and Penny. Ritual handshake. Her hand was very small and slender, fine-boned, long fingers. Faint pattern of freckles across nose and cheekbones. Perfume too musky-heavy for her, too liberally applied. I could detect no evidence of a removed ring on third finger left, no pale line or indentation of flesh.

We made the casual talk that is on one level, while we made speculative, sensual communication on the second level. Humid looks from the lady. Pressure of round knee against the side of my thigh when she turned to talk more directly to me. Parting of lips and the tongue tip moistening. But she was too edgy, somehow, too fumbly with cigarettes and purse and lighter and drink. And her component parts did not add up to a specific identity. Wig, makeup, and perfume were garishly obvious. Dress, manicure, diction were not.

So Trav was in town to see a man interested in putting some money in a little company called Floatation Associates, and Penny was a receptionist-bookkeeper in a doctor's office. Trav wasn't married, and Penny had been, four years ago, for a year, and it didn't take. And it sure had been a rainy summer and fall. Too much humidity. And the big thing about Simon and Garfunkel was the words to the songs, *reely*. If you read the lyrics right along with the songs while the record was on, you know, the lyrics right on the record case, it could really turn you on, like that thing about Silence especially. Don't you think, honest now, that when people like the same things and have enjoyed the same things, like before they ever met, Trav, it is sort of as if they had known each other a long time, instead of just meeting? And people don't have enough chance to just talk. People don't communicate anymore somehow, and so everybody goes around kind of lonesome and out of touch, sort of.

So I played out the charade and walked her out, her elbow socketed in the palm of my hand, and she was thinking out loud of maybe some other place we could go, and rejecting each one for one reason or another as soon as she mentioned it, and I drew her into a dark alcove near the grinding roar of the central air conditioning, and after a sudden and startled rigidity and instinctive defensive tactics, she somewhat hesitantly made a presentation of her mouth, which somehow imitated avidity yet tasted prim, then she let herself be guided to 109 and ushered in, her voice getting too shrill and tight in her effort to stay loose.

"Gin?" she said. "That's your drink, isn't it? I *adore* it, but I don't like to drink it in public because I get too wildly happy and loud and everything. But could we have some, darling?"

There was a double handful of melting cubes afloat in ice water in the bottom of the ice bucket. She decided she did not want any mix with hers either. We clinked glasses and she smilingly fluttered her long plastic eyelashes at me. She took a hummingbird sip and sat and put the drink down on the rug and slipped her left shoe off and tenderly squeezed her bruised toes.

I had taken a mouthful of the Plymouth. I am a taster when I like the taste. But it was subtly wrong, just wrong enough so I knew that the hunch had been right. A bad Penny. Under pretext of taking a second swallow, I let the first slide back into the glass. It left me with an astringent prickling of the membranes of the mouth and a slight aftertaste of dust.

"Excuse," I said, and went into the bath. There, behind the closed door, I dumped the drink into a pocket I made in a face towel. It saved the ice. I rinsed glass and ice and made myself some tap water on the rocks. I flushed the toilet and stood for a few moments assembling the pieces of the procedure before I went back out. She hadn't been near the opened bottle of Plymouth, at least on this visit to my quarters.

So she or some associate had done the doctoring. Then she was there to make sure I had a drink, to take the chain off the door if necessary, assuming there was an associate in their venture. And unless you wanted to risk putting somebody so far under they might not make it back up again, it was efficient to be there to know when it took effect.

I went back out and noticed that two thirds of her drink was gone. Back among the melting cubes, I assumed. She had both her shoes off. She was sitting with her legs crossed. The hem of the white dress was hiked to midthigh. She was a little long-waisted girl. Her legs could have been called chunky had they not been beautifully shaped.

"Am I supposed to drink alone?" she asked, pouting.

"Never compete with a gulper," I said, and drained the tap water potion. I went over to the counter where the bottle and ice were and said, "In fact, I will have another one down the hatch before you finish that little piece of gin you've got left, angel."

She came over in considerable haste and came up behind me and wrapped her arms around me. "Darling, let's not drink *too* much, huh? It can spoil things for people, you know. I think we've both had . . . just exactly the right amount."

It was a helpful clue. If the idea of my having two alarmed her, then it had to be fast-acting. But I thought I might quite plausibly give her a little lesson in anxiety before I faked being overcome. So, instead of making the drink, I turned and began chuckling and wrapped my arms around her. She stood very small in her stocking feet. She tried to seem cooperative until I found the zipper at the nape of her neck and opened it in one tug all the way down to the coccyx. Chuckling blandly, I peeled the dress forward off her shoulders, and she became nervously agitated, hopping and struggling, saying, "No! No, darling! Let's be . . . Hey! More leisurely . . . Hey! . . . Please!" I pulled the dress sleeves down her arms, inhibiting her struggles. She wore a pale yellow bra with white lace. "You'll tear my . . . Wait! Don't . . ." I found the bra snap and got the edge of a thumbnail under it and popped it open, and the bra straps slid down her arms. "No! Dammit! Hey! Please!"

She got one arm out of the sleeve and tried to pull her dress back up, but as she did so I pulled the other arm free, then caught both wrists in one hand, put the other around her waist, and lifted her off the floor. When I shook her a little, still chuckling, the dress and bra slid off her and fell to the floor, and I swung her in the air and caught her, an arm around her shoulders, the other under her knees, and chuckling inanely, toted her over to the bed. She had begun a silent battle, in deadly earnest, to retain the little yellow matching panties, and finally I took pity on her and groaned as hollowly as I could and toppled heavily across her, my chest across her sturdy agitated thighs.

She was breathing hard. She pushed at me. "Hey! Wake up!" I did not move. She caught a fold of flesh on the side of my throat under the ear and gave a painful, twisting pinch. Then she pulled my hand toward her and put her fingertips on my pulse. Satisfied, she pushed at me and wormed her legs out from under me. She grunted with the effort. I kept my eyes closed. The bed shifted as she got off it. In a few moments I heard the little clicking snap of the bra catch and soon the almost inaudible purr of the nylon zipper, the rezipping divided into three segments, as it was hard to reach. Then a faint thudding of her footsteps became audible and I knew she had put her shoes back on.

She picked up the phone on the bedside stand and dialed for an outside line. She dialed a number. She waited a few moments, then said, "Okay," and hung up. Clack of her lighter. Huff of exhalation. Smell of cigarette. I identified the next move as her unlatching the door, probably to leave it ajar for whoever had the word that things were now okay in 109. The edge of the bed had caught me across the lower belly. My toes rested on the rug.

"Come *on!*" she whispered. "Come *on,* Rick darling."

Make it six or seven minutes from phone call to arrival. Male voice, after the door was gently closed. "Everything okay, honey?"

"No problems."

"Nice work. I hated the idea of you coming to his room. I was afraid maybe he'd decide he didn't want a drink, and then he's such a big, rough-looking son of a bitch, I was afraid——"

"Just like I hate the idea of your sleeping with your dear wife Janice every damned night, darling?" Her voice was bitter.

"And you know why it has to be that way."

"Do I?"

"No time to open the same damned old can of worms, Penny. Let's see if we're going to do any good."

He took me by the belt and pulled me back off the bed. I let myself tumble, completely slack. I ended up on my side, knees bent, cheek against the bristle of the rug. He pulled at my shoulder and I rolled slowly onto my back. He rolled me another half turn, face down, and I felt him work the wallet out of my hip pocket, heard the distinctive sound as he sat on the bed. Sizable, I guessed. Young voice. Physically powerful.

"Anything?" she asked.

"Not in this. Pockets of his jacket?"

"Just this stuff. Nothing."

"I better check the side pockets of his pants."

"Would there be anything in . . . in the lining of anything, or in his shoes?"

"I don't know. I'll check it if we draw a blank. The thing that bothers me is that this son of a bitch doesn't have enough on him."

"What do you mean, dear?"

"The average guy has pieces of paper on him. Notebook, notes, addresses, letters, junk like that. McGee here has got car rental papers, a plane ticket to Lauderdale, keys, drivers license, and a half dozen credit cards and . . . a little over eight hundred in cash. Here. Take these two fifties."

"I don't *want* the money!"

"We want him to think he had a ball. Here, dammit!"

"All right. But I can't see why he'd——"

"Win, lose, or draw, we rumple the hell out of that bed, rub lipstick on the pillow, squirt some of your perfume on him, undress him, and leave him in the bed. And dump the rest of that bottle into the john."

"Okay. But you know, he didn't *seem* like somebody who'd——"

"For chrissake, Penny!"

"All right. I'm sorry."

"We knew it was a big man. We know he was from out of town. We know he went to see Pike."

He checked the other pockets. Then the girl asked about the shirt pocket. He rolled me onto my back again. She was standing close. I opened my eyes just far enough to make out the shape and distance of his head as he bent over me. I hit him solidly in the side of the throat with my right fist, rolling my body to the left as I did so to give it more leverage, and then swung my legs in a wide arc at floor level. I clipped her right at the ankles and she landed flat on her back with a very large thud for a girl that size. Her friend had rolled over onto his back and back onto his knees. He got up just as I did. He was making gagging, strangling sounds. Eyes bulged. Mouth hung open. Sandy-blond with a lot of neck, shoulders, and jaw. Look of the college lineman six years later, twenty pounds heavier, and a lot softer.

But as he got his back against the wall, he pulled a blue-black and very efficient-looking revolver out of somewhere and aimed it at my middle. I stopped very suddenly and took a cautious step backward, and raised my arms, and said, "Easy now. Easy does it, friend."

He coughed and gagged and massaged his throat. He spoke in a rasping, traumatic whisper. "Back up and sit on the edge of the bed, smartass. And hold the back of your neck with both hands."

I obeyed, slowly and carefully. Penny was still on her back on the floor. She was making a horrid articulated sound with each inhalation. She had hiked her knees up.

Her clenched fists were against her breast. The fall had knocked all the wind out of her.

He went over and looked down at her. Her breathing eased. He gave her his hand and he pulled her up to a sitting position, but she shook her head violently and pulled her hand away. That was as far as she wanted to go for the moment. She hugged her legs, forehead on her knees.

"Two hours you said," he whispered. "Or three."

"He . . . he must be resistant to it. He had enough for . . . a full-grown horse."

With his eyes on me, he moved the straight chair over and placed it about five feet from me, the back toward me. He straddled it and rested the short barrel on the back of the chair, centered on my chest. "We'll have a nice little talk, smartass."

"About what? This lousy setup? I've got eight hundred on me, so take it. Wear it in good health. Leave."

She got to her feet, took one step, and nearly went down again. She hobbled over toward the head of the bed, her face twisted with pain.

"My ankle," she said. She was having a clumsy evening.

"We are going to have a little talk about Doctor Stewart Sherman, smartass."

I frowned at him, my bafflement entirely genuine. "I never heard of the man in my life. If this is some variation of the badger game, friend, you are making it too complicated."

"And we are going to talk about how you are putting the squeeze on Tom Pike. Want to deny seeing him today?"

"I went to see Maurie and Biddy, the two daughters of Mick Pearson, a friend of mine who died five years, nearly six years ago, not that it is any of your business."

There was a look of uncertainty in his eyes for just a moment. But I needed more advantage than that and, remembering their very personal little squabble, and remembering how she had reported having no trouble at all with me, I thought of an evil way to improve the odds.

"Like I said. Take the eight hundred and leave. Your broad was pretty good, but she wasn't worth eight hundred, but if that's the going rate, let me pay."

"Now, don't get cute," he said. His voice was coming back.

"Man, the very last thing I am going to be is cute. My head hurts from whatever she loaded my drink with. We had this nice little romp and then, instead of settling down, she wants to go out to some saloon. She said we could come back afterward. So I get dressed and she wants a drink, so I fix two drinks and I drink mine, and the last thing I remember is seeing her watching me in a funny way as she's putting her clothes on. Then the lights went out."

"He's making it up! It wasn't like that at all, darling!"

I raised my eyebrows in surprise and tried to look as though a slow understanding was dawning on me. I nodded. "All right. If she's all yours, buddy, then I'm making it up and it wasn't like that at all. Never happened."

The shape of his mouth was uglier. Without taking his watchful stare off me, he said to her, "How could you figure he'd wake up? How could you figure he'd tell me? A little fun on the side, darling?"

"Please!" she said. "Please, you can't believe him. He's trying to——"

"I'm trying to be a nice guy," I said. "It never happened. Okay, Penny?"

"Stop it!" she cried.

"Maybe the only way you can keep me from using this gun is by proving it did happen. Tell me . . . some things you couldn't know otherwise, smartass."

"Pale yellow bra and panties with white lace. Freckles, very faint and small but lots of them, across the tops of her breasts. A brown mole, about the size of a dime, maybe a little smaller, two inches below her left nipple and toward the middle of her, like maybe at seven o'clock. And when she was making out, she called me Rick. If you're not Rick, you've got more problems."

The blood had gone out of his face. Instead of turning his eyes, he turned his whole head toward her.

In a breathy dog-whistle squeak she said, "But he knows because . . . I never . . . when he was . . ."

"You cheap little bum," he said in a pebbly voice. "You dirty little hot-pants slut. You . . ."

And by then his head was turned far enough, and I made the long reach for the kick and put a lot of energy and hope and anxiety in it, because there was so little barrel jutting out over the back of the chair. But I hit it hard enough to numb my toes and hard enough to kick it out of his hand and over his head. It hit the wall and bounded back, spinning along the rug. He pounced very well and even came up with it, but I was moving then, adjusting stride and balance as I moved, and got my turn and my pivot at the right place and, keeping my wrist locked, put my right fist into the perfect middle of that triangle formed by the horizontal line of the belt and the two descending curves of the rib cage. He said a mighty *hawff* and sat solidly on the floor about four feet behind where he had been standing, rolled his eyes back into his head and slumped like Raggedy Andy. I scooped up the revolver and knelt beside him and checked heart and breathing. It is a mighty nerve center, and fright had added lots and lots of adrenalin to my reaction time, and it can so shock the nervous system that the breathing will stop and the heart go into fibrillation.

I saw a movement out of the corner of my eye and I lunged for the girl and caught her just as she got her hand on the door. I spun her back into the room, forgetting her bad ankle. She fell and rolled and started to get up, then lay there curled on the floor, making little smothered hopeless sounds of weeping.

Her Rick was too big to fool with, and I found a couple of wire hangers in the closet, leftovers hung in with the wooden kind that fit into nasty little metal slots so you won't steal them. I straightened one into a straight piece of wire, then held his wrists close together by grasping both his arms just above the wrist in the long fingers of my left hand. I put the end of the wire under my left thumb and then quickly and firmly wrapped it around his wrists as many times as it would go, then bent and tucked the two ends under the encircling strands. It is a wickedly effective device. And quick.

I went over to her and picked her up and sat her on the edge of the bed. She sat blubbering like a defeated child. I squatted and examined her ankle. It was solid and shapely, and beginning to puff on the outside, just below the anklebone.

"I l-l-love him!" she said. "That was a . . . a wicked . . . a wicked evil thing for you to do. That was . . . a wicked evil lie."

Her wig was askew and I reached and plucked it off. She was a sandy redhead with a casual scissor cut. Without the wig her face was in better proportion, but the eye makeup, particularly with much of it making black gutters down her cheeks, look ridiculous.

"Wick-wick-wicked!" she moaned.

"But there's nothing wicked and evil about picking me up and knocking me out with a Mickey? Go wash that goop off your face, girl. Besides, if I busted it up, maybe I did you a favor. He'll never leave Janice and marry you."

I helped her up. She went limping toward the bathroom. She stopped suddenly and stood quite still, then turned and stared at me. "That was right aft-after he came in, that about Jan-Janice! Then you were never . . . Then you just pretended . . . all along you *knew?*"

"Go wash your dirty face, honey."

When she closed the door, I emptied Rick's pockets and took the stuff over to the desk and looked at it under the light.

The identification startled and alarmed me. I had thumped and wired up one Richard Haslo Holton, Attorney at Law. He was a county Democratic committeeman, an honorary Florida sheriff, past president of the Junior Chamber, holder of many credit cards, member of practically everything from Civitan to Sertoma, from the Quarterback Club to the Baseball Boosters League, from the Civic Symphony Association to the Prosecuting Attorneys' Association.

He carried a batch of color prints of a smiling slender

dark-haired woman and two boys at various ages from about one year to six years. One does not go about needlessly irritating any member in good standing of any local power structure. I had the feeling he was going to wake up in a state of irritation.

Penny came out of the bathroom with her face scrubbed clean and with the big black lashes peeled off and stuffed away somewhere. She had stopped streaming, but she was tragic and snuffly.

Just then Mister Attorney made a sound of growling and an effort to sit up. It seemed useful to leave a small but lasting impression on both of them. So I went over and scooped him up, slung him, and dropped him in a sitting position in the black armchair. It shocked and surprised him. He was meaty and sizable. I had done it effortlessly, of course. It had given me an ache in all my back teeth, ground my vertebrae together, pulled my arms out of the sockets, and started a double hernia. But, by God, I made it *look* easy.

"Now let's all have a nice little chat," I said.

"——— your ——— ——— ——— in ——— ———!" he said.

I smiled amiably. "I can phone Mrs. Holton and ask her to come over and join us. Maybe she can help us all communicate."

So we all had a nice little chat.

8 *SEEMS THAT* Miss Penny Woertz was the loyal devoted office nurse for one Dr. Stewart Sherman, a man in the general practice of medicine. He was inclined, however, to get so involved in special fields of interest that he often neglected his general practice.

In early July, three months ago, Dr. Sherman had gone down to his office on a Saturday evening. Penny knew that he had been anxious to get his notes in shape so that he could finish a draft of a paper he was writing on the effects of induced sleep in curing barbiturate addiction.

He was a widower, a man in his middle fifties, with grown children married and living in other states. He lived alone in a small apartment and did some of his research work there and did the rest of it in one of the back rooms of his small suite of offices. The body was not discovered until Penny came to work on Monday morning at ten, as was her customary time.

The body was on the table in the treatment room. The left sleeve of the white shirt had been rolled up. A length of rubber tubing that had apparently been knotted around the left arm above the elbow to make the vein more accessible was unfastened but held there by the weight of the arm upon it. Over the countertop was an empty container and an empty syringe with injection needle attached. Both the small bottle with the rubber diaphragm top and the syringe showed traces of morphine. The drug safe was unlocked. The key was in his pocket. His fragmentary prints were found on the syringe and the bottle. Beside the empty bottle was a small wad of surgical cotton with a streak of blood diluted by alcohol on it. The autopsy conducted by the county medical examiner showed that the death, to a reasonable medical certainty, was due to a massive overdose of morphine. According to Penny, nothing else was missing from the drug safe, or from the other stocks of drugs used in the treatment of patients. But she could not tell whether anything was missing from the back room stocks especially ordered by Dr. Stewart Sherman and used in his experimentations.

She had unlocked the door when she arrived.

By then I had unwired Rick Holton. His attitude was a lot better and the wire had been painful.

He said, "At one time I was the assistant state attorney here in Courtney County. The way it works, the state attorney has a whole judicial district, five counties, so he has an assistant prosecutor in each county. It's elective. I'd decided not to run again. The state attorney is still the same guy. Ben Gaffner. The day I heard that Stew Sherman was supposed to have killed himself, I told Ben that I would just never believe it. Well, dammit, they had the autopsy, and Sheriff Turk investigated and he turned the file over to Ben Gaffner, and Ben said there was no reason in the world why he should make a jackass of himself by trying to present it to the grand jury as something other than suicide, which it damn well was—according to him."

"The doctor *couldn't* have killed himself!" Penny said.

"That's what I felt," Rick said. "So because they were closing the file, I thought what I'd do was use what time I could spare to do some digging. Ben gave me his unofficial blessing. The first time I interviewed Penny, I found out she felt exactly the same way."

So that was how their affair had started. From what I had heard while pretending to be unconscious, I knew it was going sour. And now they were very stiff with each other, harboring delicious resentments.

As I thought the tensions between them might inhibit their communicating with me, I tried to take them off the hook. I told Holton that when the taste of the gin had clued me, I decided to give her some real reason to be jumpy and maybe teach her that pretending to be a hooker could be a messy little game, so I had peeled her out of her dress and bra. "She put up a good fight," I said.

He looked a little happier. "I see. So you made me so goddamn mad at her, I gave you an opening. You're pretty good, McGee."

"If I'd known you were a member of the bar and every lunch club in town, I wouldn't have tried you. It was a very small opening and you carry a very damaging caliber. If you'd had the hammer back, I wouldn't have tried you. But why me? Like I told you, I never heard of the doctor."

He summarized what he had been able to dig up. He had an orderly mind and professional knowledge of the rules of evidence. With Penny's help he had located two people who had seen a very tall man let himself out of Dr. Sherman's offices late Saturday night. One guessed eleven thirty. The other guessed a little after midnight. Penny knew that when the doctor was working on his research projects, he would not answer the office phone. The answering service had recorded no calls for the doctor that evening. One witness said that the man had gotten into a dark blue or black car parked diagonally across the street, a new-looking car, and had driven away. That witness had the impression that the car bore Florida plates but had a single digit before the hyphen rather than the double digit designating Courtney County. He had taken affidavits and put them in his private file on the case.

"But how does Tom Pike come into the picture?" I asked.

"I was looking for motive. I heard a couple of people saying that Stew had died at one hell of an inconvenient time as far as Tom was concerned, and he might take a real bath on some of his deals. So I wondered if maybe somebody had killed the doctor just to put the screws on Tom. You see, Stew Sherman was the Pike family doctor, and when Tom started Development Unlimited two years ago, Stew invested with him in a big way. He'd always made pretty good money in his practice and on top of that he had the money his wife left when she died three years ago. Tom had put together some marvelous opportunities for Stew and the others who went in on the first deals he made. They stood to make really fantastic capital gains. Money is always a good motive. So I had a long talk with Tom. At first he didn't want to tell me anything. He said everything was fine. But when he saw what I was driving at, he got very upset and he opened up. The doctor had been fully committed on three big parcels of land east of town. Tom had put together a fourth deal, and Stew had made preliminary arrangements to borrow a large sum of money from the bank, using his equity in the first three parcels as collateral. Based on the bank's preliminary approval, Tom had gone ahead and committed the group on the fourth deal. Now not only was he going to be badly squeezed on the fourth deal, but the Internal Revenue Service had come in on an estate tax basis and froze the doctor's equities in the other three parcels, and actually could order sale of those equities in order to meet the estate tax bite. Tom told me that Doctor Sherman couldn't have died at a worse time, not only for the sake of his own estate, but also because of what it could do to the others who were in on all four syndicates. He told me that he was going to have to do one hell of a lot of scrambling to keep the whole thing from falling apart."

"I assume he made out all right."

"The word is that he squeaked through, but that it cost him. As a matter of fact, Stew's sons tried to bring some kind of action against Tom because there was a lot less left than they thought there ought to be. But there was no basis for action. I asked Tom if anybody could have killed the doctor in order to mess up the deals he had on the fire. The idea shocked hell out of him. He said he could think of some people who might have wanted to, but they would have had no way of knowing how badly it would pinch him. He agreed that it seemed very, very strange that the doctor should kill himself, but he couldn't offer any alternative."

"But some tall man has been putting the squeeze on Tom Pike?"

"That's one of those funny breaks you get, the kind that may mean something or nothing. In late August, Tom Pike drew twenty thousand in cash out of one of his accounts. A lot of real estate deals are cash deals, so it wasn't anything unusual. I found out how much by checking back, quietly, through a friend, after I heard what happened. One of my law partners mail-ordered a big reflector telescope for his twelve-year-old kid's birthday and had it sent to the office. He set it up, tripod and all, and was fooling around putting the different eyepieces on and aiming it out the office window at the shopping plaza a block away. He had it at two hundred and forty power, meaning that something two hundred and forty yards away looks like one yard away. He focused it on a car parked all alone in an empty part of the lot and when he got it sharp and clear, he found he was looking at Tom Pike standing and leaning against the car. He wondered what he was waiting for. Just then another car pulled up and a tall man got out. My partner said he had never seen him before. He had a lot of tan and looked rugged and wore a white sport shirt and khakis. Tom gave the stranger a brown envelope. The stranger opened it and took out a sheaf of bills and riffled the end of the sheaf with his thumb. My partner said he could damned near see the denomination. He then put the brown envelope into his car and took out a white envelope or package and gave it to Tom Pike, who stuffed it away so quickly my partner didn't get much of a look at it. They got into their cars and took off. He mentioned it to me a couple of days later. We were talking about a divorce action we're handling and he said maybe we should invest in a telescope and told me about spying on Tom. There could be a lot of answers. Maybe it was a cash option on ranchland or groveland. Maybe he was buying advance highway information from a road engineer. But maybe it was the tall man who was in Stew's office that night and got into the act somehow."

"So just how did you come up with me?"

"I was at the bar with a client last night when you came in with Tom's sister-in-law. She started crying and you took her out. I told my client I'd be right back. I saw you unlock One-O-nine and took a look at your plate and saw it was a rental number. I got your name at the desk. I have a cop friend I give some work to when he's off duty and he tailed you today and phoned me when you pulled into the Pike house. I met him here and he went through your room while I hung around the house phone to give him a warning call if you got back too soon. He didn't find a thing that would give us a clue. I don't have any official status, of course. And even if I did, I could still get in real trouble taking you in for a shakedown. Penny and I worked out the idea of her seeing if she could pick you up. I knew about the opened bottle from what my cop friend told me. Penny had something she thought would work fast. While you were eating I spiked your bottle."

"How did you get in?"

"With the passkey from my cop friend. He's got a master key for every big motel in the area."

I looked at them. "You people are very diligent and so on. And damned stupid. So if I didn't want to get picked up? So I wanted to come back here all by myself and kill the bottle?"

"I was five minutes away. She was going to phone me and I was going to come over, use the phone, and get you out of the room on some pretext. She was going to use the passkey and dump the bottle or steal it."

"Because," she said in a small voice, "to make one drink strong enough, I had to put enough in so that all of it would have killed you, through suppression of the sympathetic nervous system."

"Why *did* Pike give you the twenty thousand?" Holton asked.

"Amateur to the end," I said. "I never met him until today. Can I prove it? No, sir. I can't prove it. Do I want to try to prove it? No. I can't be bothered. Do you want to try to prove it? Go ahead, Holton." I spun the cylinder of his Police Positive. Full load. I handed it to him. "The doctor was probably a nice guy. And you are probably fairly nice people yourselves. But you two are a nurse and a joiner and if you found somebody who really killed the doctor, he'd probably kill the two of you also. You belong on serial television. If I had killed the doctor, I would rap your skulls, put you in the trunk of the car, and drop you into one of the biggest sinkholes I could find and cave some of the limestone sides down onto you."

He was flushed as he got to his feet, stuffing the revolver into his belt. "I don't need lectures from some damned drifter."

"Stay busier. Join more clubs."

"Do I have your permission to go, *Mister* McGee!"

"Nothing could give me more piercing delight."

"Come on, Pen."

"Go home to Janice," she said. "You've been out enough nights."

"Look, I'm *sorry* I blew my stack when he said . . . uh——"

"You were so *ready,* darling. You were just *aching* to believe something like that, something nasty. You want to think that because you got to first, second, third base, and home, anybody can. Anytime. Go to hell, Rick. You are a mean lousy little human being and you have a dirty little mind."

"Are you coming with me or aren't you?"

"I'm going to stay right here for a little while, thank you."

"Either you come with me——"

"Or you'll never forgive me, and we're through, and so on. Oh, baby, are we ever through! If there's no trust, there's no nothing at all. Good-bye, Rickie dear. All the way home to Janice you can dwell on all the nasty things you think are probably going on right here on this bed."

He spun around, marched out, and slammed the door viciously.

Her attempt to smile at me was truly ghastly. Her mouth wouldn't hold together. "Hope you didn't mind me . . . hope it was all right to . . ." Then the mouth broke and she sprang up and went, *"Waw! Hoo Oh waw,"* as she hobbled into the bathroom.

Fort Courtney was nice enough if you didn't mind it being full of sobbing women trotting into your bathroom, fifty percent of them running with a limp. I took the ice bucket outside and dumped the water out of it and scooped more cubes out of the machine. I thought of dumping out the spiked gin, then changed my mind, capped it, and put the bottle in a back corner of the closet alcove. I unwrapped a fresh glass and opened the second bottle of Plymouth and fixed myself a drink. When she finally came out, slumped, small and dispirited, I offered her a drink.

"Thanks, I guess not. I'd better be going."

"Got a car here?"

"No. Rick dropped me off. My car is over at my place. I can phone for a cab from the office."

"Sit down for a minute while I work on this. Then I'll drive you home."

"Okay." She wandered over and got a cigarette from her purse and lit it. She picked up the thick red-blond wig between thumb and finger like somebody picking up a large dead bug. She dropped it back onto the countertop and said, "Fifteen ninety-eight, plus tax, to try to look like a sexpot."

"You didn't do badly."

"Forget it. I've got freckles, straw hair, short fat legs, and a big behinder. And I'm clumsy. I keep falling over things. And people. Lucky little old me, falling for Rick Holton." She hesitated. "Maybe I'll change my mind about the drink. Okay?"

I unwrapped the last glass and fixed her one, turned, and handed it to her. She took it over to the chair. "Thanks. Why should you do me favors, though? After what I tried to do to you."

"Guilt syndrome. I clobbered your romance."

She frowned. "It hurts. I know. I walked into it expecting to get hurt. You didn't do it, really. You just brought it to a head a little quicker. He's been beginning to want out. I could feel it. He was looking for a great big reason. Jesus, you made him mad!"

"I think I was a little irritated too. I couldn't find out what your plans were unless I faked you out."

She looked into her glass. "You know something? I think I ought to get smashed. I don't have to drive. And from the way this one is making me feel numb around the mouth already, it shouldn't take much."

"Be my guest. Just don't sing." I started to get her glass but she waved me off and went over and fixed her own.

"You sure you don't mind, McGee? Drunk females are horrid. I learned that from working the emergency ward."

"Look, how can you two be so sure that the doctor didn't kill himself?"

"Perfect health. Loved his work and his little projects.

He had enthusiasm about things. Like a kid. And I know how he felt about the attempted suicides. Well, like Tom Pike's wife. It just baffled him. He couldn't understand how anybody could take their own life."

"He treated her?"

"Both times. And it was close both times. If Tom hadn't been on the ball, she would have bought it. He phoned the doctor when he couldn't wake her up, and the doctor told him to rush her down to the emergency room. He met them there and pumped her out and gave her stimulants and they kept walking her and slapping her awake until she was out of danger. The other time Tom had to break the bathroom door down. She'd lost a lot of blood. There were two of those . . . hesitation marks, they call them, on her left wrist, where she couldn't make herself cut deep enough. Then she cut deep enough the third time. It's slower bleeding from a vein, of course. She's a nice standard type, and Doctor Sherman put four pints back into her and did such a good job on her wrist I'll bet that by now the scar is almost invisible."

"Reported to the authorities?"

"Oh, yes. You have to. It's the law."

"Did you have any idea anything at all might have been bugging the doctor?"

"Gee, it's hard to say. I mean he wasn't one of those always-the-same people. When he'd get involved in some project, he'd get sort of remote, especially when things wouldn't be going well. And he wouldn't want to talk about it. So . . . *maybe* something was bothering him, because he'd been acting the way he usually did when things weren't going the way he expected. But I just *know* he wouldn't kill himself."

"Anything questionable in the autopsy?"

"Like maybe he was knocked out first? No. No sign of it and no trace of anything but morphine, and that was more than a trace."

I was slouched deep in the armchair, legs resting on a round formica table. After the silence had lasted a little while, I looked over at her. She was staring at me. She had one eye a third closed and the other half closed. She had one brow arched and she had her lips pulled back away from her rather pretty teeth. It was a strange, fixed grimace, not quite smirk and not quite sneer.

"Hi!" she said in a husky voice, and I suddenly realized that the stare had been meant to be erotic and inviting. It startled me.

"Oh, come *on*, Penny!"

"Well . . . listen. You're cute. You know that? Pretty damn cute. What I was thinking, that sumbitch was so ready to think I cheated, right? I was thinking like they say about having the name and the game too. Whoose going anyplace anyways? Friday night, iznit? Dowanna waysh . . . *waste* the li'l pill I took this morning, do I?"

"Time to take you home."

"Yah, yah, yah. Thanks a lot. You must find me real attractive, McGee. Freckles turn you off? Doan like dumpy-legged women?"

"I like them just fine, nurse. Settle down."

She came around toward me and stood and gave me that fixed buggy stare again, put her glass on the table, then did a kind of half spin and tumbled solidly onto my lap, managing to give me a pretty good chop in the eye with her elbow as she did so. It hit some kind of nerve that started my eye weeping. She snuggled into me, cheek against my chest, and gave me another breathy "Hi!"

"Penny-friend, it is a lousy way to try to get even with good old Rick. You're bold with booze. You'd hate yourself."

"D'wanna take d'vantage of a girl?"

"Sure. Glad to. You think it over and come back tomorrow night and scratch on the door."

She gave a long, weary exhalation and for a moment I wondered if she was suddenly passing out. But then in a level and perfectly articulated voice she said, "I have a good head for booze."

"Hmmm. Why the act?"

"It ain't easy, McGee, for a cold-sober girl to offer her all to the passing stranger. Maybe for some, but not for Penny Woertz. No! Don't push me up. I can tell you easier if I'm not looked at."

"Tell me what?"

"It's a bad hang-up for me. With Rick. He really *is* mean. Do you know how a guy can be mean? Cruel little things. Know why he can get away with being like that?"

"Because you're the only one with the hang-up?"

"Right. You're pretty smart. Know what I'll do now?"

"What will you do?"

"Get very firm with myself. Tell myself it was a no-good thing. Chin up, tummy in, walk straight, girl. Think of him every three minutes of every waking hour for two or three or four days, and then dial the private line in his office and humble myself and whimper and beg and apologize for things I didn't do. And be ashamed of myself and kind of sick-joyful at the same time."

"No character, hey?"

"I used to think I had lots. He got to me in . . . a kind of physical way. I think of him and get to wanting him so bad my head hums and my ears roar and the world gets tilty."

"Hmm. Humiliating?"

"That's the word. I want out. I want free. So while I was in your bathroom blubbering because he walked out, I had this idea of how to get loose, if I could work up enough nerve."

"Use me to solve your problem?"

"I thought you'd jump at the chance. Not because I'm so astonishingly lovely, something that turns all the heads when I walk by. But I've had to learn that there is some damn thing about me that seems to work pretty good. I mean if I was in some saloon with Miss International Asparagus Patch, and a man moved in on us because he drew a bead on her, a lot of the time he'd switch targets, and I've never known why it happens, but it does. That's why I was so sure I could pick you up in the bar."

"You *do* project a message."

"Wish I knew what the message reads."

"I think it says, 'Here I am!' "

"Darn it. I *like* men. As men. Six brothers. I was the only girl. I've never been able to really be a girl-girl, luncheons and girl talk and all that. But I don't go shacking

90

around. I love to make love, sure. But it never seemed to be any kind of real necessity, you know? Except now I'm hung up that way with Rick, and I don't even *like* him very much. I don't even know if . . . it would be any good at all with another man nowadays. I thought you'd be a good way to find out. I thought, once I'd pumped up the nerve, one little opening and Pow. Easier to play drunk. Hardly know you. Won't see you again. So you come on with these scruples. Or maybe my mysterious whatzit isn't on your wavelength, dear. Oh, Christ! I feel so awkward and timid and dumb. I never tried to promote a stranger before, honest."

"So if nothing much happened, wouldn't you be hung up worse than ever?"

"No. Because it would keep me from having the guts to phone him. After sleeping with you—win, lose, or draw—I'd feel too guilty. And that would give me the time to finally get over it. You see, I always have to go crawling to him. If when he doesn't hear from me, he comes after me, I don't know if I can stay in the clear. But . . . it would give me a pretty good chance."

She gave that deep long sigh once more. Strange little freckled lady, radiating something indefinable, something lusty and gutsy. Something playtime. So the world is a wide shadowy place, with just a few times, a few corners, where strangers touch. And she could be a partial cure for the random restlessness of the past weeks. Ol' Doctor McGee. Home therapy. The laying on of hands. Therapeutic manipulation. The hunger that isn't a damned bit interested in names or faces is always there, needing only a proper fragment of rationalization to emerge. So I drifted my fingertips along the sad curl of her back and found the same old zipper tab and slowly pulled it from nape to stern. She pushed up, swarmy-eyed, hair-tousled, to make the opening gift of her mouth in her acceptance.

But stopped and focused, frowned. "It's a sad story, okay. But it isn't *that* sad! It shouldn't make a strong man cry."

"I'm not. You got me in the eye with your elbow a while back."

Hers was a good laugh, belly laugh, total surrender to laughter, enough for tears, but with no edge of hysteria. While I got the lights, she hung her dress on a hanger and turned the bed down. We left the bathroom door ajar, a strip of light angling across the foot of the bed. She was constricted and muscle-taut and nervous for a time but not for long. And after more unmeasured time had gone by, I found out just what that mysterious aura was. It was clean, solid, healthy, joyous, inexhaustible girl, all clovery oils and pungencies, long limber waist and torso sophisticating the rhythmic counterpoint of solid, heated, thirsty hips, creating somehow along with release the small awarenesses of new hunger soon to rebuild.

I awakened slowly to the morning sound of her shower and drifted off again, and was awakened a little later by sun-brightness shining into the darkened room, and saw her naked by the double draperies, holding the edge away from the window while she peered out at the day. With her other hand she was foamily scrubbing away at her teeth with my toothbrush and toothpaste.

She turned away from the window and, seeing that my eyes were open, she roamed over to the bed, still scrubbing. ". . . ood oring, arley."

"And good morning to you too, tiger."

"O you O eye."

"What?"

Removed brush. "I said I hope you don't mind. Me using your toothbrush. I mean invasions of privacy are sort of relative, huh?"

"Like the old joke, it's been the equivalent of a social introduction."

When she started brushing again, I reached and caught her by the free wrist, pulled her closer. She removed brush, stared thoughtfully at me. "Really? You're serious?" She smiled. "Well sure! Let me go rench." She went into the bathroom. The water ran. The sound of spitting was *p-too, p-tooey,* like a small child. She came trotting back, beaming, launched herself into the bed, landing solidly, reaching greedily, and saying an anticipatory "Yum" with utmost comfortable satisfaction. In her own special field of expertise she was the least clumsy thing in probably the entire county.

After we were dressed, she began to be increasingly nervous about leaving a motel room at high noon on Saturday. She was almost certain Rick was out there, waiting in murderous patience. Or that a group of her friends would be strolling by the room, for some unknown reason. She put the wig on as a partial disguise. She had me go out and start the motor in the rental, open the door on her side, and tap the horn ring when I was certain the coast was clear.

She came out at a hunched-over half gallop and while scrambling into the car she gave her knee such a hell of a whack on the edge of the door that she spent the first three blocks all scrooched down, hugging her knee and moaning. Then from time to time she would stick her head up just far enough to see where we were and give me directions. She had an apartment in a little garden apartment development called Ridge Lane. After she insisted I drive around two blocks twice to make certain Rick's red convertible wasn't parked in the area, I drove into her short, narrow drive behind the redwood privacy fence and stopped a few inches behind the rear bumper of her faded blue Volkswagen in the carport. She spelled Woertz for me and said she was in the book. But I had the feeling she did not want me to call her. I had performed the required service. She did not want to trade one entanglement for another.

I remembered a question I had forgotten to ask. "By the way, what were you people hoping to find on my person, Penny?"

She shrugged. "We didn't know, really. Anything that would tie you in somehow. Papers or money or letters or notes or something. When you come to a blind alley, you're ready to try almost anything."

We sat there and suddenly both yawned at once, great luxurious shuddering jaw-creakers. Then laughed at ourselves. She kissed me, got out, and gave a squeak of pain when she put her weight on her leg. She bent and rubbed her sore knee, then limped to her door. When she had unlocked it and opened it, she smiled and waved and I backed out.

On the way back I stopped at a place as clean as any operating theater and had fresh juice, hot fresh doughnuts, surprisingly good coffee. Then, feeling a little bit ridiculous at being overly prim and fastidious, I walked a half block and bought a toothbrush before driving back to the motel. Yes, there are different degrees of personal privacy, and a toothbrush seems to be on some special level all its own, a notch above a hairbrush.

The room had been made up. Though checkout time was eleven, I was certain they would not clip me for the ensuing night, as they just weren't that busy.

But I sat and yawned and sighed, feeling too pleasantly wearied to make any decisions. The episode, I told myself, had changed nothing. A dead doctor, no matter how he died, had nothing to do with a damaged young wife who seemed to want to die.

Nothing new had been added except . . .

Except something she had said in the middle of the night after that time that had been unmistakably the most complete one for her, not any kind of thrashing wildness, or spasmodic yelping, but just very lasting and very strong, fading very slowly for her, slowly and gently. It was one of those fragmented drowsy conversations as we lay in a night tangle of contentment, sheet and blanket shoved down to the foot of the bed, the flesh drying and cooling after the moist of effort. Her deep and slowing breath was humid against the base of my throat. Round knee against my belly, her slow, affectionate fingertips tracing over and over the line of my jaw from earlobe to chin. In down-glance I could see, against the light that lay in a crisp diagonal line across the foot of the bed, a round height of her hip, semiluminous, and a steep descent to the waist where rested, in dark contrast, my large hand with fingers splayed.

"Mmmmm," she said, "so now I know."

"Search for guilt?"

"Too soon for that, darling Feel too delicious for that. Later maybe. But . . . damn it all anyway."

94

"Problem?"

"I don't know. Girl finds she can get turned way, way on, big as can be, with a nice guy that comes along. So she's kind of a lousy person."

"Glandular type, eh?"

"A lousy nympho, maybe."

"Then, I'd have to be number eight hundred and fifty-six or something."

She lay in thought for a moment and then giggled. "Counting Rick, you got one figure right. The six. The other four, I was married to one and engaged to two and head over heels with the other. Compared to some of the R.N.'s I work with and was in training with, I'm practically a nun. But my old grandma would faint dead away."

"Nymphs are concerned only with self, honey. They lose track of who the guy is. Don't know or care. A robot would suit them fine."

"I knew you were you, all along. Even more so when it got to the best part. What does that make me?"

"Serendipitous."

"Is that dirty?"

"No. That's a clean."

She stretched, yawned, shifted closer. "I keep wanting to say I love you, darling. That's for my conscience, I guess. Anyway, I like the hell out of you."

"Same here. It's the afterglow that proves it worked right."

She pushed herself up and knee-walked down and sorted out sheet and blanket and pulled them up over us, straightening and tucking and neatening, and then curled again, shivering once, fists and forehead against my chest, knees in my belly, her cheek resting on my underarm, with my other arm around her, palm against her back, fingertips wedged under the relaxed weight of her rib cage against the undersheet.

I moved back and forth across the edge of sleep, thinking of that afterglow, trying to explain it to myself. With the mink, the musk ox, the chimpanzee, and the human, the proper friction at the proper places if continued for x minutes will cause the nerve ends to trigger the small glandular-muscular explosive mechanics of climax. And afterward there is no more urge to caress the causative flesh than there would be to stroke the shaker that contained the pepper that caused a satisfying series of sneezes.

So in the sensual-sexual-emotional areas each man and each woman has, maybe, a series of little flaws and foibles, hang-ups, neural and emotional memory pattern and superstition, and if there is no fit between their complex subjective patterns, then the only product you can expect is the little frictional explosion, but when there is that mysterious fit, then maybe there are bigger and better explosions down in the ancient black meat of the hidden brain, down in the membraned secret rooms of the heart, so that what happens within the rocking clamp of the loins at that same time is only a grace note, and then it is the afterglow of affection and contentment that celebrates the far more significant climax in brain and heart.

Her voice came from far off with an echo chamber quality, pulling me back across the edge of sleep. ". . . like they say female moths give off some kind of mating signal. Gees, I don't bat my eyes and wiggle my behind and moisten my lips. But the bed patients make grabs at me. And the deliveryman from the dry cleaner. And Mr. Tom Pike, last spring."

"Pike?"

"While his wife was in the hospital for a couple of days of observation after she emptied the pill bottle. It was in the office while she was waiting for Dr. Sherman to come back from an emergency. There was nothing crude about the pass, you understand. Tom Pike is a very tasty and very careful guy. And I felt so darn sorry for him, and I respect him so much for the way he's handling the whole mess with Maureen . . . I almost got involved just out of pity."

"When was all that?"

"March, I guess. Maybe April. One thing, I knew he'd be very careful and cautious and secretive and he wouldn't go around bragging about his loving little nurse friend. I guess he'd have been a good thing, because then I wouldn't have gotten messed up with Rick."

"Think he found some other recruit?"

"I sort of hope so. Somebody sweet and nice and loving. But who would know? Somehow Mr. Pike gets to know everything about everybody, and nobody finds out much about him. It's probably even more important he should have found a friend now that Mrs. Trescott is dead."

"Why?"

"Now there's just the three of them, and kid sister has a terrible yen for him, and nobody could really blame him for giving her some very long second looks, either. And that would be as messy a triangle as you could find."

She yawned and sighed. " 'Night, sweetheart," she said.

I slid almost back into sleep and stopped on the dreaming edge of it. Little by little I became ever more aware of every single place where flesh touched flesh. She had achieved such a honeyed and luxuriant completion that in some bewitched way it seemed to mark the spent flesh with a kind of sensuous continuity, as though it had not ended at all but was still continuing in some hidden manner. I was increasingly aware of the resting engines of our bodies, our slow thump of hearts, blood pulse, suck and sag of the bellows of four lungs, breathing commingled in the cozy bed, all the incredible complexity of cells and nourishments and energy transformation and secretions and heat balance going on and on. I wondered if she slept, but at my first tentative and stealthy caress she took a deep, quick breath that caught and she arched and stretched herself, made a purr of acceptance and luxurious anticipations.

So into the tempos and climates of it again, bodies familiarized now. Fragments. Like things glimpsed at night from a moving train. Dragging whisper-sound of palm on flesh. Deep, deep, slow-thick into the clench of honey, clovery oils, nipples pebbled, lift-clamp of thigh, arythmic flesh-clap fading into tempo reattained, held long and longer and longest, then beginning quivorous hesitation at the end of deepening, richening beat, a shifting of her, mouth agape, furnace breath, tongue curl, grit of tooth against tooth, hands then cup and pull the rubberous buttocky pumping, her bellows breath whistling exploding the words against my mouth—"*Love* you. *Love* you. *Love* you." Then somehow opening more, taking deeper, pulling, demanding, a final grinding moaning agony of her, requiring me to drive, batter, cleave without mercy. Then slow toppling. The long slope. Hearts trying to leap from chests. Gagging gasps from the long run up the far side. Tumbling into the meadow. Tall grass. Clover and grass. Sag into sleep, still coupled, fall into sleep while still feeling in her depths the gentle residual claspings, small infrequent tightenings like that of a small sleeping hand when the brain dreams.

Then in the morning, as I lay watching her get dressed and knowing that soon I had to stir myself too, she looked so frowning-thoughtful, I asked her if she was still working at that lousy-person syndrome of hers.

She put her arms into the sleeves of the white dress after she had stepped into it and pulled it up. "You didn't get to me all the way, Travis, because you're some kind of fantastic lover."

"Thanks a lot."

"I mean, you know, none of that sort of tricky stuff."

She came over and turned around to be zipped. I sat up and swung my legs out and, before zipping her, kissed the crease of her back about two inches south of her bra strap.

"See?" she said.

"See what?"

"Well, that was just nice, honey. So I'm in love with you, sort of. And I wasn't in love with you that first time we made it, and so it wasn't so much, and then when I liked you more, then it got to be something else. So I've got a new philosophy about the bed bit."

"Pray tell," I had said, zipping her up, giving her a pat on the rear.

She moved away and turned, hitching at the white dress and smoothing it across her hips with the backs of her hands. "It isn't all set yet. It's sort of in bits and pieces. I'm going to live as if freckled girls have more fun. And to hell with all the whining and bleeding and gnashing my fool teeth about R. H. Holton, boy attorney. And if I've discovered that I just happen to love to make love with men I could fall in love with . . . people have to put up with a lot worse problems. Darling! *Are* you going to get up and drive me home? It gets later and later and later."

So I had taken her home. End of brief affair. You could staple all the wrong tags on it. One-night stand. Pickup. Handy little shack job for the travelin' man. Hell, Charlie, you know how them nurses are.

So maybe the only adventures that don't look trivial and tawdry are one's own.

It had been my impression that while deep in thought I had been packing up to get out of there and go back to Lauderdale. But I discovered I hadn't packed a thing. I was atop the bedspread, shoes off, practicing deep breathing. And the next I knew it was eight o'clock on that Saturday night, and I wanted two quick drinks and two pounds of rare sirloin.

9 IT WAS NOT two pounds of steak, but it was rare enough, and I had it in the Luau Room of the Wahini Lodge at about nine, after a long shower, shave, two long-lasting Plymouths on ice.

The mood was the old yin-yang balance of conflicting emotions. There was the fatuous he-male satisfaction and self-approval after having roundly and soundly tumbled the hot-bodied she-thing, with her approvals registered by the reactive flutterings and choke-throated gasps. Satisfaction in the sense of emptied ease and relaxation, with texture memories of the responsive body imprinted for a time on the touching-parts of the hands and mouth. The other half was the drifting elusive postcoital sadness. Perhaps it comes from the constant buried need for a closeness that will eliminate that loneliness of the spirit we all know. And for just a few moments the need is almost eased, the deeply coupled bodies serving as a sort of symbol of that far greater need to stop being totally alone. But then it is over, the illusion gone, and once again there are two strangers in a rumpled bed who, despite any affectionate embrace, are as essentially unknown to each other as two passengers in the same bus seat who have happened to purchase tickets to the same destination. Maybe that is why there is always sadness mingled with the aftertastes of pleasure, because once again, as so many times before, you have proven that the fleeting closeness only underlines the essential apartness of people, makes it uncomfortably evident for a little while. We had fitted each other's needs and could have no way of knowing how much of our willingness was honest and how much was the flood of excuses the loins project so brilliantly on the front screen of the mind.

The loins tell you it is always bigger than both of anybody.

Suddenly, I remembered the hundred dollars that Holton had made Penny stuff into her purse, and smiled. I would hear from her sooner than expected, because when she came across it and remembered, she would be in a horrid haste to get it back to me, as it would make a very sordid footnote to the swarmy night.

And so when I went back to my room at ten thirty something and saw the red light on the phone winking, I was certain it would be Penny Woertz. But it was a very agitated Biddy, expressing surprise that I was still in Fort Courtney and asking me if I had seen or heard from Maureen. She had somehow sneaked down the stairs and out through the back of the house while Tom was in the living room working at the desk, and while Bridget had been out picking up odds and ends at one of the Stop 'n' Shop outlets. She had been gone since a little before seven. "Tom has been out hunting her ever since. I phoned everyplace I could think of and then I left too, about quarter to eight. Right now I'm at a place out near the airport and I happened to think she might come there to the motel, because she knew you were staying there."

"Police looking too?"

"Well, not specifically. But they know she is around and if they see her, they'll take her in. Travis, she's wearing a pink chambray jumper with big black pockets and she's probably barefoot."

"Driving a car?"

"No, thank God. Or maybe it would be better if she did. I don't know. She probably did the same as last time, walked over to Route Thirty and hitched a ride. She doesn't have any trouble getting a lift, as you can imagine. But I am so afraid that some . . . sick person might pick her up."

"Can I help?"

"I can't think of anything you could do. If she does show up there, you could call nine-three-four, two-six-six-one. That's Tom's answering service. We keep calling in every fifteen minutes or so to see if there's word of her."

"Are you with him?"

"No. We can cover more places this way. I usually run across him sooner or later."

"Will you let me know when you find her?"

"If you wish. Yes. I'll phone you."

I hung up wondering why they didn't think about the bottom of the lake. She's had a try at about everything else except jumping out a high window. What was the word? Self-defenestration. Out the window I must go, I must go, I must go . . .

Then some fragment of old knowledge began to nudge at the back of my mind. After I had the eleven o'clock news on the television, I couldn't pay attention because I was too busy roaming around the room trying to unearth what was trying to attract my attention.

Then a name surfaced, along with a man's sallow face, bitter mouth, knowing eyes. Harry Simmons. A long talk, long ago, after a friend of a friend had died. He'd added a large chunk onto an existing insurance policy about five months before they found him afloat, face-down, in Biscayne Bay.

I sat on the bed and slowly reconstructed the pattern of part of his conversation. My thought about the lake and the high window had opened a small door to an old memory.

"With the jumpers and the drowners, McGee, you don't pick up a pattern. That's because a jumper damned near always makes it the first time, and a drowner is usually almost as successful, about the same rate as hangers. They get cut down maybe as rarely as the drowners get pulled out. So the patterns mostly come from the bleeders and the pill-takers and the shooters. Funny how many people survive a self-shooting. But if they don't destroy a chunk of their brain, they get a chance at a second try. Like the bleeders cut themselves again, and the pill-takers keep trying. It's always patterns. Never change. They pick the way that they want to go and keep after it until they make it. A pill-taker doesn't turn into a jumper, and a drowner won't shoot himself. Like they've got one picture of dying and that's it and there's no other way of going."

All right, then say that Harry Simmons might *probably* admit a very rare exception. But Maurie Pearson Pike had opted for the pills, the razor, and the rope. Three methods.

I felt a prickling of the flesh on the backs of my hands. But it was a clumsy fit, no matter how you looked at it. The suffering husband making a narrow save each time. Or the kid sister? Was there a third party who could get close enough to Maurie?

What about motive? The big ones are love and money. The estate was "substantial." What are the terms? Check it out through soft-voiced D. Wintin Hardahee. And noble suffering Tommy *had* made the discreet pass at Freckle-Girl. So on top of that we have a dead family physician labeled suicide, and he had treated Maureen, and does that make any sense or any fit? Penny believed with all her sturdy heart that Dr. Stewart Sherman could not have killed himself.

The tap at my door had to be Penny bringing back the two fifty-dollar bills, and as I went toward the door I was uncomfortably aware of a hollow feeling in the belly that was a lustful anticipation that maybe she could be induced to stay awhile.

But there were two men there, and they both stared at me with that mild, bland, skeptical curiosity of the experienced lawman. It must be very like the first inspection of new specimens brought back to the base camp by museum expeditions. The specimen might be rare or damaged or poisonous. But you check it over and soon you are able to catalog it based on the experience of cataloging thousands of others over the years, and then it is a very ordinary job from then on, the one you are paid for.

The big, hard-boned, young one wore khakis, a white fishing cap with a peak, blue and white sneakers, and a white sport shirt with a pattern of red pelicans on it. It was worn outside the belt, doubtless to hide the miniature revolver that seems to be more and more of a fad with Florida local law. The smaller older one wore a pale tan suit, a white shirt with no tie. He had a balding head, liver spots, little dusty brown eyes, and a virulent halitosis that almost concealed the news that his young partner had been wearing the same shirt too long.

"Name McGee?"

"That's right. What can I do for you?" I was stripped to my underwear shorts and barefoot.

"Well, for a starter, just turn around real slow with your arms out, then you can go stand by the window." He flipped his wallet open and gave me the glimpse of the little gold badge. "I'm Stanger," he said, and, indicating the younger one, "he's Nudenbarger. City."

"And for a starter," I said, "search warrant?"

"Not unless I have to have one, McGee. But you make

us go through the motions, everybody gets pissed off, and it's a hot night, and it all adds up the same way anyway. So you—if you want to—you can like invite us to just poke around."

"Poke around, Mr. Stanger. You too, Mr. Nudenbarger."

He checked my wallet on the countertop while Nudenbarger checked the closet, the suitcase, the bathroom. Stanger wrote down some bits of information copied off credit cards into a blue pocket notebook, dime-sized. He couldn't write without sticking his tongue out of the corner of his mouth. Credit cards hearten them. The confetti of the power structure.

"Plenty cash, Mr. McGee."

Cash and credit had earned me the "mister." I moved over and sat on the bed without permission. "Seven hundred and something. Let me see . . . and thirty-eight. It's sort of a bad habit I'm trying to break, Mr. Stanger. It's stupid to carry cash. Probably the result of some kind of insecurity in my childhood. It's my blue blanket."

He looked at me impassively. "I guess that's pretty funny."

"Funny peculiar?"

"No. Being funny like jokes. Being witty with stupid cops."

"No. The thing about the blue blanket——"

"I keep track of Beethoven's birthday, and the dog flies a DeHavilland Moth."

"What's that?" Nudenbarger asked. "What's that?"

"Forget it, Lew," Stanger said in a weary voice.

"You always say that," Nudenbarger said, accusingly indignant.

It is like a marriage, of course. They are teamed up and they work on each other's nerves, and some of the gutsy ones who have gone into the dark warehouse have been shot in the back by the partner/wife who just couldn't stand any more.

Stanger perched a tired buttock on the countertop,

other leg braced with knee locked, licked his thumb, and leafed back through some pages in the blue notebook.

"Done any time at all, Mr. McGee?"

"No."

"Arrests?"

"Here and there. No charges."

"Suspicion of what?"

"Faked-up things. Impersonation, conspiracy, extortion. Somebody gets a great idea, but the first little investigation and it all falls down."

"Often?"

"What's often? Five times in a lifetime? About that."

"And you wouldn't mention it except if I checked it would show up someplace."

"If you say so."

"You have been here and there, McGee, because for me there is something missing. Right. What do you storm troopers want? What makes you think you can come in here, et cetera, et cetera, et cetera. But you don't object at all."

"Would it work with you, Stanger?"

"Not lately. So okay. Would you say you left about noon and got back a little after one today?"

"Close enough."

"And sacked out?"

"Slept like death until maybe eight o'clock."

"When you make a will, Mr. McGee, leave a little something to Mrs. Imber."

"Who is she?"

"Sort of the housekeeper. Checking on the job the maids do. Opened your door with her passkey at four o'clock, give or take ten minutes. You were snoring on the bed."

"Which sounds as if it was the right place to be."

"A nice place to be. Let me read you a little note. I copied this off the original, which is at the lab. It goes like this: . . . By the way, it was sealed in an envelope and on the outside it said Mr. T. McGee, One-O-nine. So we check some places and find a place with a One-O-nine with a McGee in it. Which is here, and you. It

105

says: 'Dear Honey, What do I say about the wages of sin? Anyway, it was one of his lousy ideas and over-looked, so here it is back. Woke up and couldn't get back to sleep and went into the purse for a cigarette and found this. Reason I couldn't get back to sleep? Well, hell. Reasons. Plural. Memories of you and me . . . getting me a little too worked up for sleepy-bye. And something maybe we should talk over. It's about something SS said about memory and digital skills. Have to go do a trick as a Special at eight, filling in for a friend. I'll drop this off on the way. No man in his right mind would pick a girl up in the hospital lot at four fifteen on Sunday morning, would he? Would he? Would he?' "

Stanger read badly. He said, "It's signed with an initial. P. Nobody you ever heard of?"

"Penny Woertz."

"The hundred bucks was the wages of sin, McGee?"

"Just a not very funny joke. Private and personal."

Nudenbarger stood looking me over, a butcher selecting a side of beef. "Get chopped up in the service?"

"Some of it."

Nudenbarger's smirk, locker-room variety, didn't charm me. "How was she, McGee? Pretty good piece of ass?"

"Shut up, Lew," Stanger said with weary patience. "How long did you know Miss Woertz, McGee?"

"Since we met in the bar last night. You can ask the man who was working the bar. His name is Jake."

"The room maid said you must have had a woman in here last night. So you confirm that it was the nurse. Then you took her back to her apartment at about noon. Did you go in with her?"

I did not like the shape of the little cloud forming on the horizon in the back of my head. "Let's stop the games," I said.

"She mention anybody she thought might be checking up on her?" Stanger asked.

"I'll give you that name after we stop playing games."

Stanger reached into the inside pocket of his soiled tan suitcoat, took an envelope out, took some color Polaroids out of it. As he handed them to me he said, "These aren't official record. Just something I do for my own personal file."

He had used a flash. She was on a kitchen floor, left shoulder braced against the base of the cabinet under the sink, head lolled back. She wore a blue and white checked robe, still belted, but the two sides had separated, the right side pulled away to expose one breast and expose the right hip and thigh. The closed blades of a pair of blue-handled kitchen shears had been driven deep into the socket of her throat. Blood had spread wide under her. Her bloodless face looked pallid and smaller than my memory of her, the freckles more apparent against the pallor. There were four shots from four different angles. I swallowed a heaviness that had collected in my throat and handed them back to him.

"Report came in at eight thirty," he said. "She was going to give another nurse a ride in, and the other nurse had a key to her place because she'd oversleep sometimes. The other nurse lives in one of those garden apartments around on the other side. According to the county medical examiner, time of death was four thirty, give or take twenty minutes. Bases it on coagulation, body temperature, lividity in the lower limbs, and the beginning of *rigor* in the jaws and neck."

I swallowed again. "It's . . . unpleasant."

"I looked in a saucepan on the stove to see if she was cooking something. I picked up the lid and looked in and the sealed-up note to you was in there, half wadded up, like she had hidden it in a hurry the first place she could think of. That part about remembering you and getting all worked up would be something she wouldn't want a boyfriend to read. Think the boyfriend knew she spent the night here in this room?"

"Maybe. I don't know."

"She worried about him?"

"Some."

"Just in case there was two of them, suppose you give me the name you know."

"Richard Holton, Attorney at Law."

"The only name?"

"The only boyfriend, I'd say."

Stanger sighed and looked discouraged. "Same name we've got, dammit. And he drove his wife over to Vero Beach to visit her sister today. Left about nine this morning. Put through a call over there about an hour and a half ago, and they had left about eight to drive back. Should be home by now. This is still a pretty small town, McGee. Mr. Holton and this nurse had been kicking up a fuss about Doc Sherman's death being called suicide. That's the SS in the note, I guess?"

"Yes. She talked to me about the doctor."

"What's this about . . . let me find it here . . . here it is, 'memory and digital skills'?"

"It doesn't mean a thing to me."

"Would it have anything to do with the doctor *not* killing himself?"

"I haven't any idea."

"Pictures make you feel sick?" Nudenbarger asked.

"Shut up, Lew," Stanger said.

It was past midnight. I looked at my watch when the phone rang. Stanger motioned to me to take it and moved over and leaned close to me to hear the other end of the conversation.

"Travis? This is Biddy. I just got home. Tom found her about twenty minutes ago."

"Is she all right?"

"I guess so. After looking practically all over the county, he found her wandering around not over a mile from here. The poor darling has been bitten a billion times. She's swelling up and going out of her mind with the itching. Tom is bathing her now, and then we'll use the Dormed. Sleep will be the best thing in the world for her."

"Use the what?"

"It's electrotherapy. She responds well to it. And . . . thanks for being concerned, Travis. We both . . . all appreciate it."

I hung up and Stanger said with mild surprise, "You know the Pikes too?"

"The wife and her sister, from a long time ago. And their mother."

"Didn't she die just a while back?"

"That's right."

"They find that kook wife?" Nudenbarger asked.

"Tom Pike found her."

Nudenbarger shook his head slowly. "Now, that one is really something, I swear to God! Al, I'll just never forget how she looked that time last spring she was missing for two days, and those three Telaferro brothers had kept her the whole time in that little bitty storeroom out to the truck depot, keeping her boozed up and bangin' that poor flippy woman day and night until I swear she was so plain wore-down pooped that Mike and Sandy had to use a stretcher to tote her out to——"

"Shut your goddamn mouth, Lew!" Stanger roared.

Nudenbarger stared blankly at him. "*Now* what in the world is eating you, anyway."

"Go out and check in and see if there's anything new and if there is, come get me, and if there isn't, stay the hell out there in the car!"

"Sure. Okay."

After the door had closed gently behind the younger man, Stanger sighed and sat down and felt around in the side pocket of his jacket and found a half cigar and lit the ash end thoroughly and carefully. "Mr. Tom Pike should send that wife off someplace. Or watch her a little more close. She's going to go out some night and meet up with some bug who'll maybe kill her."

"Before she kills herself?"

"Seems like if a man has good luck in one direction, McGee, it runs real bad some other way. When she lost the second kid, something went wrong in her head. I say it would be a blessing if she had made a good job of it when she tried. Mr. McGee, I think it would be a good thing if you stayed right in town for a few days."

"I want to help if I can. I didn't know Penny Woertz very long. But . . . I liked her a lot."

He pulled on the cigar. "Amateur help? Run around in circles and get everything all confused?"

"Let's just say it wouldn't be quite as amateur as the help you're running around with right now, Stanger."

"It like to broke Lew's heart when they picked him off his motor-sickel and give him to me. What you might do, if it wouldn't put you out any, is see if Rick Holton made the trip he said he made. It's unhealthy for me to check up on a man in Holton's position. I think maybe Janice Holton would be easy to talk with, easier for you than me."

Once again I remembered Harry Simmons, and I said, "If she phones you to check on me, confirm the fact that I'm an insurance investigator looking into a death claim on Dr. Sherman."

"Going to her instead of to Holton himself?"

"Just to see if she thinks he's sincere in believing it was murder or if he's been faking it in order to snuggle up to Nurse Woertz."

He whistled softly. "You could lose some hide off your face."

"Depending on how I work up to it."

"If they'd both been in town, both Rick Holton and his wife, and they weren't together, I'd want to make sure I knew where she was at the time that girl got stuck with the shears."

"She capable of it?"

He stood up. "Who knows what anybody will do or won't do, when the moon is right? All I know is that she was Janice Nocera before she married the lawyer, and her folks have always had a habit of taking care of their own problems in their own way."

I remembered the pictures of her and the kids, the ones I had taken out of Holton's wallet. Handsome, lean, dark, with a mop of black hair and more than her share of both nose and mouth, and a jaunty defiance in the way she stared smiling into the lens.

"And I'll be checking you out a little more too," he said, and gave me a small, tired smile and went out.

10 *PAGE ONE* of the Fort Courtney *Sunday Register* bannered LOCAL NURSE SLAIN. They had a sunshiny smiling picture of her that pinched my heart in a sly and painful way.

Very few facts had been furnished by the law—just the way the body had been discovered, the murder weapon, and the estimated time of death. As usual, an arrest was expected momentarily.

It was almost noon on Sunday when I phoned Biddy. She sounded tired and listless. She said Tom had flown up to Atlanta for a business meeting and would be home, he thought, by about midnight. Yes, it was a terrible thing about Penny Woertz. She had always been so obliging and helpful when Maurie had been Dr. Sherman's patient. Such a really marvelous disposition, never snippy or officious.

"Suppose I come out there and see if I can cheer you up, girl?"

"With songs and jokes and parlor tricks? I don't think anything would work today. But . . . come along if you want to."

I pressed the door chime button three times before she finally came to the door and let me in.

"Sorry to keep you standing out here, Trav. I was putting her back to sleep."

She led the way back into the big living room, long-legged in yellow denim shorts with brass buttons on the hip pockets, and a faded blue short-sleeved work shirt. She had piled her long straight blond hair atop her head and anchored it in place with a yellow comb, but casual tendrils escaped, and when she turned and gave me a crooked smile of self-mockery, she brushed some silky strands away from her forehead with her fingertips. "I'm the total mess of the month, Travis. Would you like a drink? Bloody Mary? Gin and tonic? Beer?"

"What are you having?"

"Maybe a Bloody would be therapeutic. Want to come help?"

The big kitchen was bright and cheerful, decorated in blue and white. The windows looked across the back lawn toward the lake.

She got out the ice and ingredients and I made them. She leaned against the countertop, ankles crossed, sipped and said, "If I suddenly fall on my face, don't be alarmed. I did a damfool thing last night after we got her settled down. I had to get my mind off . . . everything and I went out to the boathouse and painted a fool thing I'll probably paint out. It was five before I went to bed and Tom woke me up at eight when he left."

"Can I have a look at it?"

"Well . . . why not? But it isn't anything like what I usually do."

We carried our drinks. There was an outside staircase to the big room over the boathouse, which she had fixed up as a studio. A window air-conditioner was humming. She turned on a second one, then went over and turned on an intercom and turned the volume up until I could hear a slow rhythmic sound I suddenly identified as the deep and somewhat guttural breathing of someone in deep sleep.

She said, "Maurie can't wake up, actually, but I just feel better if I can hear her." The studio had a composite smell of pigments and oils and thinner. The work stacked against the walls and the few that were hung were semi-abstract. Obviously she had taken her themes from nature, from stones, earth, bark, leaves. The colors were powerful. Some of the areas were almost representational.

She waved toward them. "These are the usual me. Kind of old hat. No op and pop. No structures and lumps and walk-throughs."

"But," I said, "one hell of a lot of overpainting and glazes, so you can see down into those colors."

She looked surprised and pleased. "Member of the club?"

"Hell, woman, I even know the trick words that mean absolutely nothing. Like dynamic symmetry."

"Tonal integrity?"

"Sure. Structural perceptions. Compositionally iconoclastic."

She laughed aloud and it was a good laugh. "It's such terrible crap, isn't it? The language of gallery people and critics, and insecure painters. What are *your* words, Professor McGee?"

"Does a painting always look the same or will it change according to the light and how I happen to feel? And after it has been hung for a month, will it disappear so completely the only time I might notice it would be if it fell off the wall?"

She nodded thoughtfully. "So I'll buy that. Anyway . . . I seldom do the figure. But here is my night work."

It was on an easel, a horizontal rectangle, maybe thirty inches by four feet. At dead center was a small clearing, a naked female figure sitting, jackknifed, huddled, arms around her legs, face buried against her knees, blond hair spilling down. Around her was angry jungle, slashes of sharp spears of leaf, vine tangle, visceral roots, hints of black water, fleshy tropic blooms against black-green. It had a flavor of great silence, stillness, waiting.

We studied it and could hear the deep sonorous breathing of the sleeping sister. Biddy coughed, sipped her drink, said, "I think it's too dramatic and sentimental and . . . narrative."

"I say let it sit. You'll know more about it later."

She put her drink down, lifted it off the easel, and placed it against the wall, the back of the canvas toward the room. She backed off. "Where I can't see it, I guess."

She showed me more of her work and then she turned the intercom off and one of the air-conditioners. We walked back to the house. "Another drink and maybe a sandwich?"

"On one condition."

"Such as?"

"Quick drink and simple sandwich and then you go fall into the sack. I am reliable, dependable, conscientious, and so on. If you're needed for anything, I'll wake you up."

"I couldn't let you do——"

"Hot shower, clean sheets, blinds closed, and McGee taking care."

She covered her yawn with the back of her fist. "Bless you, bless you. I'm sold."

After we ate, she led me upstairs and down the carpeted hallway to Maureen's room. Maureen slept on her back in the middle of a double bed. The room was air-conditioned to coolness. She wore a quilted bed jacket. The sheets and pillowcases were blue with a white flower pattern. The blanket was a darker blue. Her face and throat were puffed, red-blotched. There was a mixture of small odors in the silence, calamine and rubbing alcohol and perfume. Flavors of illness and of girl. She wore opaque sleep-glasses in spite of the room being darkened.

Biddy startled me by speaking in a normal conversational tone. "I'm going to keep her asleep until at least six o'clock. Oh, she can't hear us. Not while the Dormed is on."

As she took me over to the bed to show me what she meant, I saw the small electric cord that led from the heavy pair of glasses to a piece of equipment on the bedside stand. It looked like a small ham radio receiver. There were three dials. A tiny orange light winked constantly. She explained that it was an electrosleep device invented in Germany and distributed in England and the United States by one of the medical supply houses. There were electrodes in the headset, covered with a foam plastic, two which rested on the eyelids, and one at the end of each earpiece where they made contact with the mastoid bone behind each ear. She said that you moistened the foam rubber pads with a salt solution and put the headset on the patient. The control unit was a pulse generator that sent an extremely weak electrical impulse—in fact a thousand times weaker than the current a flashlight bulb requires—through the sleep centers in the thalamus and hypothalamus.

"It's perfectly safe," she said. "It's been used on thousands and thousands of patients. You just adjust the strength and the frequency with these two dials. The other is the on and off switch. Dr. Sherman got it for us and trained me in how to use it. You see, he was afraid of the side effects of making her sleep with medication, in her condition, whatever it is. We do have to give her shots when she gets too upset, but this is usually enough."

"What does it feel like?"

"Very . . . odd. No discomfort at all. All I felt was a kind of flickering in my eyes. Not unpleasant, really. I was trying to fight it. I was telling myself that this certainly wouldn't put me to sleep. And then there wasn't the flickering sensation anymore, and kind of . . . a slow warm delicious feeling all over me, like sinking slowly in a hot sudsy perfumed tub. And I was gone! It is marvelous sleep, really. Deep and sweet and refreshing. Once she's asleep, you can take them off and the Dormed sleep will just turn into absolutely natural sleep. Or like now, I'm leaving it on at very low strength, and she will sleep on and on until I take them off. You could parade a brass band through here, and she'd sleep like a baby. It's a marvelous invention. It's a portable unit, with a neat little gray suitcase thing it fits into, with a place for the salt solution and all."

"Is there anything I have to do about it while you sleep?"

"Nothing. Well . . . what I do isn't necessary. I just come in and look at her and see if that little light is going on and off. It hasn't ever stopped or anything. And only once did she ever move her head enough to move the headset out of place."

"But you'd feel better if I did the same thing?"

"I guess so. Yes."

"Off with you, then."

We went into the hall and she pointed out her door. "Just knock until I answer. Don't settle for a mumble.

Get a real answer." She looked at her watch. "And don't let me sleep past five o'clock. Okay?"

"Five o'clock."

"If you get hungry or thirsty or anything———"

"I know where things are. Bug off, Bridget. Sleep tight."

In thirty minutes the house was filled with that special silence of Sunday sleep. Little relays and servo devices made faint tickings and hummings. Refrigerator, deep freeze, air-conditioning, thermostats, electric clocks. Kids water-skied the lake, outboards droning, a faint sound through the closed windows.

Where do you look when you have no idea what you are looking for? An alcove off the living room apparently served as a small home office for Tom Pike. The top of the antique desk was clean. The drawers were locked, and the locks were splendid modern intricate devices, unpickable, except in television drama. On a hallway phone table I found a black and white photograph in a silver frame. Helena, Maureen, and Bridget on the foredeck of the *Likely Lady*. Boat clothes, sweaters for cool sailing. Mick Pearson's girls, all slender, smiling, assured, and with the loving look that could only mean that it had been Mick's eye at the finder, Mick's finger on the shutter release.

So roam the silence and up the padded stairs, long slow steps, two at a time. A closed door at the back of the house, unlocked, opening into a master bedroom. Draperied window-wall facing the lake. One end was sitting room, fireplace, bookshelves. An oversized custom bed dominated the other end. It seemed too sybaritic, a bit out of key with the rest of the house. Two baths, two dressing rooms. His and hers. Sunken dark blue tub in hers, square, with clear glass in the shower-stall arrangement. Strategic mirroring there, as on the walls nearest the oversized bed.

The big bed was neatly made, so on Sunday, at least, Biddy was maid, cook, and housekeeper. Maureen's bath had been cleared of the daily personal things. Winter clothing in her dressing room closets. Bottles of perfume and lotion on her dressing table just a little bit dusty. But he lived here, very neatly. Sport shirts here, dress shirts there. Jackets, slacks on one bar. Suits hanging from another. The shoe-treed shoes on a built-in rack. Silk, cashmere, linen, Irish tweed, English wool, Italian shoes. Labeling from Worth Avenue, New York, St. Thomas, Palm Springs, Montreal. Taste, cost, and quality. Impersonal, remote, correct, and somehow sterile. Apparently no sentiment about an ancient sweater, crumpled old moccasins, baggy elderly slacks, or a gummy old bathrobe. When anything showed enough evident signs of wear, it was eliminated.

I searched for more clues to him. Apparently he did not have anything wrong with him that could not be fixed by an aspirin or an Alka Seltzer. He did not leave random notes to himself in the pockets of his suits and jackets. He did not seem to have a single hobby or a weapon or a book not devoted to economics, law, securities, or real estate.

So I gave up on Tom Pike and walked quietly down the hall and into Maureen's room. The deep breathing was just the same. She had not moved. The little orange light on the face of the control unit of the Dormed went off and on as before. I went to the side of the bed. Her arms rested at her sides, atop the blanket. I cautiously picked her left hand up. It was warm and dry, and complete relaxation gave it a heaviness, like the hand of a fresh corpse. The back of the hand was scratched, and welted with insect bites. I turned the inside of the wrist toward what light there was and, bending close to it, I could make out the white line of scar tissue across the pattern of the blue veins under the sensitive skin. I placed the hand the way it had been and looked down at her. The heavy glasses made her look as if both eyes had been bandaged. I could see the slow, steady beat of a tiny pulse in her throat. Even welted and mottled, dappled with the dry orange-white spots of lotion, she was a cushioned and luxurious and sweetly sensuous animal.

Sweet outcast. All the lovely, wifely tumbling in that outsized bed, mirrored hoyden, romping in sweet excitements with the lean and beloved husband. But then paradise is warped and the image becomes grotesque. Instead of babies, two sudden agonies, and two little bloody wads of tissue expelled too soon from the warm black safety of the womb. Then a world gone strange, like something half dreamed and soon forgotten. Exchange the springy bed for the sacking on the floor of the little storage room at the truck depot where, booze-blind, lamed, and sprung, you are kept at the rough service of the Telaferro brothers. Excuse me, my dear, while I pry around your outcast room looking for answers to questions I haven't thought of. Or one I have: Would you really rather be dead?

But there was nothing. There was a steel cabinet in the bathroom, resting on a bench, securely locked. Medicines, no doubt. There seemed to be nothing left in the bedroom or bath that she could hurt herself with. There was a rattling purr at the end of each exhalation. Her diaphragm rose and fell with the deep breathing of deep sleep.

I was glad to leave her room and leave the sound of breathing. Somehow it was like the coma that precedes death. I went down and found a cold beer, turned on the television set with the volume low, and watched twenty-two very large young men knocking one another down while thousands cheered. I watched and yet did not watch. It was merely a busy pattern of color, motion, and sound.

Blue handles of kitchen shears. Helena climbing naked in the red light of the Exuma sun, rising to teeter on the rail, then find her balance, then dive into the black-gray water of the cove at Shroud Cay and then surface, seal-sleek, hair water-pasted flat to the delicate skull contours. Penny Woertz snuggling against me in the night, her back and shoulders moist with exertion, making little umming sounds of content as her breath was slowing. Biddy sobbing aloud as she trotted into my bathroom, her running a humble, awkward, clumsy, bovine, knock-kneed gait. Memory and digital skills. The bleeders don't jump, and the hangers don't bleed. Twenty thousand to a tall man. Jake saying "Bon voyage." The *Bama Gal* erupting into the sunlight after all the weeks on the murky bottom.

Tom Pike lifting his face from his hands, eyes streaming. Mick thumping the cabin trim with a solid fist as he showed me the honest way the *Likely Lady* had been built. Substantial means more than comfortable and less than impressive. Maurie streaking greasy fingers across the rounded, pneumatic, porcelain-gold of her thigh. Rick Holton flexing and rubbing his wrists after I'd unwound the tight bite of the hanger wire. Blue handles of kitchen shears. Penny's clovery scents. Five dozen silk ties with good labels. Orange light winking. An umber-orange mole, not as big as a dime. Huddled nude in a Gauguin jungle.

The mind is a cauldron and things bubble up and show for a moment, then slip back into the brew. You can't reach down and find anything by touch. You wait for some order, some relationship in the order in which they appear. Then yell Eureka! and believe that it was a process of cold, pure logic.

Finally, on my fourth visit to the electrosleep bedside, it was exactly six o'clock, so I gently removed the headset, put it aside, and turned the Dormed off. I watched her, ready to go awaken Biddy if Maureen woke up. For several minutes she did not move. Then she rolled her head over to one side, made a murmurous sound, then rolled all the way over onto her side, pulled her knees up, put her two hands, palms together, under her cheek, and soon was breathing as deeply as before.

As the room got darker I turned on a low lamp on the other side of the room. I sat in a Boston rocker near the bed, watching the sleeping woman and thinking that this was probably where Biddy sat and watched her, while she thought about the marriage and thought about her own life.

At a little after eight I knocked on Biddy's door. After the second attempt I heard a groggy, querulous mutter. I waited and knocked again and suddenly she pulled the door open. She had a robe around her shoulders and she held it closed with a concealed hand. Her hair was in wild disarray and her face was swollen with sleep.

"What time is it!"

I told her it was a little after eight, that I had un-hooked Maurie from her machine at six, and that she was still sleeping. She yawned and combed her hair back with her free hand. "The poor thing must have been really exhausted. I won't be a minute."

When she was dressed, she sent me downstairs, saying she'd bring Maurie down in a little while. I found the light switches. As I was making a drink the phone rang. It was just one ring. No more. And so I decided Biddy had probably answered it upstairs. As I was carrying my drink into the living room it rang again, and once again it was just one ring.

Soon they came down. Maurie wore a navy blue floor-length robe with long sleeves and white buttons and white trim. She was scratching her shoulder with one hand and the opposite hip with the other, and complaining in a sour little voice. "Just about eaten to pieces. How do they get in with the house all closed up?"

"You'll just make them worse by scratching, dear."

"I can't help it."

"Say hello to Travis, dear."

She stopped at the foot of the stairs and smiled at me, still scratching, and said, "Hello, Travis McGee! How are you? I had a very good nap today."

"Good for you."

"But I itch something awful. Biddy?"

"Yes, honey."

"Is he here?" Her tone and expression were apprehensive.

"Tom went on a trip."

"Can I have peanut butter sandwiches, Biddy, please?"

"But your diet, dear. You're almost up to a hundred and fifty again."

Her tone was wheedling, sympathy-seeking. "But I'm real tall, Biddy. And I'm *starving*. And I had a good nap and I itch something awful!"

"Well . . ."

"Please? *He* isn't here anyway. *He* won't know about it. You know something? Some son of a bitch must have kicked me or something. I'm so sore right——"

"Maureen!"

She stopped, gulped, looked humble. "I didn't mean to."

"Please try to speak nicely, dear."

"You won't tell *him?*"

Biddy took my glass and they went out into the kitchen. In a little while Maureen came walking in very slowly and carefully, carrying my fresh drink. I thanked her and she beamed at me. Somehow she had managed to get a little wad of peanut butter stuck on the end of her nose, possibly from licking the top off the jar. She went back. I heard them talking out there but could not hear the words, just the tone, and it was like a conversation between child and mother.

When they came back in, Maureen pulled a hassock over in front of the television set. Biddy plugged a set of earphones into a jack in the rear of the set and Maureen put them on eagerly and then was lost in the images and the sound, expression rapt, as she ate her sandwiches.

Biddy said, "She loves to watch things Tom can't stand."

"Does she remember running away last night?"

"No. It's all gone now. Slate wiped clean."

"She won't say Tom's name?"

"Sometimes she will. She's so terribly anxious to please him, to have him approve of her. She just gets . . . all tightened up when he's here. Really, he's wonderfully kind and patient with her. But I guess that . . . a child-wife isn't what a man of Tom's intelligence can adjust to."

"If you think of her just as a child, she's a good child."

"Oh, yes. She's happy, or seems happy, and she likes to help, but she forgets how to do things."

"It doesn't seem consistent with suicide attempts, does it?"

She frowned. "No. But it's more complex than that, Travis. There's another kind of child involved, a sly and naughty child. And the times she's tried, she's gotten into the liquor and gotten drunk first. It's almost as if alcohol creates some kind of awareness of self and her condition, removes some block or something. We keep it all locked up, of course, ever since the first time. But the time she locked herself in the bathroom and cut her wrist, I'd forgotten and left a half quart of gin on the countertop with the bottles of mix. I just didn't see it, somehow. And she sneaked it upstairs, I guess. Anyway, the empty bottle was under her bed. Then the time Tom found the noose, we know she got into something, but we don't know what it was or how. Vanilla extract or shaving lotion or something. Maybe even rubbing alcohol. But of course she couldn't remember. It's quite late. Can I fix you something to eat?"

"I think I'll be moving along, Biddy. Thanks."

"I owe you, my friend. I was irritated you let me sleep so long. But I guess you knew better than I how badly I needed it. I was getting ragged around the edges. The very least I can do is feed you."

"No thanks, I . . ."

She straightened, head tilted, listening, and then relaxed. "Sorry. I thought it was that damned phone again. I think something's wrong with the line. For the last two or three months every once in a while it will give one ring or part of a ring and then stop, and there won't be anybody there. Just the dial tone when you pick it up. Did you say you would stay?"

"I'd better not, thanks just the same."

Maureen's good-night was a smile and a bob of the head and a hasty return to the color screen where a vivid-faced girl was leaning over a wire fence amid a throng, cheering a racehorse toward the finish line. The only sound was the insectile buzzing that escaped from Maureen's padded earphones.

As I walked to the car in the drive I heard the clack behind me as Biddy relocked the heavy front door.

11   *SUNDAY DINNER* was finished by the time I got to the motel dining room, but they could provide steak sandwiches. There was one whispering couple on the far side of the room and one lonely fat man slumped at the bar. Both the couple and the fat man were gone when I went to the bar for a nightcap. I sat on the far stool by the wall, where Penny had been sitting when I had first seen her.

Jake, the bartender, wore an odd expression as he approached me. "Evening, sir. Look, if I got you in any kind of jam——"

"I told Stanger he could check it out with you, that I met her right here Friday night."

He looked relieved. "What happened, he mousetrapped me. He came up with this thing about we let them come in and hustle, we could lose the license. And one thing and another, he worked it around to you and that girl, and I thought he had been tipped and I couldn't exactly deny it, so I said sure, they left together, but how could I know they weren't friends or something already. Honest to God, sir, I didn't know it was the same one in the paper this morning until he said so. Then I'm left hanging, wondering if you were some kind of crazy that took her home and . . . there are some very ordinary looking guys who are very weird about hustlers. But I couldn't imagine you doing . . . Anyway, when I saw you come in, I felt better, I don't know why."

"I think maybe some Black Jack on one rock."

"Yes, sir, Mr. McGee." When he served it with a proper flourish, he said, "Jesus, I've felt half sick ever

123

since. And . . . I guess you've got a right to feel a lot sicker than me." The implied question was very clear.

"Jake, we walked out of here and shook hands and sang one small hymn and said good-night."

He flushed. "I'm sorry. It's none of my business. I was just thinking she didn't have the right moves, you know? So what she is doing is trying to get even with a boyfriend who's cheating on her by doing some swinging herself, so she takes you home and the next day she tells him how she got even, and he can't stand it. She's laughing at him. He grabs the first thing and——"

"Stares in horror at what he's done and, sobbing his heart out, dials the cops."

"It's just that you try to figure out what happened."

"I know, Jake. I'm sorry. Everybody plays that particular game. That's because we always want to know why. Not so much how and who and when. But why."

"Can I ask you something? Did you stop in your room before you came in to eat?"

"No. I parked in front. The question implies I've been away from the place. So somebody has been trying to get me."

He looked uneasy. "Well, it's Mr. Holton. He comes in off and on and he's never any trouble. He's a lawyer. He was here about five o'clock looking for you. He had two quick ones and he came back about quarter to six. He'd have some and then go looking for you and come back. I let him have more than I would somebody else, on account of he's local and a good customer and he's always treated me good. Well, he finally got mean and loud and I finally had to cut him off. From the way he walked out . . . maybe a half hour before you came in to eat . . . he could have passed out in his car by now. Or maybe he's still on his feet and waiting for you by your room. He began telling me, toward the end, that he was going to whip your ass. Looking at you, I think maybe it wouldn't be so easy to do, unless he sucker-punched you, which he acted mad enough to do. I thought you might want to keep your eyes open on your way back to the room."

It earned him the change from a five for the one drink.

I decided to walk around to 109 rather than drive, as I had planned. I went the long way around and moved onto the grass and kept out of the lights. I stopped and listened and looked and finally discerned a burly shadow standing near a tall shrub and leaning against the white motel wall. I reconstructed the memory of what he had done with the revolver when he got it back. He had shoved it into his belt on the left side, under his jacket, well over toward his hip, grip toward the middle, where he could reach it easily with his right hand. I squatted and figured out a plausible route and then pulled my shoes off and circled and ducked quickly and silently through two areas of light, and then crawled slowly and carefully on hands and knees into the shelter of the foliage just behind him and to his right. As I neared him I heard his bad case of hiccups, a steady solid rhythmic case, each one a strangled, muffled sound due to his effort to stay quiet enough to ambush me. From then on I made each move on the hiccup, a jerky progress as in the most ancient motion pictures. At last, unheard, I was on my hands and knees right behind him and slightly to his right, just where a large and obedient dog would be. I inched my knees closer and put my weight back and lifted both hands. On the next hiccup I snapped my hands out and grasped his heavy ankles and yanked his legs out from under him, giving enough of a twist so that he would land on his left side. As he landed I scrambled onto him, felt the checkered wooden grip, and yanked the revolver free and rolled across the grass with it and stood up.

He pushed himself slowly to a sitting position, rolled up onto his knees, put his hands on the wall, and slowly stood up. He turned and put his back against the wall and shook his thick head.

"Bassard," he said thickly. "Dirry stud bassard."

"Settle down, Richard. I cured your hiccups."

He grunted and launched himself at me, swinging wildly while he was still too far away to punish anything but the humid night air. I ducked to the side and stuck a leg out and he went down heavily onto his face. And once again, with the painful slowness of a large damaged bug, he got himself up onto his feet, using a small tree as a prop.

He turned around and located me. "Wages of sin," he mumbled. "My lousy ideas. Memories. All worked up. I read it, you bassard. Made her sore at me, you tricky bassard. Kept her here and soft-talked her an' pronged her, you lousy smartass."

And with a big effortful grunt he came at me again. As he got to me I dropped, squatting, fingertips on the grass. As he tripped and spilled over my back I came up swiftly and he did a half turn in the air and landed flat on his back. He stared at the sky, breathing hard. He coughed in a shallow gagging way.

"Sick," he said. "Gonna be sick."

I helped him roll over. He got onto hands and knees, crawled slowly and then stopped, braced, vomited in dreadful spasms.

"So sick," he moaned.

I got him onto his feet, and with one arm across my shoulders, my arm around his clumsy waist, I got him into the room. Once in the bathroom he was sick again. I held his stupid head, then sat him on the closed lid of the toilet and swabbed the mud and vomit off him with a wet towel. He swayed, eyes half closed. "Loved that girl. Loved her. Lousy thing. I can't stand it." He opened his eyes and looked up at me. "Honest to God, I can't *stand* it!"

"We better get you home, Rick."

He thought that over and nodded. "Best thing. Bad shape. Who cares anymore? Janice doesn't give a shit. Penny the only one cared. Gone. Some sumbitch killed her. Some crazy. Know it wasn't you. Wish it had been you. Fix you good."

"Where do you live, Holton?"

"Twenny-eight twenny, Forest Drive."

I got his car keys from him and the description of his car. and went around to the front and drove it back to the room. I went in and brought him out and helped him

126

into the red convertible, and got behind the wheel. He muttered directions.

When I had to stop for a light, he said, "Sorry I had to smack you around, McGee. You know how it is."

"Sure. I know how it is."

"Get it out of my system. Hated you. Shouldna layed my girl, my wonnerful freckly nurse-girl. But man to man, shit, if she wanned it, she wanned it, and why should you turn it down, huh? Great kid. Greatest piece of ass in the worl'. You're a nice guy, McGee. I doan wanna like you, you sumbitch, but I do. Hear that? I do."

I had to shake him awake to get more directions. When I turned into the asphalt drive, he was asleep again. It was a cement-block house, one story, white with pink trim, a scraggly yard, house lights on, a gray Plymouth station wagon in one half of the carport.

I turned away from the carport and stopped near the front door. The outside light went on and the door opened and a lean, dark-haired woman looked out through the screen door.

I got out and came around the car. "Mrs. Holton?"

She came out and looked at her sleeping husband. She wore dark orange slacks, a yellow blouse, and she had a bright red kerchief tied around her slender, dusky throat. Gypsy colors.

"Unfortunately, yes. Who are you?"

"My name is McGee."

I had the feeling that it startled her slightly and I could think of no reason why.

"I'll help you get him in."

She reached and took hold of his jaw and turned his head slightly. She raised the other hand, held it poised for a moment, and then whip-cracked her lean palm across his face twice, very quickly and with great force. It brought him struggling up out of the mists, gasping and looking around.

"Hey! Hey there, Janice doll! This here is Travis McGee, my ver' good buddy. He's going to come in and have a li'l drink. We're all going to have a drink. Right?"

As he struggled to get out of the car I took him by the

arm and levered him out. We supported him, one on either side, and after we got him through the door, she gave directions in a voice strained with effort. She turned on the light of what was obviously a guest room. We sat him on the bed and he sat with his eyes closed, mumbling something we could not understand. When he started to topple over backward, I grabbed him by the shoulders and turned him so that he landed on the pillow. She knelt and unlaced his shoes and pulled them off. I picked his legs up and swung them onto the bed. She loosened his belt. When he gave a long, ragged snore, she looked at me and made a mouth of distaste. I followed her as she walked out. She turned the lights off and closed the guest room door.

I followed her into the living room. She turned, standing more erect, and said, "Thanks for your help. This doesn't happen often. That is not an excuse or an apology. Just a statement of fact."

I worked the revolver out of my trouser pocket and gave it to her. "If it happens at all, he shouldn't run around with this thing."

"I'll put it away and tell him he must have lost it. Thank you again."

"May I use your phone to call a cab?"

She stepped to the front window and looked across the street. "My friend is still up. She'll come over and listen for the kids while I take you in."

"I don't want to trouble you, Mrs. Holton."

"I'd like some air. And you've been to a lot of trouble."

She went to the phone in the foyer and dialed, then had a brief low-voiced conversation. We went out and got into the car. She asked me to wait for a moment. When the door opened in the house across the street and a woman came out and started across, she told me to start up. She waved and called, "Thanks a lot, Meg."

"Perfectly okay, Jan. Take your time, honey."

Janice Holton untied the kerchief and put it over her dark hair and fastened it under her chin. From her manner it was going to be a swift and silent trip.

"I guess what racked your husband up was having some person or persons unknown kill his girl friend."

Out of the corner of my eye I could see that she had turned quickly and was staring at me. "I couldn't care less what . . . racks him up, Mr. McGee. I feel sorry for the girl. As a matter of fact I regret never having had a chance to thank her."

"Thank her?"

"For letting me out of bondage, let's say."

"Unlocked your chains?"

"You're not *really* interested in the sordid details of my happy marriage, are you?"

"It just seemed like a strange way to put it."

"I find myself saying some very strange things lately."

"Right at the bottom of the certificate, Mrs. Holton, there's the fine print that says you live happily ever after."

I suppose that you could call it role-playing, maybe in the same sense that the psychologists who use group therapy use the term. Or you could call it, as Meyer does, my con-man instinct. Okay, call it a trace of chameleon blood. But the best way to relate to people is to fake their same hang-ups, and when you relate to people, you open them up. So I lie a little. Instant empathy. To crack her facade I had to make out like an ex-married, so I spoke with the maximum male bitterness.

"You sound like you had the tour too, Mr. McGee?"

"Ride the rolly-coaster. Find your way through the fun house. Float through the tunnel of love. Sure. I had a carnival trip, Mrs. Holton. But the setup tends to do a pretty good job of gutting the husband. I believed the fine print. But she turned out to be a bum. So I end up paying her so much a month so she can keep on being a bum. So I'm a little bitter about the way the system works."

"For a girl married to a lawyer, it doesn't exactly work out that way. I believed the fine print too, Mr. McGee. I considered it an honorable estate, an honorable contract. And, by God, I worked at it. I knew after the first year it wasn't going to be the way . . . you hope it will be. So I tried to understand him. I think Rick feels

129

that he is . . . unworthy of being loved. So he can't ever believe anyone loves him, really. So he has a thousand mean snide little ways of spoiling things. He loves the boys, I know. But any kind of . . . family ceremony, something for warmth and love and fun—oh, can he ever clobber everybody. Tears and shambles and nastiness, and everything you try to plan . . . birthdays, anniversaries, he has such a cruel way of making things turn sour. But I was stuck with it. I *thought* I was stuck with it. You know, if you're a grownup, you add up the ledger. A successful man, a faithful man, not a drunk or a chaser. But then . . . the sneaky business with Miss Woertz changed the ledger."

"And let you out of bondage?"

"Kept me from agonizing over . . . making the marriage work. Sort of . . . canceled all my vows."

"Did you find out about her quite recently?"

"Oh, no. I found out practically as soon as it started. He started that crusade about finding out what *really* happened to Doctor Sherman. You know about that?"

"He told me about it. Was that just to help cover up the affair with the nurse?"

"Oh, no. He's sincere about it. But when it threw them together, he sure put in a lot of hours in so-called investigation. Somebody called me up and told me about it, in a very nasty whisper. I couldn't tell if it was a man or a woman. I didn't want to believe it, but I knew it was true, somehow. Then I saw all the little clues." She gave a mirthless laugh. "The most convincing one was the way he became so much sweeter to me and the boys."

"So are you going to divorce him?"

"I don't know. I don't love him anymore. But I haven't got a dime of my own. And I just don't know if I could get enough alimony and child support if I bring suit."

I turned in at the Wahini Lodge and parked away from the entrance lights, over near the architectured waterfall and the flaming gas torches.

"You're too darned easy to talk to, Mr. McGee."

"Maybe because we just wear the same kind of battle

scars. I had to get out of my setup just as fast as I could."

"Any kids?"

"No. She kept saying later, later."

"It makes a difference, you know. It's a pretty nice house, nice neighborhood, good school. There's medicine and dental work and shoes and savings accounts. It's an arrangement, right now. I do my part of the job of keeping the house going. But I won't ever let him touch me again. It would turn my stomach. He can find himself another playmate. I don't give a damn. And we don't have to socialize, particularly."

"Can you live the rest of your life like that?"

"No! I don't intend to. But I have a friend who says that we . . . says that I had better just sort of go along with it as is for the time being. He is a dear, gentle, wise, understanding man. We've been very close ever since I found out about Rick. His marriage is as hopeless as mine but in a different way. I'm not having an affair with him. We see each other and we have to be terribly careful and discreet because I wouldn't want to give Rick any kind of ammunition he could use if and when I try to get a divorce. We don't even have any kind of special understanding about the future. It's just that we both . . . have to endure things the way they are for a while."

"Then, I guess the family outing Rick told me about, the trip to Vero Beach yesterday, must have been pretty grim."

She had turned in the bucket seat to face me, her back against the door, legs pulled up. "Was it ever! Like that old thing about what a tangled web we weave. I didn't have any idea he'd want to spend any part of Saturday with his wife and children. I'd told him I was going to drive over and see June and leave the boys off with my best friend on the way. She lives twenty miles east of here. Her boys are just the same ages, practically. I'd fixed it with June to cover for me in case Rick phoned me there for some stupid reason. And I was going to drive to . . . another place close by and spend the day with my friend. But out of the clear blue Rick decided to come too! I didn't see how in the world he could have found out anything. But he was so ugly I decided he must have had a little lovers' spat with his girl friend. When I left the boys at my friend's place, I had a chance to phone my sister and warn her, while Rick was out in the car, but I couldn't get hold of my friend to call the date off. Rick was in a foul mood all day." Again the mirthless laugh. "What a lousy soap-opera!"

I could not leave at that moment because it would give her the aftertaste of having been pumped, of having talked too much. So I invented a gaudy confrontation between me and the boyfriend of a wife I never had. I spun it out and when I was through, she said, "It's wretched that people have to be put through things like that just because a wife or a husband is too immature to . . . to be plain everyday faithful. Do you ever run into her? Is she still in Lauderdale?"

"No. She moved away. I have no idea where she is now. I send the money to a Jacksonville bank. If I want to find out where she is, all I'd have to do is stop making payments. Look, do you want to come in for a nightcap?"

"Golly, where did the time go? Meg is a good neighbor, but I don't want to take too much advantage. Mr. McGee?"

"Travis."

"Travis, I didn't mean to sound like a long cry of woe, but it's made me feel better somehow, comparing bruises with somebody."

"Good luck to you, Janice."

"And to you too." I had gotten out. She clambered over to the driver's seat, snapped the belt on, and pulled it back to her slender dimension. "Night, now," she called, and backed out and swung around and out onto the divided highway, upshifting skillfully as she went.

I projected a telepathic suggestion to her unknown friend. Grab that one, man. Richard Haslo Holton was too blind to see what he had. She's got fire, integrity, courage, restraint. And she is a very handsome lively creature. Grab her if you can, because even though there are quite a few of them around, hardly any of them ever get loose.

No messages, no blinking red light on the phone. The maid had turned the bed down. Small hours of the morning. When I put the light out, a freckled ghost roamed the room. I said good night to her. "We'll find out, Miss Penny," I told her. "Somehow we'll find out and you can stop this wandering around motel rooms at night."

12

I HAD A hell of a night. Hundreds of dreams and from what little I could remember of them, they all had the same pattern. Either somebody was running after me to tell me something important and I could not stop running from them or understand why I couldn't stop, or I was running headlong after somebody else who was slowly moving away no matter how hard I ran, moving away in a car or a bus or a train. Sometimes it was Penny, sometimes Helena. I woke with an aching tiredness of bone, a mouth like a cricket cage, grainy eyes, and skin that seemed to have stretched so that it was too big for me and wanted to hang in tired, draped folds.

After endless toothbrushing and a shower that did no good I phoned the Fort Courtney Police Department and left word for Stanger that I had called.

My breakfast had just been served when he settled into the chair across the table from me and told the waitress to bring him some hot tea.

"You look poorly, McGee."

"Slept poorly, feel poorly."

"That's my story, every morning of my life. You get yourself a swing and a miss with Janice Holton?"

"They took the trip to Vero Beach together. And you could confirm it by finding out who she left the kids with, an old friend twenty miles from here, in the direction of Vero Beach. And Holton is serious about believing somebody killed Doctor Sherman. The Holton marriage has bombed out. She knew about the nurse. She's going through the motions for the sake of the kids until she can find some way to land on her feet. And I think she will, sooner or later."

He blew on his hot tea and took a sip and stared at me and shook his head slowly. "Now, aren't you the one! By God, she cozies up pretty good to some damn insurance investigator."

"I didn't have to use it. You gave me a better approach."

He aimed his little dusty brown eyes at me. "I did?"

I put my fork down and smiled across at him. "Yes, indeed you did, you silly half-ass fumbling excuse for a cop."

"Now, don't you get your——"

"You *knew* Holton was screwing her, Stanger. You *knew* that the note you found made it clear to anybody who can read simple words that she and I had something going for us. So what did you think Holton would do after he saw the note or a copy of it? Chuckle and say, Well, well, well, how about that? You probably know even that the ex-assistant state attorney carries a gun. But did you make any effort to tip me so I wouldn't get shot? Not good old Stanger, the lawman. Thanks, Stanger. Anytime I can do any little thing for you, look me up."

"Now, wait a minute, goddamn it! What makes you think he read the note?"

"Some direct quotes sort of stuck in his mind. He recited them."

He drank more of his tea. He found a third of a cigar on his person, thumbnailed the remains of the ash off it, held a match to it.

"He try to use the gun?"

"He didn't get the chance. I was tipped. I found him staked out and waiting, so I sneaked up on him and took it away. I don't know whether he was going to use it or not. Give him the benefit of the argument and say he wouldn't. He knew I hadn't put the shears in her neck. He knew I was cleared of that. Let's say he resented the rest of it, though. Incidentally, I gave the gun to his wife and she seemed to think it would be a good idea to tuck it away. Maybe there shouldn't be a gun in that happy household."

"So you took the gun away from him and?"

"I yanked his legs out from under him to get it. Then I had to trip him onto his face, and then I had to block him and somersault him onto his back. The last one took it out of him. He'd been drinking. It made him sick. I drove him home in his car. We became dear old buddies somehow. Drunks are changeable. He was passed out by the time I got him home. I helped get him to bed. She had a neighbor watch the kids while she drove me back. She's known about the affair since it started. He sleeps in the guest room. I like her."

He held up the hand with the cigar in it. He held it up, palm toward me, and said, "I swear on the grave of my dear old mother who loved me so much she didn't even mind me becoming a cop that I just can't figure out how the hell Rick Holton got hold of that note. Look, as an ex-prosecutor he's got a little leverage. Not too much but some. I think he would know where to look, who to bug, *if* he knew there *was* a note. But *how* could he know? Look, now. The Woertz woman knew because she wrote it. I knew because I found it. Jackass Nudenbarger knew because he was with me when I found it. You knew because I read it to you. And down at the store, two men. Tad Unger did the lab work and made photocopies. Bill Samuels acts as a sort of clerk-coordinator. He sets up the file and keeps it neat and tidy and complete to turn over to the state attorney if need be. He protects the chain of evidence, makes the autopsy request, and so on."

Had I thought for a moment, I would have realized there had to be an autopsy. They would want to know if a murdered unmarried woman was pregnant, if there was any sign of a blow that had not left any surface bruises, contusions, or abrasions, if she was under the influence of alcohol or narcotics, if she had been raped or had had intercourse recently enough to be able to type the semen. And the painstaking, inch-by-inch examination of the epidermis would disclose any scratches, puncture wounds, minor bruises, bite marks. And there would be a chemical analysis of the contents of the stomach, as death stops the normal digestive processes.

"You all right?" Stanger asked softly.

"I'm just perfect. When did they do the autopsy?"

"They must have been starting on it when I was talking to you in your room Saturday night."

"And those two men, Unger and . . ."

"Samuels."

"They wouldn't volunteer any information about the note?"

"Hell no. The days of volunteering any information to anybody about anything are long gone. Order yourself more coffee. Don't go away. Be right back."

It took him ten minutes. He sat down wearily, mopped his forehead on a soiled handkerchief. "Well, Bill Samuels was off yesterday and Holton came in about eleven in the morning. A clerk named Foster was on duty and Holton told him that the state attorney, Ben Gaffner, had asked him to take a look at the note that had been found in the Woertz girl's apartment. So Foster unlocked the file and let him read the photocopy. It still doesn't answer the question."

"Can I give it a try?"

"Go ahead."

"Would Holton know you were on the case?"

"Sure."

"Would he know he wouldn't be able to get much out of you?"

"He'd know that."

"Would he know who's working with you?"

"I guess he'd know . . . Oh, goddamn that motorsickel idiot!"

He told me that as long as I'd had the grief of it, I might as well have the pleasure of seeing the chewing process. I signed the check for my breakfast and his tea and followed him out.

The car was parked in the shade. Nudenbarger, now in a sport shirt with green and white vertical stripes, was leaning against it smiling and talking to a pair of brown hefty little teen-age girls in shorts. He saw us coming and said something. The kids turned and looked at us, then walked slowly away, looking back from time to time.

"All set?" he asked, opening the car door.

Stanger kicked it shut. "Maybe on the side you could rent that mouth. People could store stuff in it. Bicycles, broken rocking chairs, footlockers. Nice little income on the side."

"Now just a minute, Al, I——"

"Shut up. Close that big empty stupid cave fastened to the front of your stupid face, Nudenbarger. Stop holding the car up. I just want to know how stupid you are. Every day you become the new world's champion stupid. How did you get mousetrapped into talking about the note the nurse left?"

"Mousetrapped? I wasn't mousetrapped."

"But you talked about it, didn't you?"

"Well . . . as a mattter of fact——"

"After I told you you had never heard of any note?"

"But this was different, Al."

"He just walked up and asked you what we found in the apartment?"

"No. What he said was that he was upset about her being killed. He was out to the place real early yesterday. I'd just got up and I was walking around calling the dog. He said he and his wife were very fond of her and grateful to her. He said he didn't want to get out of line or step on any toes, but he wondered if maybe outside investigators ought to be brought in, and he thought he might be able to arrange it. Al, I know how you feel about anything like that, so I told him it looked like we could make it. He asked if we had much of anything to go on, and I said we had that note and told him what I could remember of it and said that the fellow she wrote it to, meaning you, McGee, had checked out okay."

"What kept you from falling down laughing?"

"About what, Al?"

"That line about him and his wife being fond of the little nurse. And grateful to her? Jesus!"

"What's wrong with that?"

"Why in the world would Janice Holton be grateful to Penny Woertz?"

"Who said anything about Janice Holton?"

"Didn't you say Holton told you that——"

"Holton! It was Mr. Tom Pike that stopped at the place. I haven't said one damn word to Mr. Holton. Mr. Tom Pike only had a couple of minutes. He was on his way to the airport and he was taking the shortcut, the back road past my place, and saw me and stopped because, like he said, he was upset about the girl getting killed. Now you agree it was different? Do you?"

The anger sagged out of Stanger. "Okay. It was different. He's the kind of guy who'd want to help any way he can. And the nurse helped take care of Mrs. Pike. Now, dammit, Lew, did you say one word to anybody else about any note?"

"Never did. Not once. And I won't, Al."

"You shouldn't have told Pike either."

Stanger turned to me. "Back where we started. Look, I'll get it out of Holton and if I think you ought to know, I'll let you know, McGee."

I motioned to him and took him out of earshot of Nudenbarger. "Any more little errands on the side, as long as I'm stuck here?"

He scowled, spat, scuffed his foot. "I've got men ringing every doorbell in the whole area around that Ridge Lane place. Somebody had to arrive and kill her and leave in broad daylight. Somebody had to see something on Saturday afternoon. I've got men going through the office files of Doc Sherman that went into storage when he died, and the files that were taken over by the doctor who took over Sherman's practice, Doctor John Wayne. Hell of a name, eh? Little fat fellow. Sherman treated some crazies when he was researching barbiturate addiction. So we don't want to rule out the chance of an ex-patient going after the office nurse. She'd been working as a special-duty nurse, so I got hold of the list of patients she took care of ever since the doctor died, and we're going through those. On top of that I've got a good man digging into her private life, every damned thing he can find, the ex-husband, previous boyfriends. Nothing was stolen from the apartment. She lived alone. Those are good solid front doors and good locks on the kitchen doors. I think she would have to know somebody to let them in. No sign of forcible entry. From the condition of the bed, she was sleeping and got up and put the robe on and let somebody in. No makeup. A man or woman could have shoved those shears into her throat. We've got a blood pattern, a spatter pattern. Whoever did it could have gotten some on them from the knees down. To reconstruct it, she put both hands to her throat, staggered back, fell to her knees, then rolled over onto her back. She hadn't been sexually molested. There were indications she'd had intercourse within from four to six hours from the time of death. She wasn't pregnant. She was going to start her period in about three days. She had a slightly sprained ankle, based on some edema and discoloration. There was a small contusion just above the hairline at the center of her forehead and a contusion on her right knee, but these three injuries had occurred a considerable time before death. We're processing a court order to get into her checking account records and her safety deposit box. Now if you can come up with something I just haven't happened to think of, McGee . . ."

It was a challenge, of course. And I was supposed to be overwhelmed by the diligence and thoroughness of the law.

"What about delivery and service people? Dry cleaners, laundry, TV repairs, phone, plumber, electrician? What about the apartment superintendent, if any?"

He sighed heavily. He was upwind of me and even outdoors he had breath like a cannibal bat. "Son of a gun.

Would you believe me if I told you that was all in the works, but I just forgot to mention it?"

"I'd believe you, Stanger. I think you might be pretty good at your job."

"I'll write that in my diary tonight."

"What about the nurses' day room at the hospital? She'd probably have a locker there. There might be some personal stuff in it."

He sighed again and took out his blue notebook and wrote it down. "One for you."

"Maybe there's another one too. If there is, can I check it out? I have . . . a personal interest in this, you know."

"If there's another one, you can check it out."

"I don't think a registered nurse would be doing the billing and the bookkeeping and keeping the appointment book. So there probably had to be another girl working for Sherman, part time or full time."

He squinted at the bright sky. He nodded. "And she was on vacation when he killed himself. Just now remembered. Okay, go ahead, dammit. Can't recall her name. But Doctor Wayne's office girl would know. Just don't try to carry the ball if you come up with anything. Report to me first."

"And you tell me what you find out from Holton."

"Deal."

He trudged toward the waiting car. I went back inside and used a pay phone in the lobby to call Dr. Wayne's office. The answering service told me they opened the office at noon on Mondays.

I went back to 109. The cart was outside the door, the maid just finishing up. She was a brawny, handsome black woman. Her skin tone was a flawless coppery brown, and across the cheekbones she looked as if she had an admixture of Indian blood.

"Be through here in a minute," she said.

"Take your time."

She was making up the bed. I sat on the straight chair by the desk module that was part of the long formica countertop. I found the phone number for D. Wintin

Hardahee and as I wrote it down I saw the maid out of the corner of my eye and for a moment thought she was dancing. When I turned and looked at her, I saw that she was swaying, feet planted, chin on her chest, eyes closed. She lifted her head and gave me a distant smile and said, "Feeling kind of . . . kind of . . ." Then she closed her eyes and toppled forward. Her head and shoulders landed facedown on the bed and she slipped and bounded loosely off and landed on the floor, rolling onto her back.

Suddenly I knew what must have happened. I went to the closet alcove and bent and picked the doctored bottle of gin out of the corner where I had put it and, stupidly, forgotten it. There were a couple of fresh drops of colorless liquid on the outside of the bottle, on the shoulder of it. Any moisture would have long since dried up in the dehumidifying effect of the air conditioning. I licked a drop off with my tongue tip. Plain water. So she had taken a nice little morning pickup out of the bottle and replaced it with tap water.

I went to her and knelt beside her. Her pulse was strong and good, and she was breathing deeply and regularly. She wore a pale blue uniform trimmed with white. Over the blouse pocket was embroidered, in red, "Cathy."

After weighing pros and cons and cursing my idiocy for leaving the gin where somebody might find it, I went looking for another maid. There was a cart on the long balcony overhead, in front of an open door to one of the second-floor units. I went up the iron stairs and rapped on the open door and went in. The maid came out of the bathroom. She was younger than Cathy, small and lean, with matte skin the shade of a cup of coffee, double on the cream. She wore orange lipstick, had two white streaks bleached into her dark hair, and a projection of astonishingly large breasts. Her embroidery said "Lorette."

"Sir, I just now started in here. I can come back if——"

"It isn't my room. Are you a friend of Cathy's?"

"You looking for her, great big strong girl, she's working the downstairs wing right under here, mister."

141

"I know where she is. I asked you if you're a friend of hers."

"Why you asking me, mister?"

"She might need a friend to do her a favor."

"She and me, we get along pretty good."

"Would you come down to Room One-O-nine?"

She looked very skeptical. "What she wants to do and what I want are a couple of different things, mister. I do maid work, period. I don't hold it against her, but she ought to know by now if she wants a girl for anything else, she can go call that fat Annabelle or that crazy kid they got working in the kitchen."

"I got back to my room a couple of minutes ago, Lorette. Your friend Cathy tapped one of my bottles. She thought it was gin. It was sleeping medicine. She's down there passed out. Now, if you don't give a damn, say so."

Her eyes were round and wide. "Cold stone passed out? You go on down, please, and I'll come right along quick."

Ten seconds after I was back in the room, she pushed the door open and stood on the threshold, staring in at Cathy.

"It's like you said?" she asked. "You didn't mess with her any kind of way, did you?"

"There's the bottle over there. Go take a slug and in a little while you can lie down right beside her."

She made up her mind and pulled the door almost closed as she came in. She dropped to her knees and laid her ear against Cathy's chest. Then she shook her and slapped her. Cathy's sleeping head lolled and Cathy made a little whine of irritation and complaint.

"Can you cover for her?" I asked.

She sat back on her heels and nibbled a thumb knuckle. "Best thing is get Jase to bring a laundry cart and he'p load her in and put a couple sheets over her and put her in an empty." She stared suspiciously up at me. "That's no kind of poison, is it? She'll come out of it okay?"

"In two to three hours, probably."

She stood up and stared at me, head tilted. "How come you don't just call the desk?"

"Would they fire her?"

"They sure to hell would."

"Lorette, if I'd had that bottle locked up in my suitcase and she'd gone digging around in there and tapped it, then I might have called the desk. Maybe I would have called anyway if she'd been giving me sloppy service since I've been here. But she's kept this place bright as a button, and I plain forgot that bottle and left it on the closet floor over there where any maid would find it. So I share the blame."

"And maybe you don't want to have to tell a lot of folks how come you keep your sleeping medicine in with the gin?"

"I think you're a nice bright girl and you can cover for her without any trouble at all."

"Because it's slack right now I can do hers and mine both, what rooms we got left. But one more thing. If you turned her in, could she rightly say that you've been messing with her some?"

"No. She couldn't say that."

"Then, I'll be back in just a little while."

It was five minutes before she came back. She held the door open for a tall young boy with enormous shoulders, who pushed a laundry hamper on wheels into the room. He parked it beside Cathy and picked her up easily and lowered her into it. Lorette covered her with a couple of rumpled sheets and said, "Now Annabelle will be waiting right there in Two eighty-eight, Jase. You just put Cathy on the bed there and let Annabelle tend to her, hear?"

"Yump," said Jase, and wheeled her out.

"Finish up fixing your bed for you, mister."

"Thanks."

As she was finishing she giggled. She had a lot of lovely white teeth. She shook her head. "That ol' girl is sure going to wonder what in the world happened to her."

"Explain the situation, will you?"

"Surely. If you're not checking out, she'll be coming by to say thank you tomorrow, I expect." She paused at the door, fists in the pockets of her uniform skirt. "It's important Cathy shouldn't get fired, mister. She needs the job. She lives with her old mother, and that old woman is mean as a snake. All crippled up with arthritis. She about drove Cathy's man away, I guess. There's three little kids, and Cathy could manage all right on the job money, but she'll see a dress and keep thinking about it until she just has to have it, no matter what, and she'll put it on layaway, and then she'll have to use the money for other things at home, and she'll be afraid she'll lose the dress and what she paid on it, and then, well, she'll take chances she wouldn't otherwise and do things she wouldn't otherwise. She's older than me but lots of ways she's like a kid. This place does a lot of commercial trade, and what she does, when you unlock a number and it's a single in there, he's maybe just waking up or he's getting dressed, she gives a big smile and says something like good morning, sir, sure sorry if I disturbed you. And he looks her over and says, Honey, you come on right in here, and, well, she does. Then it's ten dollars or twenty to keep from losing the dress, but she's going to get caught someday and lose this good job. The reason I'm telling you all this is on account of from what I said about her messing around, I didn't want you thinking she was nothing but a hustler. It's only sometimes with her, and even if I wouldn't go down that road, it doesn't mean she isn't no friend of mine. She's my friend. She used to let me hold her first baby. I was ten years old and she was fifteen. And . . . thanks for coming and telling one of us."

She left and I screwed the bottle cap tight and put the doctored—and watered—gin in my carry-on suitcase, wondering all the while if it wouldn't be a sounder idea to pour it out.

D. Wintin Hardahee was with a client. I left the motel number and room number. He called back ten minutes later, at eleven o'clock.

"I was wondering if maybe I could scrounge a little more information from you, Mr. Hardahee."

"I am very sorry, Mr. McGee, but my work load is very heavy." The soft voice had a flat and dead sound.

"Maybe we could have a chat after you get through work."

"I am not taking on any new clients at this time."

"Is something the matter? Is something wrong?"

"Sorry I can't be more cooperative. Good-bye, Mr. McGee." Click.

I paced around, cursing. This nice orderly prosperous community was getting on my nerves. A big ball of tangled string. But when you found a loose end and pulled, all you got was a batch of loose ends. It seemed like at least a month ago that I had thought to check out Helena's estate arrangements. I thought maybe Hardahee could work it through his New York classmate. But Hardahee wasn't going to work out anything for me. So what could turn him off so quickly and so completely? Lies? Fear?

I stretched out on the bed and let the confusing cauldron bubble away, giving me glimpses of Penny, Janice, Biddy, Maureen, Tom Pike, Rick, Stanger, Tom Pike, Helena, Hardahee, Nudenbarger, Tom Pike.

Pike was getting pretty damned ubiquitous. And little bits of conversation kept coming back. I heard parts of the night talk with Janice Holton and something bothered me and I went back over it and found what bothered me, then slowly sat up.

She had asked about my imaginary wife. "Do you ever run into her? Is she still in Lauderdale?"

Review. I had not said one damned word about Lauderdale. Holton had checked the registration. So he knew. But was there any reason for him to have said word one about it to his wife? "Look, darling, my girl friend wanted to stay in the motel room with some jerk from Lauderdale named McGee."

Not likely.

Backtrack. A little look of surprise at hearing my name. Surprise to find me with her husband.

Possibility: Friend of Biddy's. Had met her in supermarket or somewhere. Biddy spoke of an old friend named McGee from Lauderdale.

Or: In the process of checking me out Saturday evening, and checking Holton out, Stanger made some mention of me to Janice Holton. "Do you know, or do you know if your husband knows, anybody named Travis McGee from Fort Lauderdale?"

Possible, but I didn't like the fit. They were like limericks that do not quite scan, that have one syllable too much or one missing. My brain was a pudding. I walked across to a shopping plaza, bought some swim pants in a chain store, came back and put them on and padded out to the big motel pool. There was a separate wading pool full of three- and four-year-olds, shrieking, choking, throwing rubber animals, and belting each other under the casually benign stare of four well-greased young mothers. So I dived and did some slow lengths of the main pool and then gradually let it out, reaching farther, changing the kick beat, stretching and punishing the long muscles of arms, shoulders, back, thighs, and belly, sucking air and blowing out the little layers of sedentary staleness in the bottoms of my lungs. I held it just below that pace at which I begin to get too much side roll and begin to thrash and slap, and then brutalized myself by saying, Just one more. And one more. And one more. Finally I lumbered out, totally whipped, heart way up there close to a hundred and a half, lungs straining, arms and legs weak as canvas tubes full of old wet feathers. I dried my face on the bath towel I'd brought from the room and then stretched out on it to let the sunshine do the rest.

Meyer calls it my "instant I.Q." In a sense it is. You oxygenate the blood to the maximum and you stimulate the heart into pumping it around at a breakneck pace. That enriched blood goes churning through the brain at the same time that it is nourishing the overworked muscle tissues. Sometimes it even works.

But I put my fat, newly enriched, humming head to work on the Janice-Lauderdale problem, and its final report was, "Damned if I know, fella."

So I went back to 109 and before I dressed, I tried the

office of the fat little John Wayne, M.D., got hold of a cheery, cooperative lady who told me that Dr. Stewart Sherman's receptionist and bookkeeper was Miss Helen Boughmer, and she did not know if she was working or not, but I could reach her through the phone listed for Mrs. Robert M. Boughmer. She asked me to wait a moment and gave me the number to write down.

Mrs. Robert M. Boughmer was very firm about things. "I'm sorry, but I couldn't possibly call my daughter to the phone. She is not well today. She is in bed. Does she know you? What is this all about?"

"I'd like a chance to ask her some questions about an insurance matter, Mrs. Boughmer."

"I can definitely say that she is not interested in buying any insurance and neither am I. Good-day."

"Wait!" I missed her and had to call again. "Mrs. Boughmer, I am an insurance investigator. I am investigating a policy claim."

"But we haven't had any accidents with the car. Not for years."

"It's some information on a death claim."

"Oh?"

"On Doctor Sherman. Just a few routine questions, ma'am."

"Well . . . if you'll promise not to tire Helen, I think you might be able to talk to her at about four o'clock, if you'll come here to the house." I said I would. It was at 90 Rose Street, and she told me how to find it. "It's a little white frame house with yellow trim, on the right, on the second corner, with two big live oak trees in the front yard."

After I hung up, I phoned the Pike place and Biddy answered.

"Well, hello!" she said. "Yes, Maurie is doing just fine, thank you. We were just about to have a swim before lunch."

"I wondered if I could come out and talk to you about something after lunch."

"Why not? What time is it? Why don't you make it

about two thirty or quarter to three? She'll be having her nap then. Will that be okay?"

I said it was just fine. I dressed and had lunch at the motel and then went strolling through the rear areas looking for Lorette. There was a service alley behind the kitchen. When I walked along it, past a neat row of garbage cans, I came to an open door to a linen storage room. I looked in and saw Lorette, still in uniform, sitting on a table laughing and talking and swinging her legs. There were two older black women in there, not in uniform. The rubber-tired maid carts were aligned against the wall near a battered Coke machine and a row of green metal lockers.

She saw me and the talk and laughter stopped. She slid off the old wooden table and came and stood in the doorway, her face impassive, her eyes down-slanted. "You want something, sir?"

"To ask you something," I said, and walked on to a place where the roof overhang shaded a portion of the alley and a flame vine was curling up a post that supported the overhang. She had not followed me. I looked back and she shrugged and came slowly toward me. She put her hands in her skirt pockets and leaned against the wall.

"Ask me what?"

"I didn't know if you could talk in front of those other women. I wanted to know how Cathy is."

"Jes fine." Her face was blank and she let her mouth hang slightly open. It made her look adenoidally stupid.

"She come out of it okay?"

"She gone on home."

It was all too familiar and all too frustrating. It is the black armor, a kind of listless vacuity, stubborn as an acre of mules. They go that route or they become all teeth and giggles and forelock. Okay, so they have had more than their share of grief from men of my outward stamp, big and white and muscular, sun-darkened and visibly battered in small personal wars. My outward type had knotted a lot of black skulls, tupped a plenitude of black ewes, burned crosses and people in season. They see just the outward look and they classify on that basis. Some of them you can't ever reach in any way, just as you can't teach most women to handle snakes and cherish spiders. But I knew I could reach her because for a little time with me she had been disarmed, had put her guard down, and I had seen behind it a shrewd and understanding mind, a quick and unschooled intelligence.

I had to find my way past that black armor. Funny how it used to be easier. Suspicion used to be on an individual basis. Now each one of us, black or white, is a symbol. The war is out in the open and the skin color is a uniform. All the deep and basic similarities of the human condition are forgotten so that we can exaggerate the few differences that exist.

"What's wrong with you?" I asked her.

"Nothin' wrong."

"You could talk to me before. Now you've slammed the door."

"Door? What door, mister? I got to get back to work."

Suddenly I realized what it might be. "Lorette, have you slammed the door because you know that this morning I stood out in front of this place talking to a couple of cops?"

There was a sidelong glance, quick, vivid with suspicion, before she dropped her eyes again. "Don't matter who you talkin' to."

"Looked like a nice friendly little chat, I suppose."

"Mister, I got to go to work."

"That housekeeper here, Mrs. Imber? If she hadn't happened to look into 109 on Saturday afternoon and saw me there sacked out, it wouldn't have been any nice friendly conversation with the law. And it wouldn't have happened out in front of this place. It would have been in one of their little rooms, with nobody smiling. They would have been trying to nail me for killing that nurse."

She turned and leaned against the shady wall, arms folded, her face no longer slack with the defensive tactic of improvised imbecility. She wore a thoughtful frown, white teeth biting the fullness of her underlip. "Then it was that nurse girl with you in the room Friday night, Mr. McGee?"

"That's how I got acquainted with the law, with Stanger and Nudenbarger."

"The way I know you had a woman with you, Cathy she told me Stanger asked her if when she did the room she saw any sign you'd had a woman in there. That was before you helped her some. No reason to try to save any white from the law anytime. She said you surely had a party. So it was a lucky thing about Miz Imber checking the room, I guess."

"Yes, indeed."

Her brown-eyed stare was narrow and suspicious. "Then, what call have you got to fool around with those two law?"

"I liked the nurse. If I can help find out who killed her, I'd buddy up to a leper or a rattlesnake. It's a personal matter."

Her eyes softened. "I guess being with someone you like, being in the bed with them, and they're dead the next day, it could be a sorrowful thing."

It struck me that this was the first sympathetic and understanding response I'd had from anyone. "It's a sorrowful thing."

With a sudden thin smile she said, "Now, if she was so nice and all, how come she was giving it away to such a mean honk lawyer like that Mr. Holton? Surprised I know? Man, we keep good track of everybody like Holton."

"What's your beef with him?"

"When he was prosecutor, he got his kicks from busting every black that come to trial, busting him big as he could manage. Ever'time he could send a black to Raiford State Prison, it was a big holiday for him, grinning and struttin' around and shaking hands. The ones like that, they can't get anybody for yard work or housework, at least nobody worth a damn or a day's pay."

"She didn't like Holton, Lorette. She was trying to break loose. Being with me was part of the try. Didn't you ever hear of any woman with a hang-up on a sorry man?"

There had been antagonism toward me when she had talked of Holton. I was on Holton's team because of my color. But by telling her how it was between Penny and Rick, I had swung it all back to that familiar lonely confusing country of the human heart, the shared thing rather than the difference.

"It happens. It surely happens," she said. "And the other way around too. Well, yes, I heard you was with those two this morning. Lieutenant Stanger, he isn't so bad. Fair as maybe they let him be. But the one called Lew, he likes to whip heads. Don't care whose, long as it's a black skull. Stanger don't stop him, so the day they go down, they both go down like there was no difference at all."

"I wanted to ask you how Cathy made out. I had no way of knowing how much she drank out of that bottle."

Her stare was wise, timeless, sardonic. "Why, now, that big ol' gal is just fine. Big strong healthy gal. On account of you didn't get her fired, she might be real thankful to you. How thankful do you want she should be, man?"

"Dammit, why do you think that's what I've got in mind?"

She laughed, a rich, raw little sound, full of derision. "Because what the hell else could you want from black motel maids? Sweepin' and cleanin' lessons? A walk in the park? A Bible lesson? Those women back in that room, now. I know exactly what they're thinking. They got it all figured that finally, somehow a whitey got to me, and probably tomorrow I switch with Cathy, one of mine for her One-O-nine, because I decided to be motel tail and pick up some extra bread. Those women know there's not another damn thing in the world about me or Cathy you could be after. And that's how it is."

"And that is exactly what you believe about me?"

"Mister, I don't know *what* to believe about you, and that's the truth."

"I hunted you up because I wanted to see how Cathy made it. And I wanted to ask a favor."

"Like what?"

"I've seen a lot of towns like this one. Enough to know that the black community knows everything that happens in the white community. Maids and cooks and yard men make one of the best intelligence apparatuses in the world."

"Sneaky niggers listening to everything, huh?"

"If I happened to be black, you can damn well bet I'd keep track, Mrs. Walker. Just to keep from getting caught in the middle of anything. I would have to be just that much faster on my feet, just to get a job and keep a job. I'd listen and I'd know."

She tilted her head as she looked up at me. "You almost know where it is, don't you, man? If you were black, now, wouldn't you be too smart to be a yard man?"

"Exactly the same way that if you were white, you're too smart to be a motel maid."

"So what makes you think I'm so stupid I'd get myself messed up in some white killing by coming to you with anything I hear about it?"

"Because I liked that nurse. Because without special help the cops might plumber this one. Because you can follow your hunch, which tells you I'd never make any attempt to bring you into it at all. But the big reason you'll do it is because it's one of the last things in the world you ever thought you'd do."

She snickered. "My grandma kept telling me, she'd say, 'Lorrie, when you got your haid in the lion's mouth, just you lay quiet. You keep forgetting and it's gone get you in bad trouble.'"

"So?"

"Mr. McGee, I got to do the late checkouts. Cathy wasn't all as fine as I said. She said she felt far off. She worked slow and her tongue sounded thick and she said she felt like her skull was cracked open up on top. So Jase drove her on home, and I got two of her late rooms and three of my own to do up."

"Will you think about it, at least?"

With an enigmatic smile she walked away slowly. She had her hands in the pockets of the uniform skirt. She scuffed her heels and went a dozen steps, then stopped and looked back at me over her shoulder, her smile merry and impudent.

"I might see if there's a thing worth knowing. But if there was and I told you and you told somebody I told you, if they come to me about it, they're going to come up onto the dumbest black girl south of George Wallace."

Nobody looks far enough down the road we're going. Someday one man at a big button board can do all the industrial production for the whole country by operating the machines that make the machines that design and make the rest of the machines. Then where is the myth about anybody who wants a job being able to find it?

And if the black man demands that Big Uncle take care of him in the style the hucksters render so desirable, then it's a sideways return to slavery.

Whitey wants law and order, meaning a head-knocker like Alabama George. No black is going to grieve about some nice sweet dedicated unprejudiced liberal being yanked out of his Buick and beaten to death, because there have been a great many nice humble ingratiating hardworking blacks beaten to death too. In all such cases the unforgivable sin was to be born black or white, just as in some ancient cultures if you were foolish enough to be born female, they took you by your baby heels, whapped your fuzzy skull on a tree, and tossed the newborn to the crocs.

And so, Mrs. Lorette Walker, no solutions for me or thee, not from your leaders be they passive or militant, nor from the politicians or the liberals or the head-knockers or the educators. No answer but time. And if the law and the courts can be induced to become color-blind, we'll have a good answer, after both of us are dead. And a bloody answer otherwise.

13 *I STOPPED* in the driveway at 28 Haze Lake Drive at ten of three. As I got out of the car motion caught my eye and I saw Biddy waving to me from the window of the studio over the boathouse.

She opened the door as I got to the top of the outside staircase. She seemed to be in very good spirits. She wore baggy white denim shorts and a man's blue work shirt with the sleeves scissored off at the shoulder seam. The seams came about four inches down her upper arms. She had a little smear of pale blue pigment along the left side of her jaw and a little pattern of yellow spatter on her forehead. The familiar slow heavy breathing was coming over the intercom.

"Maybe it's the extra sleep you let me have, Travis. Or maybe because it's a lovely day. Or maybe because Maurie seems so *much* better."

"Electrosleep?" I asked, gesturing at the speaker.

"Oh, no. Just to get her to sleep and then I took it off. It's more natural that way, even though I don't really think she gets quite as much rest out of it."

I looked at the canvas she was working on. "Seascape?"

"Well, sort of. It's from the sea oats that used to grow in front of the Casey Key place, the way you could see the blue water through the stems and the way they waved in the breeze. It's coming along the way I want it. We can keep talking while I work."

"So she's much better?"

"I'm sure of it. Strange how maybe something changed for her when she was lost and we were trying to find her.

At least she didn't go off and let somebody buy her too many drinks and get into some kind of nasty situation. I guess she must have been wandering around in the brush. But she doesn't remember anything about it. She just seems to . . . have a better grip on herself. Tom is terribly pleased about it. I even think it might be all right to take her to the opening tomorrow night, but Tom is dubious."

"Opening of what?"

"Maybe you noticed that big new building at the corner of Grove Boulevard and Lake Street? Twelve stories? Lots of windows? Well, anyway, it's there and it's new, and it's a project Tom has been working on for almost a year now. He organized the investment group and got the land lease. The Courtney Bank and Trust will move into the first four floors next week, or start moving next week. Almost all the space is rented already. Tom is moving his offices to the top floor. It's really a lovely suite of offices, and the decorators have been working like madmen to get it done in time. So tomorrow night it's sort of a preview of the new offices of Development Unlimited, a party with bartender and caterer and all, beginning just at sundown. He thinks it will be too much for her, but if she is as good tomorrow as she is today, I really think we ought to try it. If she begins to act as if she can't handle it, I can always bring her home. She is sleeping well now, because I made her swim and swim and swim."

I looked down into the back lawn and saw a chin-whiskered man in overalls and Mennonite hat guiding a power mower.

"What did you want to ask me about, Trav?"

"Nothing of any importance. I wondered if you know a Mrs. Holton. Janice Holton?"

"Is she sort of . . . dark and vivid?"

"Yes."

"I was introduced to her once, I think. But I really don't know her. I mean I would speak to her if I saw her, but I haven't seen her in weeks and weeks. Why?"

"Nothing. I met her Sunday night after I left here, and she looks like somebody I used to know. I didn't get to

155

ask her. I thought you might know something about her, like where she's from, so I could figure out if she's the same one."

"I really don't know a thing about her except she seems nice. She must have had quite an impact on you, if you came all the way out here to ask me that."

"I didn't. I just had some odds and ends. That's one of them. I wondered about something else. I don't mean to pry. But remember, I'm sort of an unofficial uncle. Did your mother leave you enough to get along on?"

She rolled her eyes. "Enough! Heavens. When she knew she needed the first operation, back before Maurie became so sick with that miscarriage, she told each of us how she had set things up and asked us if we wanted anything changed while she still had time. Some enormously clever man handled her finances after Daddy died, and made her a lot of money. There are two trust accounts, one for me and one for Maurie. After estate taxes and legal costs and probate costs and all that, there'll be some fantastic amount in trust for each of us, close to seven hundred thousand dollars! So as soon as it's settled and the Casey Key house is sold and all, we'll start getting some idiotic amount like forty thousand a year each. I had no idea! It's tied up in trust until each of us reach forty-five, or until our oldest child gets to be twenty-one. If we have no children, then of course we just have access to the whole amount when we're forty-five. But if we do, then each child gets a hundred-thousand-dollar trust fund when it gets to be twenty-one, and because, by the time you're forty-five, you certainly know there aren't going to be any more kids, the same amount is sequestered—is that the word?—for your kids, like if you have five all under twenty-one, then a hundred thousand would be set aside for each one for their trust funds, and you would get what's left over."

"What happens if either of you die?"

"All the money would be left in trust for the kids, if I was married and had any. And if not, the trust would just sort of end and Maurie would get the amount that's in trust. God, Travis, it is such a horrid feeling thinking these past weeks what would happen if Maurie did manage to kill herself. Hundreds of thousands of dollars directly to me, and all that income from the trust. It's spooky, because I never knew and I never thought of myself that way. I knew there would be some, of course. But past a certain point it just gets ridiculous." She turned from the painting, brush in hand, and smiled at me. "Dear Uncle, you do not have to worry about my finances." Her face saddened abruptly. "Mother just didn't have much of a life, the last six years of it. After we got back to the Key, after my father died, we'd take long walks on the beach, the three of us, every morning. She talked to us. She made us understand that Mick Pearson just could not have ever accepted a neat, tidy, orderly, well-regulated little life. He had to bet it all, every time. And I remember that she said to us that if she'd only had five years of him, or ten, or fifteen instead of twenty-one, she would still have settled for that much life with him instead of forty years with any other man she'd ever met. She said that was what marriage was all about and she hoped we'd both find something just half as perfect."

"Did she have her first operation here?"

"Yes. You see, Maurie was almost five months pregnant and she'd lost the first baby at six months. It was an absolutely stupid accident the first time. She drove down to pick up a cake she'd ordered for Tom's birthday and it was in July two years ago, and she was driving back in a heavy rain and she started to put on the brakes and the cake started to slide off the seat, and she grabbed for it and when she did, she stomped harder on the brake and the car slid and she went up over the curb and hit a palm tree, and the steering wheel hit her in the stomach, and about three hours later, in the hospital, she aborted and the baby was alive, actually, a preemie, but less than two pounds, and she just didn't make it. It was very sad and all, but Maurie told me on long distance there was no point in my coming down. She recovered very quickly. So I guess mother thought she'd better come over and keep Maurie from running into any palm trees so she would have her first grandchild. After she was here a week or so, she noticed some bleeding and had a checkup and they decided they'd better operate. She had Doctor William Dyckes, and he is fabulously good. When we knew she was going to be operated on, I came down to be with her and do what I could. Then, three days after she was operated on, Maurie went into some kind of kidney failure and had convulsions and lost her second baby, and hasn't been right since. While they were both in there, I flew up and packed and closed my apartment and put stuff in storage and had the rest shipped down."

"When was all that?"

"A year ago last month. Or a lifetime ago. Take your pick. Doctor Bill operated on Mother again last March. And then she died on the third of this month." She frowned. "Only eleven days ago, Trav! But it seems much longer ago. And it was, of course. They kept her so doped, trying to build her up at the same time, for the operation. She was so tiny and shrunken. She looked seventy years old. You'd never have known her. And she was so . . . damn brave. I'm sorry. Excuse me. What the hell good is bravery in her situation?"

"Was there any chance?"

"Not the faintest. Bill explained it to Tom and me. I had to give permission. He said he thought it might help her to do another radical, take out more of the bowel, cut some nerve trunks to ease the pain. He wasn't kidding me. I know he didn't give her much chance of surviving it. But . . . he liked Mom. And she might have lasted for another two months, even more, before it killed her."

I sat and made casual talk for a little while, watching her at work. She asked me to come to the party Tuesday evening. I said I might if I didn't have to leave town before then. She said that if Tom wasn't tied up, the three of them were going to drive down to Casey Key next Sunday, and she would look for that information about the *Likely Lady*.

I found the Boughmer house at 90 Rose Street without difficulty, but it was twenty after four when I walked up the porch steps and rang the bell. The blinds were closed against the afternoon heat. A broad doughy woman appeared out of the gloom and looked out at me through the screen. She wore a cotton print with a large floral design. She had brass-gold hair so rigidly coiffed it looked as if it had been forged from a single piece of metal.

"Well?"

"My name is McGee, Mrs. Boughmer. I called about talking to your daughter on that insurance matter?"

"You're not very businesslike about arriving on time. You don't look like a business person to me. Do you have any identification?"

I had found three of the old cards and moved them into the front of the wallet before I got out of my car. Engraved, fancy, chocolate on buff. D. Travis McGee. Field Director. Associated Adjusters, Inc. And a complex Miami address, two phone numbers, and a cable address.

She opened the door just far enough for me to slip the card through. She studied it, ran the ball of her thumb over the lettering, opened the door, and gave it back to me.

"In here, please, Mr. McGee. You might try the wing chair. It's very comfortable. My late husband said it was the best chair he ever sat in. I will go see about my daughter."

She went away. It was a small room with enough furniture and knickknacks in it for two large rooms. The broad blades of a ceiling fan turned slowly overhead, humming and whispering. I counted lamps. Nine. Four floor and five table. Tables. Seven. Two big, four small, one very small.

She came marching back in, straight as a drill sergeant. A younger woman followed her. I stood up and was introduced to Helen Boughmer. Thirty-three, maybe. Tall. Bad posture. Fussy, frilly, green silk blouse. Pale pleated skirt. Sallow skin. Very thin arms and legs fastened to a curious figure. It was broad but thin. Wide across the shoulders, wide across the pelvis. But with imperceptible breasts and a fanny that looked as if it had been flattened by a blow with a one-by-ten plank. Pointed nose. Mouse hair, so fine the fan kept stirring it. Glasses with gold metal frames, distorting lenses. Nervous mannerisms with hands and mouth. Self-effacing. She sat tentatively on the couch, facing me. Mom sat at the other end of the couch.

"Miss Boughmer, I'm sorry to bother you when you're not feeling well. But this is a final report on some insurance carried by Doctor Stewart Sherman."

"What policy? I knew all his policies. I was with him over five years. I made all the payments."

"I don't have those details, Miss Boughmer. We do adjustment work on contract for other companies. I was just asked to come up here and conduct interviews and write a report to my home office on whether or not, in my best opinion, the doctor's death was suicide."

"She was on her vacation," Mom said.

"Well, I was spending it right here, wasn't I?"

"And is there anything wrong with having a nice rest in your comfortable home, Helen?" She turned toward me. "It's a good thing she didn't spend her hard-earned money going around to a lot of tourist traps, because she certainly hasn't worked a day since her precious doctor died. She doesn't even seem to want to look for work. And I can tell you that *I* certainly believe in insurance, because we wouldn't be living here right now the way we are if Robert hadn't been thoughtful enough to protect his family in the event of his death."

Helen said, "I just don't know what insurance it could be. He cashed in the big policies because he wanted the money to invest with Mr. Pike. And the ones he kept, they'd be so old I guess they'd be past the suicide clause waiting period, wouldn't they?"

I had to take a wild shot at it. "I'm not sure of this, Miss Boughmer, but I have the feeling that this could have been some sort of group policy."

"Oh! I bet it's Physicians' General. That's a term policy and he had no value to cash in, so he kept it. And I guess there could be a suicide clause for the life of the policy. Do you think so?"

"I would say it's possible." I smiled at her. "There has

to be *some* policy where the problem exists, or I wouldn't be here, would I?"

"I guess that's right," the receptionist-bookkeeper said.

"There was no note left by the deceased and no apparent reason for suicide. And the company is apparently not interested in taking refuge in a technicality if the claim should be paid to the heirs. Would you say it was suicide, Miss Boughmer?"

"Yes!"

Her tone had been so wan the sudden emphasis startled me.

"Why do you think so?"

"It's just like I told the police. He was depressed, and he was moody, and I think he killed himself. They interviewed me and typed it out and I signed it."

"I've interviewed Mr. Richard Holton and, prior to the tragic murder of Miss Woertz last Saturday, I talked to her about it too. They were both most vehement in saying that it could not possibly have been suicide."

"Like you said at first," her mother said, "crying and raving and ranting around here, making a fuss like you didn't make when your poor father died. You told me fifty times your wonderful doctor couldn't have ever killed himself. You were going to find out what happened to him if it took the rest of your life, remember? And not two days later you decided all of a sudden that he *had* killed himself."

She sat with her hands clasped on her lap, fingers interlaced and rigid, head downcast. She looked like a child praying in Sunday school.

"After I thought it over I changed my mind," she said, and I found myself leaning forward to hear her.

"But Miss Woertz didn't change *her* mind."

"That's got nothing to do with me."

"Is it your impression that Miss Woertz was a stable, rational human being, Miss Boughmer?"

She looked up swiftly and down again. "She was a very sweet person. I'm sorry she's dead."

"Hah!" said Mom. "To this child *everybody* is a very sweet person. She's easily led. She'll believe anybody.

Anybody with half an eye could see that Penny Woertz was a cheap, obvious, little thing. Why, she couldn't have cared one way or another whether Doctor Sherman killed himself or was murdered."

"Mom!"

"Hush up, Helen. All the little Woertz person wanted to do was dramatize. One of the ladies in my garden club, a very reliable lady, and she's never had to wear glasses a day in her life, saw that nurse and Mr. Holton, a married man, embracing and kissing each other in a parked car in the lot at the hospital just over three weeks ago, practically under one of the streetlights in the parking lot. Do you call that rational and stable, Mr. McGee? I call it sinful and wicked and cheap."

"Mom, please!"

"Did she ever try to take any of that work off your shoulders? Did she? Not once did she ever——"

"But that wasn't her *job!* I did my job and she did hers."

"I *bet* she did. I bet she did more than her job. I bet there was more going on between her and your marvelous doctor than you could ever see, the way you think she was so sweet and wonderful."

The girl stood up quickly and wavered for a moment, dizzy. "I don't feel so good. I'm sorry. I don't want to talk about it any more."

"Then, you go to bed, dear. Mr. McGee didn't mean to tire you. I'll be up in a little while to see if there's anything you need."

She stopped in the doorway and looked toward me, not quite at me. "Nobody can ever make me say anything else about the doctor. I think he killed himself because he was moody and depressed."

She disappeared. "I'm sorry," Mrs. Boughmer said. "Helen just isn't herself these days. She's been a changed girl ever since that doctor died. She worshipped the man, God knows why. I thought he was a little on the foolish side. He could have had a marvelous practice if he'd had any energy or ambition. He was all right until his wife died three years ago. Then he sort of slacked off. She wouldn't have put up with all those stupid projects of his. Research, he called it. Why, he wasn't even a specialist. And I think the drug companies are doing all the research anybody needs."

"Your daughter hasn't looked for work since?"

"Not after she got through straightening out all the files for Dr. Wayne to pick up and trying to collect the final bills. But there doesn't seem to be much point in people paying doctor bills to a dead doctor, does there? No, she just seems to feel weak. She doesn't seem to have the will or the energy to go out and find another job. She's a good hard worker too. And she was a very good student in school. But she's always been a quiet girl. She always liked being by herself. Thank the Lord we have enough to live on. I have to scrimp and cut corners with her not working, but we get by."

"She seemed certain that the doctor hadn't killed himself?"

"Positive. She was like a maniac. I hardly knew my own daughter. Her eyes were wild. But I think it was the second day she was at the office, cleaning things up, she just came home late and went to bed and didn't want anything to eat. She hardly said a word for days. She lost a lot of weight. Well, maybe she'll start to perk up soon."

"I hope so."

14 *NINE THIRTY* Monday evening. Stanger was suddenly standing at my elbow at the bar at the motel and suggested it might be better if we talked in my room. I gulped the final third of my drink and walked around with him. The air was very close and muggy. He said a storm would help, and we might get one in the night.

Once we were in the room, I remembered something I kept forgetting to ask him. "Holton has some buddy on the force who opens motel doors for him and such like. Who is that?"

"Not on the city force. That's Dave Broon. Special investigator for the Sheriff's Department. Slippery little son of a bitch for sure. The sheriff, Amos Turk, didn't want to take him on in the first place. That was about seven years back. But there was political pressure on Amos. Dave Broon has a lot of things going for him all the time. You want a nice little favor done, like maybe some chick starts putting the pressure on you threatening to go to your wife, Dave is your boy. He'll check her out, scare her to death, and put the roust on her, but then when Dave wants something out of you, he's got the names, dates, and photostats of the motel register, so you do him a favor. He's built up a lot of political clout around this part of the state. Lot of the lawyers use him on special little jobs because he's careful and he keeps his mouth shut."

"Next question. Is D. Wintin Hardahee his own man?"

"God, you do get around some, McGee. Far as I know, he is. Soft voice, but don't mess with him. Hard-nosed and honest. Nobody tells him what to do."

"And what about Holton and the note?"

"Don't I get to ask any questions?"

"And you'll get answers. What about Holton?"

"That boy was so bad hung this morning he couldn't move his eyeballs. Had to turn his whole head. Kept sweating a lot. Cut his face all up shaving it. What happened was they got in from Vero Beach Saturday night after ten. Car radio was busted. He had a beer and went right to bed and he said he hadn't had much sleep Friday night. Drove around for a long time after he left here. Parked by the Woertz apartment for a while, but she didn't come home. Got in at three, he thinks. So he slept heavy Saturday night. Got up about ten thirty Sunday morning. His wife was already up. He was sitting on the edge of the bed when the phone rang. Picked it up and said hello. No answer for a moment and he thought it was the same kind of trouble they've been having with the line. Ring once and no more. Then he said somebody whispered to him. He didn't get it at first. They repeated it and hung up. Couldn't tell if it was a man or a woman. It made no sense to him. The whisper said, 'The police found a note she left for her new lover.' Some damfool prank, he thought. Then he saw the front page of the paper, and without breakfast or a word to anybody he came downtown and conned Foster into letting him see the note. Hunted around for you. Got ugly drunk. Might have shot you. Told me he'd given it some serious thought."

He stared over at me. "What the hell is wrong with you?"

"It goes clunk, Stanger. Things float around loose in your head and then there is a clunk, and they've lined up and make sense."

"Let me in on this clunk."

"Did you mention to Janice Holton anything about a certain McGee from Fort Lauderdale?"

"Not word one."

"Phone rings once and that's all. In the Holton house and in the Pike house too."

"Slow and steady, man. Try speaking American."

"Janice has a nice warm wonderful tender man she sees on the sly. Nothing physical about the relationship, she says. She found out about Holton and Penny from somebody who whispered the news to her over the phone."

"Do tell!"

"Lover's code, Stanger. The sneak play. You have a place you meet. A nice safe place. So you call up and let the phone ring once and you hang up. The other party looks at his or her watch. Five minutes later it rings again. Meet me at five o'clock at the usual place if you can, honey. Or eight minutes later, or two minutes later, or twelve minutes later for noon or midnight. So Tom Pike told her about me, some casual thing about a man named McGee who'd known his wife, sister-in-law, and mother-in-law in Lauderdale nearly six years ago, and who came to lunch. Maybe my coming to lunch busted up a tryst. She let it slip casually without thinking."

"So who whispers? Tom Pike for chrissake?"

"It doesn't make much sense."

"When Holton got his call from the whisperer, Tom Pike was flying to Jacksonville. Okay, so Nudenbarger told him about the note, but what would be the point? I mean even if he could make the call. Get Holton all jammed up? What for? Tom Pike isn't the kind to walk out on his marriage, fouled up as it is. And if he's got Janice Holton on the string, what is he proving or accomplishing?"

"Janice was supposed to have a big date with him Saturday, out of town, I guess. But Rick fouled it up by going along, and she couldn't get word to Tom that she was stuck with her husband and would actually have to go see her sister over in Vero Beach."

Stanger said thoughtfully, "I'm not going to fault those two, not for one minute, McGee. Janice is a hell of a lot of woman. Two sorry marriages, and they weren't the ones who made the marriages sorry. Jesus! It's a lot better than if he got involved with the kid sister."

"Who happens to be in love with him."

"Think so?"

"Sure of it."

"Then, Janice could be a kind of escape valve. Well, Tom Pike would step slow and careful, and if we hadn't . . . *you* hadn't added it up, I'll bet a dime nobody would have ever found out about it. I'd say one thing, if it isn't like you say physical, it must be a pretty good strain on them. That Janice is more than something ready. It's going to *get* physical, friend. What have we got? Some damn whisperer trying to make trouble for people."

"Al, out of the whole town, who would you pick as the whisperer? Not by any process of logic. Just by hunch."

"I guess the one I told you about. Dave Broon."

"On somebody's orders?"

"Or playing a personal angle. Turk puts him on a case, he's cute. He's got good moves. He comes up with things. And he's lucky. That's a help in cop work. But he doesn't give a goddamn about whether anything is right or wrong, anybody is legal or illegal. It isn't his business to find new work for the sheriff. If he spotted the mayor's wife shoplifting, he'd follow her home and invite himself in for a drink and a little chat. That kind."

"Could he have found out about that note without you knowing he found out about it?"

"Oh, hell yes. Far as I know he might have the leverage on somebody so that he gets a dupe of every photocopy of any evidence they run through our shop. This whole city and county is a big piece of truck garden to Dave Broon. He goes around plowing and planting and fertilizing, and harvesting everything ripe."

"How is he with bugs?"

"Not an expert but maybe better than average. He has good contacts. If it was something tricky, he'd bring in one of the experts from Miami. He can afford it."

"So we could be bugged?"

"It's possible," he said. "But not likely."

"He isn't too bright, Stanger. Not bright enough to be alarming."

"Dave alarms me, friend."

I showed him the toilet kit and the toothbrush, and the two twenties under the soap dish, and explained the situation. At first it bothered Stanger that if Broon was reasonably sure he had not left any traces, why should he advertise by taking the money? I finally made him see that taking it was the lesser of the two risks, because if I did have some way of learning that my room had been gone over carefully, finding the money untouched would alert me that it was not just petty theft.

"Broon has a family?"

"Never has. Lives alone. Lives pretty good. Recently moved to a penthouse apartment on a new high-rise out by Lake Azure. Usually got some broad living there with him. Big convertible, speedboat, big wardrobe. But on the job he dresses cheap and drives a crummy car. I've worked with him sometimes. He has a way of making the suspect choke up and then get in a big hurry to tell all."

"Description?"

"Five seven, maybe a hundred and forty pounds. Knocking fifty but does a good job of looking thirty-five. Blond, and I think it's a dye job and a hairpiece. Keeps himself in good shape. Works out a lot. Manicures, massages, sunlamp in the winter. Either his teeth are capped or it's a hell of a good set of plates. Gets good mileage out of the accents he uses. All the way from British to redneck. He's in so solid with the party, he just about sets his own work week, and there's not a damned thing Amos Turk can do about it. Couple of years ago one of Turk's big deputies took a dislike to the way Dave was goofing off and making him do the work. Dave was giving away fifty pounds, better than six inches in height and reach, and at least twenty years. They went out into the parking lot. I guess it took six minutes. Didn't even muss up Dave's hair. Then they picked the deputy up and put him in a county car and took him over to the hospital. He never has looked exactly the same and he calls Dave by the name of Mr. Broon, sir. Just say he's tough and he's careful and he's smart enough. The odd job he's best at is if somebody needs a little extra leverage to use on somebody else. Then they get hold of Dave Broon and tell him to see what he can come up with. And it's a rare human person there isn't something about that you can put to use, if you know what it is."

Then I gave him a complete rundown on my talk with Helen Boughmer. He said it sounded as if something or somebody had scared her, and I did not tell him that his appraisal seemed to belabor the obvious.

He reported no progress to speak of on the murder of the nurse. He said, "Trouble with that damned place, the architect laid out those garden apartments for privacy. They kind of back up to little open courts, and there's so many redwood fences it's like a maze back in there. If whoever killed her came to the back door, which might be the way it was because of her being found in the kitchen, I might as well give up on shucking my way through the neighborhood. No fingerprints, but come to think of it, in thirty-one years of police work I've never been on a case yet where there was a single fingerprint that ever did anybody any good or any harm in the courtroom."

He sat in moody silence until I said, "It seems to be tied in to the death of Doctor Sherman."

"Please don't tell me that. I've got a file on him that you can't hardly lift. And there's nothing to go on."

"Maybe Penny Woertz had some casual little piece of information and she didn't know it was important."

"You're reaching, McGee."

"Maybe she'd even told it to Rick Holton and it didn't mean anything to him either, yet. If somebody could play on his jealousy and get him to shoot me after she'd been killed, that puts the two of them out of circulation. Maybe Helen Boughmer knows something too, but somebody has done such a good job of closing her mouth, I don't think she'll be any good to you."

"Thanks. You try to give me a motive for one murder by hooking it up to another one last July. I am going to keep right on thinking the doc injected himself in the arm."

"Got any reason why he did that?"

"Conscience."

"Had he been a bad boy?"

"Nobody is ever going to prove anything on him, and it wouldn't do much good now anyway. But let me tell you something. I have lived a long time and I have seen a lot of things and I have seen a lot of women, but I *never* saw a worse woman in my life than Joan Sherman. Honest to Christ, she was a horror. She made every day of that doctor's life pure hell on earth. Damn voice onto her like a blue heron. She was the drill instructor and he was the buckass private. Treated him like he was a moron. One of those great big loud virtuous churchgoing ladies with a disposition like a pit viper. Full of good works. She was a diabetic. Had it pretty bad too but kept in balance. I forget how many units of insulin she had to shoot herself with in the morning. Wouldn't let the doctor shoot her. Said he was too damned clumsy with a needle. Three years ago she went into diabetic coma and died."

"He arrange it?"

Stanger shrugged. "If he did, he took such a long time to figure it out, he didn't miss a trick."

"Want me to beg? Okay. I'm begging."

"Back then the Shermans lived about six miles out, pretty nice house right in the middle of ten acres of groveland. We were having a telephone strike and things got pretty nasty. They were cutting underground cables and so on. She'd had her car picked up on a Friday to be serviced, and they were going to bring it back Monday. Because of the phones out that way being out, he thought he'd better drive in Sunday morning and see to some patients he had in the hospital. Besides, he had to pick up some insulin for her, he told us later, because she used the last ampule she had that morning. He'd pick up a month's supply at a time for her. He made his rounds and then he went to his office and worked awhile. Nobody would think that was strange. He stayed away from her as much as he dared and nobody blamed him. He said he was supposed to get back by five because a couple was coming for drinks and dinner. But he lost track of the time. The couple came and rang the bell and the woman went and looked in the window and saw her on the couch. She looked funny, the woman said. The husband broke in. No phone working. They put her in the car and headed for the hospital. They met Doc Sherman on his way out and honked and waved him down. She was DOA. They say he was a mighty upset man. There was a fresh needlemark in her thigh from her morning shot, so she hadn't forgotten. He said she never forgot. They did an autopsy, but there wasn't much point in it. I don't remember the biochemistry of it, but there just aren't any tests that will show whether you did or did not take insulin. It breaks down or disappears or something. County law checked the house. The needle had been rinsed and put in the sterilizer. The ampule was in the bathroom wastebasket. There was a drop or so left in it. That tested out full strength. The doctors decided there had been a

170

sudden change in her condition and so the dose she was used to taking just wasn't enough. Also, they'd had pancakes and maple syrup and sweet rolls for breakfast. He said she kept to her diet pretty well, but Sunday breakfast was her single exception all week. Now, tell me how he did it. That is, if he did it."

After a few minutes of thought, I had a solution, but I had been smartass too often with Stanger, so I gave up.

It pleased him. "He brought home an identical ampule of distilled water, maybe making the switch of the contents in his office. Gets up in the night and switches the water for the insulin. She gets up in the morning and shoots water into her leg. Before he goes to the hospital, he goes into the bathroom, fishes the water ampule out of the wastebasket, takes the needle out of the sterilizer, draws the insulin out of the one he filched and shoots it down the sink, puts the genuine ampule in the wastebasket, rinses the needle and syringe, and puts it back into the sterilizer. On the way into town he could have stopped, crushed the ampule under his heel, and kicked the powdered glass into the dirt if he wanted to be real careful. I think he was careful, and patient. I think maybe he waited for a lot of years until the situation was just exactly right. I mean maybe you could stand living with a terrible old broad like that if you knew that someday, somehow, you were going to do it just right. Nice?"

"Lovely. And doesn't leave you anyplace to go."

"It's the reason I was willing to lean a little bit toward suicide. Stew Sherman was a pretty right guy. And killing is sort of against everything a doctor learns in school and in his practice."

"And what if somebody else figured it out too and trapped the doctor somehow into admitting it?"

"Strengthens the suicide solution."

"Sure does."

"And I couldn't come up with a single motive for murder. His dying didn't benefit anybody in any way, McGee."

"Right back where we started?"

"I don't know. Sure like to know why that Boughmer

girl changed her mind so fast. Or who changed it for her. Isn't she one sorry thing though? Just imagine what she'd look like if you stripped her down to the buff."

"Please, Al."

He chuckled. "When I was little, we had a scrawny little old female cat out at the place. Had some Persian in her, so she looked pretty good. Picked up some kind of mange one spring, and in maybe ten days every last living hair fell off that poor beast. Honest to God, you'd look at her and you wouldn't know whether to laugh or cry. McGee, now I know that Helen is a sad, ugly, nervous woman, and I'm ashamed of myself, but if I can get to her when her mother can't pull out of the line and block for her, I think I could scare that Helen so bad she just wouldn't know what in the world she was telling me. Suppose I just do that. Tomorrow, if I can. What are you figuring on doing?"

"I might try to have a talk with Janice Holton and see if I guessed right about the boyfriend."

"So what if you did?"

"It will prove it wasn't somebody else instead of Tom Pike. So we can mark that part of the file closed."

"Anything else?"

"Find out if I can why Hardahee brushed me off."

"If he doesn't want to see you, you're not going to see him."

"I can give it a try. By the way, how are your contacts in Southtown?"

"As good as anybody's, which doesn't mean much. You think there's some Negra mixed up in this mess?"

"No. But Southtown supplies this city with cooks and maids and housekeepers and yard men. Waiters, waitresses, all kinds of manual labor. There can't be much going on among the white middle classes that they don't know about."

"You know, I think about that a lot. If I could ever tap that source, I think I'd have fifty percent of my job licked. They hear a hell of a lot, see a lot, and guess the rest. Sometimes I get a little help. But not lately. Sure God not lately. Those movies that have Southren law

172

officers in them give us a pretty bad smell, regardless of how you handle yourself. I try to level with them, but shit, they know as well as I do there's two kinds of law here, two kinds of law practically everyplace. One of them kills a white man, they open the book to a different place from where a white man kills a Negra. Rape is a different kind of word there in Southtown too. Put it this way. A neighborhood where you got lots of garbage collection, good pavement, good water, good mail service, good streetlights, nice parks and playgrounds, rape and murder are great big dirty ugly scary words. Sorry, friend. None of them are on my side and I can't think of a way to change it one bit."

It was late. We had talked a long time. He leaned and rubbed the final sodden inch of cigar out in the glass motel ashtray. We were quiet. He was a strange one, I thought. A man softened and souring in his years, looking used up, but he wasn't. There are many kinds of cop. This one was a good kind. Flavor of cynical tolerance, grasp of all the unchanging human motivations, respect for the rules and procedures of cop work.

He laughed softly. "Just thinking about Southtown, one Christmastime long back. Maybe nineteen forty-eight, forty-nine. I'd been three years in the paratroopers, so I got appointed Sanny Claus by the City Council, jump into the park a day or two before Christmas, and the toys would come down on the next swing around, in a cargo chute. Kids swarming all over."

It gave me a grotesque mental picture of Santa Stanger lifting some little blond supplicant onto his red velvet knee, and with one Ho Ho Ho of that venomous breath turning her crisp and sere as a little autumn leaf.

"One year Sid dropped me too damn high. Maybe seven thousand. Supposed to make it last longer. Wind started gusting strong and I tried to spill some air to get down far enough so I could use the shrouds to steer me into the park. But I could see right away I couldn't even come close. So I rode the wind and it carried me all the way to Southtown. Sid made his next swing around pretty low and dumped the chute with the toys upwind of the park and put them right where I was supposed to already be. But I was by then steering myself into a field right behind Lincoln School right in the heart of Southtown. Landed good and collapsed the chute and balled it up and slipped out of the harness, and then I looked around and standing around me in a big silent circle there's more dang colored kids than I ever seen in one place before. All big-eyed, just looking. There I am saying Merry Christmas!!! and saying Well, Well, Well! and saying You been good little boys and girls? and they just look. All of a sudden I can hear old Boyd coming to get me—he's been dead for years—with that siren on high scream all the way, the gusty wind blowing the sound of it around. Ten seconds later I could see just a few of those colored kids way in the distance, just the ones too little to run so fast, and twelve seconds later there wasn't a kid in sight, and I was all alone in that field when Boyd came showboating up to me, making a skid turn that stopped him where I could reach out and touch the door handle. Took me back to the park and I spread that sack of toys so fast they didn't get the pictures for the paper. They took a toy away from a pretty little girl and gave it to me to give back to her, so they got their picture, and that was the last time. The next year I said I had a bad ankle, and they didn't have anybody wanted to jump, so from then on they didn't do it anymore. I used to wonder what those little colored kids thought, hiding behind things and under things, and seeing the cop car pick up Sanny Claus. Maybe it didn't puzzle them at all, them thinking anybody can get arrested anytime."

He stood up and yawned. "Be getting along."

I walked out into the night with him and said, "Al, I have one little ice-cold patch on my back, the size of fifty cents, just under the left shoulderblade. It seems to happen when there are things I should know and don't know, and find out later."

"With me, the back of my neck gets a kind of cool feel."

"I didn't bring a handgun."

He thought that over and said, "The check I ran on

174

you, nobody said you were about to become a director of any kind of bank, but nobody could say you should have been busted if they'd had more evidence either. How do I know you wouldn't be a problem to yourself and anybody who happened to come along?"

"You'd have to make a guess."

He took me to his car and unlocked the trunk. He said, "You took this off Holton and gave it to his wife and told me and I took it off her, so we'll leave it that you took it off him and you'll get around to turning it in to me later on, because I haven't talked about it or filled out the forms yet, and not having to fill out forms is a blessing these days."

"Remember, I phoned you about it and you said bring it in as soon as I had a chance?"

"Remember clear as' day, McGee." He watched me as I turned toward the light, swung the cylinder out and checked the full load, used the ejector to spill the six rounds into my hand, snapped the cylinder back, checked the knurled safety to be certain it would not fire either double action or with the hammer back while on safe, then dry-fired it four times into the turf, twice on double action, twice with hammer back, to check the amount of trigger pull and trigger play, swung the cylinder out, reloaded, put it on safe, and thrust it inside my shirt and inside the waistband of my slacks, metal cool against the bellyflesh.

He got into the car and drove away. I saw pink lightning, a pale competition for city neon, then heard deep, fumbling thunder, a hesitant counterpoint to the truck sounds. There was just a hint of rain freshness in the wind.

Third time I'd gotten my hands on this same .38. Forgive me, Miss Penny, for tricking you and then badmouthing you that first time to get it away from your lover. You see, I didn't know you then, knew nothing about your silly honest earnest heart. Who were you staring at when you fell to your knees on the kitchen floor, putting your hands in disbelief to the blue handle of the shears? Did you think it some monstrous mistake and wanted only a chance to explain? But no chance. Tumbled and bled and died. Always tripping, falling, hurting yourself. Freckled clumsy girl.

Two portly tourists, male and female, she in a slack suit that matched his sport shirt, came plodding down the walk. They were in the floodlight pattern and did not see me in the shadows.

She was speaking in a thin and suffering voice. ". . . but no, you can't stand it to have anybody think for one stinking minute that you aren't rolling in money and so you have to tip every grubby little waitress like she was some kind of queen bee, and all it is, Fred, is just currying favor, trying to be a big shot, just showing off with the money we both saved to take this vacation, but if you have your way, the way you throw it around, we'll have to go home——"

"Shaddap!"

"They laugh at you when you tip too much. They think you're a fool. You lose all respect when you——"

"Shaddap!"

She began again, but they were too far away from me to hear her words. The tune was the same, however.

15

UP EARLY ON Tuesday. Fifteenth day of October. Pull the cords and slide the draperies away, feel crisp pile of miracle motel rug under the toes. Wonder who the hell I am. That is the blessing of morning routines—soap, brush, towel, lather, paste, razor. Each morning you wake up a slightly different person. Not significantly. But the dreams and the sleep-time rearrange the patterns inside your head. So what you see in the mirror is almost all you, and three percent stranger. It takes the comfort of routine to fit yourself back into total familiarity.

Even the little concerns are therapeutic. Does that tooth feel a little bit hollow? Seems like a lot of hair coming out. Little twinge in the shoulder when you move the arm just so. Sudden sideways unexpected glimpse in the mirrored door. Belly a little soft? Pat yourself, wash the hide, scrape the beard, brush teeth and hair. Little comforting attentions. Recognition symbols. Here I am. Now then. Me. The only me in existence.

Came walking slowly back from breakfast, marveling at how this tidy prosperous community of Fort Courtney kept producing more and more unknowns, making all its secret equations ever more insoluble. The doctor's wife, slick little Dave Broon, Hardahee's change of attitude, the strangeness of Helen Boughmer, the whisperer, and all the other little fragments of this and that. The diffusion was too wide. No new fact, no sudden inspiration, was going to link everything together into any pattern I could understand. So find one chunk of it, break it down, find out all the why and the who and the what-for.

There was a maid cart outside 109. The door was open. I went in and found Cathy doing the bathroom, Lorette Walker making up the bed.

" 'Mawnin', suh," they said. I sat in the armchair and waited and watched. Brisk work, sidelong downcast glances, a kind of humble knowing arrogance. Two to a room, one of the classic defensive maneuvers of the Negro motel maids across twenty states, where, as an indigenous morning recreational device, they are, when young enough and handsome enough, fair game for paper salesman, touring musician, minor league ballplayer, golf pro, stock car driver, mutual fund salesman.

After all, it is the only situation where white male and black female meet in the context of bedroom, and the quarry cannot exactly go running to the management to complain about a guest. Other defensive devices are the switchblade in the apron pocket, the kitchen knife taped to the inside of the chocolate thigh, the icepick inside the fold of the uniform blouse. Some, after getting tricked, trapped, overwhelmed by a few shrewd, knowing, determined white men, become part-time hustlers. Others cannot accept or adjust. Classic tragedy is the inevitable unavoidable tumble from some high place, where the victim has no place to turn, toppled by some instrument of indifferent fate. A high place is a relative thing. Pride of any kind is a high place, and any fall can kill.

"I see you didn't get fired, Cathy," I said as she came out of the bathroom with the towels.

She cast a swift and wary look at Lorette and then said, "No, suh. Thank you kindly."

There was a silence. I saw that they had begun to dust areas already dusted and were making other busy movements without improving anything. Lorette Walker, her back to me, said, "I can take off now, and this here girl can finish up."

"You look finished. You can both take off."

Lorette straightened and turned to face me, swinging that stupefying bosom around. "You want us both leaving, after I went to all the trouble of telling this here girl she should leastway give you the chance to collect on that favor you did her?"

Cathy stood at semiattention, staring at the wall beyond me, Indian face impassive. She was a big brawny woman, wide through the shoulders and hips, nipped narrow at the waist, with strong dark column of throat, husky shapely legs planted, her body looking deep and powerful through the belly and loins.

"Cathy?" I said.

"Yassa."

"There's no point in Mrs. Walker making us both uncomfortable. So why don't you just take off?"

Cathy looked toward Lorette, eyebrows raised in question. Lorette said something to her in a slurred tone. Cathy scooped up the sheets and towels and with one swift and unreadable glance at me, went out and pulled the door shut. I heard the fading jingle of the service cart as she trundled it away.

Lorette came over and sat on the bottom corner of the

bed, facing me, studying me. Small and pretty brown face, coffee with double cream, with no highlights at all on the smooth matte skin, with eyes so dark the pupils and irises merged. She fished cigarettes and matches from her skirt pocket, lit one, crossed slender legs as she exhaled a long plume. There was challenge and appraisal in her stare.

"Black turn you off, man?"

"Not at all. Suspicion does, though. It's an ugly emotion."

"And ugly living with it or having to live with it. Maybe you don't want it from Cathy on account of it would hurt your chance of making it with me, you think."

"How did you ever guess? I forced poor Cathy to drink that doctored gin, and I arranged to have the nurse killed, just so you and I could meet right here and arrange the whole thing. Take a choice of places, honey. Guatemala City? Paris? Montevideo? Where do I send your ticket?"

She was simultaneously angry and amused. Amusement won. Finally she said, "There's just one last thing I got to be sure of. Tell me, are you any kind of law at all? Any kind?"

"Not any kind at all, Lorette."

She shrugged, sighed, and said, "Well, here I go. Out where the nurse lived there's a white woman in number sixty, pretty close by. She's got her a Monday-Thursday cleaning woman, half days. Last Monday the cleaning woman got there and found a note from the woman she'd be away a week, don't come Thursday. The woman works in an office job. The cleaning woman didn't work Thursday and went there yesterday, Monday, like always. She can tell the woman that lives there isn't back yet, but somebody has been in there. Friend, maybe. Somebody lay on the bed a time. One person. Left a head mark in the pillow, wrinkled the spread. Something was spilled, and somebody used her mop, pail, things like that, and didn't put them back exactly the same. Scrubbed up part of the kitchen floor, part of the bathroom floor, and burned up something in the little fireplace those apartments have got, and she said to her it looked like ashes from burning cloth, and she couldn't find some of her cleaning rags anyplace. Don't know what good it is to you. Maybe something or nothing."

"I suppose she cleaned the place as usual and swept out the fireplace?"

"That's what she did. She told me the name of that woman, but I plain dumb forgot it."

"Never mind. I can find out."

"The cleaning woman, she said it's not far from the kitchen door of that place to the kitchen door of the nurse place. Down the walk and around a corner, behind a fence the whole way, a big high pretty fence with little gates in it to little private yards."

"Thanks. Did you get anything else?"

"There's a lot of people in Southtown who plain wouldn't tell anybody anything, black or white. Or they tell a little and hold back some if they think you want to know bad enough to lay a little bread on them. It isn't on account of being mean. Somehow there's never enough money to even get by on. Maybe if . . ."

I worked my wallet out of my hip pocket and flipped it over onto the bed by her hip. With the half-cigarette dangling from the corner of her mouth, head aslant to keep the smoke out of her eyes, she opened it and thumbed the corners of the bills. "Take what you think you might need."

"And if I just take it all, man?"

"It would be because you need it."

Bright animosity again. "Never come into your mind I was cheating you?"

"Mrs. Walker, there's seven hundred and something in there. I've got to go along with the value you put on yourself, and you've got to go along with the value I put on myself."

She stared at me, then shook her head. "You some kind of other thing for sure. Look. I got two hundred. Okay? Bring you change, prob'ly."

She started to get up, undoubtedly to bring the wallet back to me, but then out of some prideful and defiant impulse, she settled back and flipped it at me. I picked it out of the air about six inches in front of my nose, and slipped it back into the hip pocket. She folded the bills and undid one button of the high-collared uniform blouse and tucked the money down into the invisible, creamy, compacted cleft between those outsized breasts. She re-buttoned and gave herself a little pat.

She made a rueful mouth. "Talk to you so long out in the back, and now I've been in here with the door shut too long, and I tell you that everybody working here keeps close track."

She got up and took the ashtray she had used into the bathroom and brought it back, shining clean, and put it on the bedside table.

"Going to make me some nice problem," she muttered.

"Problem?"

"Nothing I can't handle. I'm kind of boss girl, right after Miz Imber. Up to me to keep them all working right. Lot of them may be older, but nobody can match me for mean. Can't tell them why I spent all this time in here with you alone. So they're going to slack off on me, thinking that on account of I suddenly start banging white, I lost my place. Oh, they'll try me for sure. But they'll find out they're going to get more mean than they can handle from ol' Fifty Pound."

"Fifty pound?"

Even with that dusky skin her sudden furious blush was apparent. "It's nothing, mister. Anyplace like this, sooner or later somebody'll give the boss gal some kind of special name. The one they give me, it comes from the way I'm built, that's all. Somebody saw me walk by and said, 'There she go. Ninety pound of mean. Forty pound of gal and fifty pound of boobs.' So it's Fifty Pound. Used to fuss me, but I don't mind now."

"See what you can find out, Lorette, about a man who works for the sheriff. Dave Broon."

She looked as if she wanted to spit. "Now, that one is all mean. Mr. Holton, he's part-time mean. Mr. Broon, he wants to know something, maybe a deputy picks up some boy out in Southtown and then Mr. Broon visits with him. When they bring the boy back, he walks old and he talks old, and he keeps his head down. But he doesn't say a thing about Mr. Broon. One thing I know, he's rich. Big rich. It's in other names but he owns maybe forty houses in Southtown. Rains through the roof. Porch steps fall off. Three families drawing water from one spigot, but the rent never goes down. It goes up. Cardboard paper on the busted windows. Tax goes up on other places, never goes up on Mr. Broon's houses."

"You told me that the Holtons couldn't get domestic help because of Holton's attitude toward your people. I know that Mr. Pike and Miss Pearson have been trying to get somebody to look after Mrs. Pike. I noticed they have the yard work done by a white man. Any special reason for that?"

She stood by the door and all expression had left her face. "It's something went on long ago, three years, maybe more, just after that house was built and him new married. Had a live-in couple quartered over the boathouse. Young couple. Good pay. They drank some kind of poison stuff that you spray on the groves. Para . . . para . . ."

"Parathion?"

"Sounds right. Both died in the hospital. Mr. Pike paid for a nice funeral."

"Accident?"

"Not with the bag right there on the floor next to the table and the powder still stuck to the spoon. Put it in red wine and drank it. Must have seen it in the movies, because they busted the glasses, threw them at the wall."

"So?"

"So the man had been in Southtown three days before. Quiet boy. Got stinking smashed pig drunk. Cried and cried and cried. So drunk nobody could hardly understand him. Something about signing a paper so they wouldn't have to go to jail. Something about some nasty thing somebody was making his wife do on account of they signed the paper. And about not being able to stand it. Nobody knows the right and wrong of it. Nobody knows what happened."

"But the Pikes can't get any help out there?"

"They maybe could have. People were thinking on it. Then just before they let Mr. Pike get out of the broker business instead of putting the law on him, he was trying to learn to play golf, and he hit a colored caddy with a golf stick. Laid his head open. Mr. Pike give up trying the game after that. Gave Danny a hundred dollars and paid the hospital. Nobody else seen it. Mr. Pike said Danny walked the wrong way at the wrong time."

"Into his backswing?"

"That's what it was, the way they said it. Danny said he had a cold and he sneezed and Mr. Pike missed the ball entire and come at him with his eyes bugged out, making crazy little crying sounds, and Danny turned to run and he knows Mr. Pike couldn't run that fast, so he figures Mr. Pike threw it at him. Then those that had any idea of working out there, they decided against it."

"Why were they going to put the law on him when he was in the brokerage house?"

She looked astonished. "Why, for stealing! How else you going to get in trouble in that kind of job? Mr. McGee, I've *got* to get back on the job. See you tomorrow I guess. You don't see me, it'll mean I didn't get anything much tonight out home."

I could get in touch with neither Janice Holton nor D. Wintin Hardahee, so I backtracked to pick up a loose end that would probably turn into nothing. I placed a call to Dr. Bill Dyckes, the surgeon who had operated on Helena Pearson Trescott. A girl in his office told me he was operating but would probably phone in when he was through, so I did not leave a message but drove over to the hospital to see if I could make contact with him there.

A very obliging switchboard girl put a call through to the doctors' lounge on the third floor in the surgical wing and caught him there and motioned me to a phone. I said I was an old friend of Helena Trescott and just wanted to ask him a couple of questions about her. He hesitated and then told me to come on up, and gave me directions.

He came out of the lounge and we walked down the corridor to a small waiting room. He wore a green cotton smock and trousers and a green skullcap. There was a spray of drying blood across the belly of the smock, and he smelled of disinfectants. He was squat and broad and younger than I had expected. His hands were thick, with short, strong-looking fingers, curly reddish hair on his wrists, backs of his hands, and down to the first knuckle of the fingers.

He dropped heavily onto a sofa in the waiting room, sighing, stretching, then pinching the bridge of his nose. He looked up at the wall clock. "Next one'll be all prepped by eleven fifteen, and please God it will be nice, straight, clean, and simple because I'm scheduled for a son of a bitch this afternoon. What'd you want to know about Mrs. Trescott, Mr. McGee?"

"Did she ever have any chance at all?"

"Not by the time I went in the first time. Big juicy metastasized carcinoma right on the large bowel with filaments going out in every direction. Got the main mass of it and as much more as I could. Left some radioactive pellets in there to slow it some."

"Did you tell her she wouldn't make it?"

"I tell each one as much as I think they can safely take, when it's bad news. I realized later I could have told her the works. But I didn't know her well enough then to know how gutsy and staunch she was. So I said I thought I'd gotten it all, but I couldn't be sure, so we'd go into some other treatment to make sure. I didn't tell the daughters because I figured she could read them loud and clear. Told Tom Pike so that he could help cushion it for the girls when the time came."

"Then, how was she the second time?"

"Downhill. Had to go in to clear a stoppage. Damned jungle in there by then. Nothing like the anatomy books. Malignant is quite a word. Turned a good experienced operating-room nurse queasy. Then by the last time there wasn't anything about her that wasn't changed by it, in one way or another, except her eyes. Great eyes on that woman. Like the eyes of a young girl."

"Too bad that Maureen is in such condition now."

"I didn't get in on that. It isn't something you go after

with a knife. But just about everybody else has had a piece of the action. She's had every test anybody around here has ever heard of, and some I think they made up. It would take two men to lift her lab files."

"Does it boil down to some specific area?"

"If by that you mean her head, yes. If you mean neurology, yes. No physical trauma, no tumor, no inhibition of nourishment. Something is screwing up the little circuits in there, the synapses. Tissue deterioration? Rare virus infection? Some new kind of withdrawal that's psychologically oriented? Some deficiency from birth that didn't show until now? Secretion imbalance? Rare allergy? My personal guess, which nobody will listen to because it's not my field, is that the trouble is in some psychiatric area. That fits the suicide impulse. But the shrinkers have gone through that and out the other side, they say. Series of shock treatments, no dice. Sodium Pentothal, no dice. Conversation on the couch, nothing. I thought you were interested in Mrs. Trescott."

"In the whole family, Doctor Dyckes."

"And I just sit here and open up like the family Bible, eh? And you take it all in, just like it was the most ordinary thing in the world to listen to a doctor violate the ethics of his profession."

"I . . . I thought you were responding to an expression of friendly interest and concern, Doctor, and——"

"Bullshit, McGee. Wanted to see if you handled yourself with any kind of sense at all. You do. Know why I'm talking to you about a patient . . . and the patient's family?"

"I guess you want to tell me why."

He brooded for a long time, eyes half closed. "Trying to find the words for what she did for me. Even when there wasn't anything left of her but the pain and her eyes, I'd go sit by her bed when things went wrong for me, like when I lost a young one that I'd prayed I wouldn't lose. Dammit, I was borrowing guts from Helena Trescott. Leaning on her. We talked a lot, up until the time I had to keep her too far under. One night she told me about a man named Travis McGee. She said that you might show up someday and you might ask a lot of questions. 'Tell him how it was, Bill. Don't pretty it up. Trust him. Tell him what you know about my girls. I'm going to ask him to help Maureen, I think.' So, friend, she's the one who made it easy for you. Not your persuasive charm. Okay?"

"Okay. Thanks."

"So where were we?"

"The next thing I was going to try to do was to get you to give me your opinion of Doctor Sherman."

"Too bad about Stew. Good man. Vague spots here and there but generally solid. I mean in the medical knowledge sense. Damned fool about money, like most doctors. We're the prize pigeons of the modern world. Gold bricks, uranium mines in Uganda, you hold it up and we'll buy it."

"I understood he invested in Development Unlimited."

"Which may be as good as gold. The guys who have gone in swear by Tom Pike. Maybe they're getting rich. Good luck to them. I turned down my golden opportunity. I was pretty interested there for a while."

"What put you off it?"

"My brother. He and his wife were down visiting us. He's a big brain in financial circles in New York. Taught economics at Columbia, then got into securities analysis and real estate investment with a couple of the banks. Then he started a no-load mutual fund a few years ago. A hedge fund. They watch him like eagles up there, trying to figure out which way he's going to jump next. I was invited to one of those little get-in-on-the-ground-floor dinners Tom puts on from time to time. Stag. Took my brother along. Tom made quite an impressive talk, I thought. Had me about to grab for my checkbook. When we got home, Dewey told me what was wrong with the things Tom said. It boiled down to this. Tom used some wonderful terms, some very tricky ideas, a lot of explanations of tax shelters and so on. But my brother explained that it didn't hang together. As if he'd memorized things that wouldn't work in the way he said he was using them. Dewey said it was like a ten-year-old kid explaining Einstein to a roomful of relatives who never got past the tenth grade. The words were so big that, by God, it had to be good and had to be right. Dewey told me to stay out. Any spare change I have, I put in his mutual fund. And little by little he's going to make me rich. He promises me he will. You know, I hope he was wrong about Tom Pike. Because if Tom is goofing, a lot of men in Fort Courtney are going to get very, very badly hurt. Look, I better go scrub. Nice to talk to you. She was one very special woman, that Mrs. Trescott."

I tried Hardahee again and struck out. But Janice Holton was home and said sure, I could stop by if I wanted to. I parked in front on the circular drive and went up and rang the doorbell. As I was waiting she came around the side of the house and said, "Oh. It's you. I'm fixing some stuff around in the back. Want to come around? I don't want to leave it half done."

She had newspapers spread on the grass, under a metal chaise, a piece of lawn furniture originally pale blue. The blue paint had been chipped off by hard use. She was giving it a spray coat of flat black DeRusto from a spray can. She wore very brief and very tight fawn-colored stretch shorts, and a faded green blouse with a sun back, and ragged old blue boat shoes. I stood in the shade within comfortable conversation range. She had a deep tan. She moved swiftly and to good effect, limber as a dancer when she bent and turned, and able to sit comfortably as a Hindu, fawn rear propped on the uptilted backs of the boat shoes. She was sweaty with sun and effort, her back glossy, accenting the play of small hard muscles under her hide as she moved.

She turned, tossing her black hair back, and said, "I ran off at the mouth Sunday night. It isn't like me. I must have been lonely."

"Funny. I had the feeling I talked too much. Had the feeling I'd bored you, Janice."

"Excuse me, but I forgot your first name."

"Travis."

"Okay, Travis. So we were a couple of refugees or

187

something. And excuse me for something else. Meg got a glimpse of you and thought you looked *very* interesting. You know, she *has* been covering for me, but she doesn't know who I've been seeing. She decided it had to be you, so I didn't say yes and I didn't say no. She thinks it is awfully sophisticated for you to bring my husband home drunk so we can put him to bed and go out together. Hmmm. Have I missed anything?"

"That brace over there on the left, under the seat."

"Where? Oh, I see it. Thanks."

She covered the last blue neatly and precisely and straightened up, cocked her head to the side, shook the paint bomb. The marble rattled around inside. "Just about completely gone. I *love* to have something be just enough instead of too much or too little. Want a drink or a cold beer or anything? I've been promising myself a beer."

She led me into the cool house and the cheerful kitchen. She tried to thrust a glass upon me, then admitted that she too preferred it right from the bottle. She leaned against the sink, elegant ankles crossed, uptilted the bottle, and drank until her eyes watered.

"Hah!" she said. "Meg probably saw you drive up. She'll think this is terribly *soigné* too, a little visit just before lunch. She's probably lurking about in the shrubbery, panting."

"As long as I'm nominated, don't you think I ought to know where we've kept all these other assignations?"

"Not assignations. Just to be together. And talk. Talk about everything under the sun. Hold hands like school kids. Cry a little sometimes. Hell! Why shouldn't a man be allowed to cry?"

"They do, from time to time."

"Not enough. Not nearly enough. Well, we had to meet where there would be absolutely no chance of anyone seeing us together."

"Pretty good trick."

"Not terribly difficult, really. We'd arrange a time and both drive to the huge parking lot at the Courtney Plaza and once we had spotted each other, you'd drive out and

I would follow you and you would find a place where we could park both cars and then sit together in one of them and not be seen. Out in one of the groves, or on a dark residential street, or out near the airport, someplace he . . . you thought we'd be safe."

"How would we arrange the date in the first place?"

"You won't have to know that."

"Is that what we were going to do last Saturday? Spend the whole day, or most of it, sitting around in some damned automobile holding hands and crying?"

"Please don't make cheap fun of it."

"Sorry."

"Saturday it might have become something else. Second phase of the affair, or something. Maybe it's just as well Rick spoiled it. I keep yearning for someplace where we could be really alone, really safe. Someplace with walls around us and a roof over us, and a door that will lock. But not a motel, for God's sake. I don't think I could stand a motel. And that would be a risk. You see he . . . he's in a position where a lot depends upon people having total confidence in him. It would be more than just . . . the appearance of infidelity."

"He's a banker?"

"You may call him a banker if you wish. He found a place for us for Saturday. He couldn't get away until about noon. So I was going to drive back and wait for him in the parking lot of a small shopping center north of town, then follow him to the place. He said it was safe and private and nobody would know. He said that not even the person who lived there would ever know we'd been there. So I guess we both knew that if we were ever alone together in a place like that, nothing could help us or save us."

"But good old Rick decided to make the Vero Beach trip."

"He was in horrible shape Monday morning, so stiff and sore and lame he could hardly get out of bed. And terribly hung over, of course. When I told him I'd taken his friend, McGee, back to the Wahini Lodge, he stared at me and then laughed in the most ghastly way. We're not speaking, of course. Just the absolute essentials."

She came and took my empty bottle and dropped the two of them into the tilt-lid kitchen can. "Again I'm doing all the talking, Travis. You have a bad effect on my mouth. Was there something you wanted to see me about, particularly?"

"I guess I've had you on my mind, Janice."

She stared at me, and her frown made two vertical clefts between her dark brows, over the generous nose. She shook her head slowly. "Uh-uh, my friend. If you're thinking what I think you're thinking. Help the embittered lady get her own back? Eye for an eye, and all that? What's the next part of the gambit? Healthy young woman deprived of a sex life, et cetera, et cetera? No, my dear. Not even to keep Meg happy by confirming her suspicions."

"Now that you bring it up, the idea has some merit, I guess. I've had you on my mind for a different reason."

"Such as?"

"Suppose I named your boyfriend by name. The dear, kind, tender, sensitive, wonderful and so on."

"You can't, of course. What are you getting at?"

"But if I did, would you feel you had to go to him and tell him that somebody knows?"

"On a hypothetical basis? Let me see. If you did name him, what would be your point, really, in wanting to be certain? What would you be after?"

"A clue to what kind of man he is."

"He is a marvelous man!"

"Does everybody think so?"

"Of *course* not! Don't be so dense! Any man who has strength and drive and opinions of his own will make enemies."

"Who'll badmouth him."

"Of course."

"Okay, his name is . . . Tompestuous K. Fliggle, Banker."

"Travis, you *are* an idiot."

"These are idiotic times we live in, my dear."

And the little inadvertent muscles around her eyes had clued me when I hit the first syllable of the invented name, which was as far as I cared to go.

At a few minutes past noon I read the nameplate on the mailbox at 60 Ridge Lane. Miss Hulda Wennersehn. The name of the real estate firm that managed the garden apartments was on a small sign at the corner. From the first drugstore phone I came to, I called the real estate offices and was switched to a Miss Forrestal. I told her I was with the credit bureau and would appreciate some information on Hulda Wennersehn. She pulled the card and said that Miss Wennersehn, age fifty-one, had been in number sixty for four years and had never been in arrears. I asked if Miss Wennersehn was employed by an insurance company and she said, "Oh, no, unless she changed jobs and didn't inform us. Of course, she'd have no reason to inform us, actually. But we have her as working for Kinder, Noyes, and Strauss. That's a brokerage firm. She works as a cashier." So thank you, my dear.

So I phoned the brokerage house and the switchboard girl told me that, my goodness, it had been at least two years since Miss Wennersehn had worked there. She was working for a real estate company. She gave me the phone number. On a hunch I asked her if a Mr. Tom Pike had ever been with the firm, and she said that he had, but that had been some time ago. The number she gave me turned out to be Development Unlimited.

"Miss Wennersehn? I'll transfer you to . . . oh, excuse me, sir. She is still up at our Jacksonville office. Shall I see if I can find out when she'll be returning?"

I thanked her and told her not to bother.

I went back to the motel to see if there were any messages. Stanger was waiting for me.

16

SOMETHING HAD changed Stanger, tautened him, given him nervous mannerisms I had not noticed before. We went to 109. He moved restlessly about. I phoned for sandwiches and coffee.

When I asked him what was wrong, he told me to let him think. He paused at the big window and stood with his hands locked behind him, teetering from heel to toe, looking out at people playing in the pool.

"I could maybe go with one of those security outfits," he said. "Gate guard. Watchman work."

"You get busted?"

"Not yet. But maybe that's what they'll want to do."

"Why?"

"That Mrs. Boughmer was off on some kind of garden club tour. I finally got the daughter to let me in. Went into my act. Want to warn you you're in serious trouble. Withholding information about a capital crime. Maybe I can help you if you level with me now. And so on and so on. Until she split open."

"What was her problem?"

He turned and walked over and sat heavily in the armchair. "She was bellering and squeaking and sobbing. Spraying spit. Words all jammed together she was trying to say them so fast. Grabbing at my hands. Begging. Confessing. Jesus!"

"Confessing what?"

"That poor dim ugly girl was in love with Doc Sherman. Not so much romance and poetry. Passion. Hot pants. You saw her. Any man ever going to lay a hand on her? So there was something she was doing, God only knows what. Last to leave. Lock the doors. Leave the office lights on. Go into the dark treatment room. Do something in there. She wouldn't say what. Something, according to her, that was nasty and evil. Went on for years, I guess. Some kind of release. No idea what Broon was after or how he got in. She was working on the files after Sherman had died, a few days later. She was in the treatment room and the lights suddenly went on and Broon is in the doorway watching her. Told her to put her clothes back on and he'd talk to her in the office. Apparently, McGee, he convinced that poor sick sad homely woman that there was some law, crime against nature, jail her as a degenerate or some damned thing. Told her that if she ever tried to tell anybody Sherman didn't kill himself, he'd have her picked up and taken in right away. He took some kind of 'evidence' away with him. How the hell was I supposed to know she was so close to the edge? All of a sudden she went rigid as a board, bit through her lip, started whooping and snapping around, eyes out of sight. Followed the ambulance in. Some kind of breakdown. Left a neighbor woman on the lookout for Mrs. Boughmer. Probably Dave Broon slipped the lock on the rear door that night and came easing in."

"That won't be anything to bust you for, Al."

"It isn't that. It's what comes next. Maybe."

"Which is?"

"Dave Broon. I've come right up to it with him. Too many years, too many things. No way to nail him according to the rules I'm supposed to follow. We're supposed to be on the same ball club. He gives the whole thing a bad smell. Maybe there's a time when you don't go by the book. Look, I've got to have somebody with me. The things I'm thinking scare me. I've got to have somebody stop me if I can't stop myself."

"Maybe you'd better think it over."

"Meaning you don't want any part of it."

"If you want me with you, okay. But just for the hell of it, before we see him, can you get a decent check on where he was the night Sherman died, and where he was the afternoon Penny Woertz died?"

"I don't know about last Saturday, but I remember he was up in Birmingham to bring a prisoner back when Sherman died. Anyway, let me see where that fancy little scut might be."

He moved to the bed and used the bedside phone. He would mumble greetings, ask about Broon, listen, hang up, dial another number. He made at least eight calls. He got up and said, "Guess I'll have some time to think it over. He's been here and there, but nobody's got a fix on him in the past hour or so. Might be hanging around the courthouse. He's got cronies over there who feed him little bits of information, probably for cash on the line. Or he could be at city hall for the same reason. Or he could be holed up in that so-called penthouse with a new playmate. Hasn't had one around for a while, so he's due."

He left, saying he would get in touch and pick me up so I could go with him to talk to Dave Broon. After he had gone, I put the lunch tray outside the door so no one would have any reason to come in after it. And before I left, I used one of the oldest and simplest tricks to warn me if anyone came into the room by way of the door while I was gone. I wadded up a sheet of the motel stationery and, as I left, I leaned over and reached back through the opening and placed it on the rug, close to the door, a precise placement because I could measure it by the length of my forearm, from the crook of elbow to the thumb and finger in which I held it. The door opened inward. Anyone entering would brush it away with the door. Even if they had the wit to try to replace it, they could never put it in the same identifiable position as before. When a door opens outward, it is easiest to close it against a bit of matchstick or toothpick inserted at some precise spot and broken off so that it is barely visible from outside the door. But a careful workman can defeat this protection, or the hair and chewing gum device, or the carbon-paper gimmick.

The day blackened, the sky cracked open, and the rain came down, storm gusts whipping the spray of the rebound and the mist of the hot streets, tearing brown fronds off the cabbage palms, shredding the broadleaf plantings, swinging signs and traffic lights. Same kind of storm wind that had made the *Likely Lady* rock her weight against the anchor lines, creaking and grunting. It had been cozy below.

I tried Hardahee. She said he had left for the day, and I could not tell if she was lying. I found Rick Holton's law office. The girl took my name and disappeared. She came back and led me down a paneled corridor. He had a big desk with a window wall behind it that looked out onto a little enclosed court paved with Japanese river stones and with some stunted trees in big white pots. Rain ran down the window wall. He had a lot of framed scrolls on the persimmon paneling of his walls, and framed photographs of politicians, warmly inscribed.

He tried the big confident junior chamber smile, but it had sagged into nothing before the girl had closed the office door.

"Sit down, McGee. Told Sally I didn't want to see anybody. Supposed to be getting through all this damned desk work. Jesus! I read things three times and don't know what I've read. Know where they're getting with the investigation? Noplace. I think it was some crazy. Hell, Penny would have opened the door to anybody. They panicked and ran. One of those lousy meaningless things. They'll pick him up for something else someday, and he'll start talking and hand them this one."

"It might open up. Stanger might come across something."

"He's good."

"Better than your friend Dave Broon?"

He shrugged. "Dave is handy for odd jobs."

"Can I get your opinion on a few things, Holton? Not legal opinion. Personal."

"For what it's worth, which isn't much lately. Everything seems to be going sour. You know, the deal with Penny was going sour. We were about ready to close the books. So why do I miss her so damn much?"

"She was pretty special."

"So Janice was very special. Past tense. I blew the whole bit. For a roll in the hay with Penny Woertz. Nowhere near as good-looking a girl as Janice. What was I trying to prove? With Janice you don't just make a sincere apology and go on from there. Done is done. Total loyalty, given and expected. I've lost her. Funny thing, driving back from Vero Beach, when I had no idea in the world Penny was already dead, I tried to tell Jan that it was something that had just sort of happened. I said it was over. I wasn't *sure* it was over, but I had the feeling that if I told Jan it was, then I'd have to make sure I kept on feeling just the way I felt when she wouldn't leave your room Friday night when I did. That was before we picked up the kids at Citrusdale. She let me talk. I thought she was really thinking it over, giving me a chance. I reached over and put my hand on her arm. You know, she actually shuddered? And she said in a polite voice to please not touch her, it made her stomach turn over. That was the end of it, right there."

"When you were waiting for me Sunday night, did you have any idea of shooting me, Holton?"

He tilted his chair back and looked up at the sound-proofed ceiling, eyes narrowed. "That was pretty dim. Jesus, I don't know. I'd read a stat of that note she wrote you. It made it pretty clear about you two. I was aware of the gun. I had the feeling that my whole life was so messed up nothing mattered too much. And you'd hit me harder than anybody ever hit me in my life. I'm still sore from it. Four days and I still hurt when I take a deep breath. I've got a lousy temper. Maybe, McGee. All things considered, I just might have. Scares me to think of it. Without Janice and without Penny, things aren't all that bad. I've got a lot of friends. I do a good job for my clients. I made a good record as an assistant state attorney and I've got a good chance of becoming county attorney next year, and that's worth a minimum forty thousand, plus other business it brings in. They say money won't buy happiness, but you can sure rent yourself some. I'm grateful to you for suckering me. And thanks for taking me home. Where's the gun anyway?"

"I turned it over to Stanger and he gave it back to me."

He was puzzled. "Why'd he do that?"

"It's just sort of a temporary loan, just a little delay in officially turning it over to him."

"When you give it back to him, tell him to hang on to it. I don't think I ought to have one around. Not for a while. Maybe not ever. But why does Al Stanger think you need a gun?"

"Just a whim, maybe."

"You mean you'd rather not say? Okay. Yesterday morning I checked out what you said about yourself. I phoned Tom Pike and he said you were an old friend of Mrs. Trescott and her daughters."

"If you could check that easily, why didn't you check before you and Penny pulled that stupid deal, that grade C melodrama?"

He blushed. "So now it seems wild and stupid. We sort of talked each other into it. If it had worked—and you have to admit it came close—then I would have maybe found out from whatever papers you were carrying on your person, the missing piece. We'd narrowed it down to one theory that looked better and better. The tall man could have been in some kind of drug traffic."

"Oh, come *on!*"

"Wait a minute now! I held back a little on you when we talked in your room. Penny followed my lead. The man seen leaving Sherman's office was carrying a case of some kind, light-colored and heavy. No controlled drugs were missing, according to the office records. But there was no control on the stuff he ordered for his experimentations. He did some animal experimentations along with the other stuff. He could have been ordering experimental compounds, couldn't he?"

"Aren't you reaching?"

"I talked to Helen Boughmer the day after he died. She was convinced that a lot of stuff might be missing from the room in back, and she was going to check the file of special orders against the inventory of what was left. *She* believed he'd been killed. And two days later, she'd changed completely. She said she had changed her mind. She said she believed he'd killed himself. She said

197

she had checked the special orders and nothing was missing. I asked her to produce the file. She claimed she couldn't find it. And she never did find it. Now somebody, dammit, had to get to her. If Sherman had killed himself, why would anybody take the time and trouble to shut her mouth. She was a changed woman. She acted terrified."

"Then, why would I come back here, if I was the one who killed Doctor Sherman? What would there be here for me?"

"Now you can say I'm reaching. Why would Tom Pike pay you twenty thousand in cash? It was one of those crazy breaks you get sometimes that one of my partners here saw him giving the money to a man who matches your description. Let's say Sherman stepped out of line when Maureen Pike was so critically ill at the time of her miscarriage, and gave her something not authorized for use on patients. Suppose he did this with Tom's knowledge and consent, and whatever it was, the side effect was some kind of brain damage? Hell, it kind of dwindles off because it doesn't seem as if it would give anybody enough leverage to pry money out of Tom Pike. But you'd seen Tom, and even if we didn't find a thing except a heavy piece of money on you, that would mean some kind of confirmation."

"Personal opinion again, please. Do you think Doctor Sherman killed his wife?"

"Ben Gaffney and I—he's the state attorney—went up one side of that and down the other. Going after him with a circumstantial case just didn't add up. We could show motive and opportunity, but there was absolutely no way to prove the cause of death. Do I think he did? Yes. So does Ben. The specialists we talked to said it was highly unlikely there could have been such a sudden deterioration in her condition that she could go into deep coma after the amount of insulin she had apparently taken. But 'highly unlikely' isn't enough to go to court with. So we closed out the investigation finally."

"Who was handling it?"

"The death occurred in county jurisdiction. Dave

Broon was handling it, under joint direction of my office and the sheriff. If Dave could have come up with something that strengthened the case, it would still have been a pretty unpopular indictment."

"Now, to get back to Sherman's death, do you have the feeling that Penny had any kind of lead at all that she hadn't told you about yet?"

He looked startled and then grim. "I see where *that* one is aimed. I don't really . . . wait a minute. Let me think." He leaned back and ground at his eyes with the heels of his hands. "I don't know if this is anything. It would have been . . . a week ago. Last Tuesday. She was working an eleven-to-six-in-the-morning shift, a postoperative case, and that was the last time she was on that one. I pulled out of here early. About quarter to four and went over to see her. She'd just gotten up. She had dreamed about Doctor Sherman. She was telling me about it. I wasn't paying much attention. She stopped all of a sudden and she had a funny expression. I asked her what the trouble was and she said she'd just thought of something, that the dream had reminded her of something. She wouldn't tell me. She said she had to ask somebody a question first, and maybe it was nothing at all, but maybe it meant something. Very mysterious about it."

"Can you remember anything about the dream?"

"Not much. Nutty stuff. Something about him opening a door in his forehead and making her look in and count the times a little orange light in there was blinking."

"But you don't know if she asked anyone that question?"

"She never brought it up again."

"While you were . . . conducting this unofficial investigation of Sherman's death, were you telling Janice about it, about things like the file the Boughmer woman wouldn't produce?"

"I guess I was telling her more than I usually would. Hell, I was trying to cover for the time I was spending with Penny. But Janice was turning ice cold, and fast. She wasn't buying it. I kept trying, but she wasn't buying it. She found out, I guess."

"Somebody told her about it practically as soon as it began."

"No kidding! Some real pal."

"Do you think she's found some other man?"

"I keep trying not to think about that. What's it to you?"

"Let's say it isn't just a case of big-nose, Holton."

"I get home and that damned Meg is either over at the house with her kids, or the kids are over at Meg's house. No note from Janice. No message, nothing. So she comes home and I say where have you been, and she says out. Looks so damned smug. But I keep telling myself that when she comes home, she doesn't have that look. You know? Something about the mouth and the hair and the way they walk. A woman who's been laid looks laid. Their eyes are different too. If she's got somebody, he's not playing his cards right. If she likes him and she's sore at me, and I know she's known about Penny, all he'd have to do would be lay one hand on her to get her going, and she'd take over from there. A lousy way to talk about the wife, I guess. But I know her. And she's no wife now. Not anymore. Never again, not for me."

"Does she think Sherman was murdered?"

"She was fond of him. She's sure of it. Not from anything I dug up or any chain of logic I explained. She operates on instinct. She says he couldn't have and to her that's it."

"So she wanted to have you find out who did it?"

"Not because she was hot to have somebody punished, but more because it would clear his name."

"What do you know about the trouble Tom Pike got into at Kinder, Noyes, and Strauss?"

"What? You jump around pretty fast. All I know is the shop talk I heard about it. He was a very hot floor man. He had people swearing by him. He went in there and built up one hell of a personal following. High fliers, discretionary accounts, a lot of trading in and out, accounts fully margined. And he's a very persuasive guy. He made a lot of money for a lot of people in this town, in a very short time. But there was one old boy who came down to retire, and he had a portfolio of blue chips. He had Telephone and General Motors and Union Carbide. He signed an agreement to have Tom Pike handle his holdings on a discretionary basis. As I understand it, Tom cashed in all the old boy's blues and started swinging with the proceeds. Fairchild Camera, Texas Instrument, Teledyne, Litton. At the end of three months the total value of the old boy's holdings was down by about twelve thousand. And Tom had made about forty trades, and the total commissions came to eight grand. The old boy blew the whistle on Tom, claiming that the agreement was that Tom would commit only twenty percent of his holdings in high-risk investments, that Tom had ignored the understanding and put the whole amount in high fliers, and had churned the account to build up his commissions. He had his lawyer send the complaint directly to the president of the firm in New York. They sent down a couple of lawyers and a senior partner to investigate. Brokerage houses are very sensitive about that kind of thing. Big conference, as I understand it. Complete audit of all trades. Tom Pike claimed that the man had told him that he was after maximum capital gains in high-risk issues and that he had other resources and could afford the risk. The man denied it. It looked as if Tom was in serious trouble. But one of the female employees was able to back up Tom's story. She said the man had phoned her to get verification of the status of his account and his buying power, and that when he had been twenty-five thousand ahead of the game, he had told her over the phone that getting out of the tired old blue chips and letting Mr. Pike handle his account was the smartest move he had ever made. The old man denied ever saying that."

"What was her name?"

"Hilda something. Long last name. The cashier."

"Hulda Wennersehn?"

"If you know about it, why are you asking me?"

"I *don't* know about it. What happened?"

"They decided that in view of Tom's knowing the man was retired and needed security, he had used bad judgment. They slapped his wrist by giving him a sixty-day

201

suspension. And they busted a couple of the more recent trades and absorbed the loss in order to build the old man's equity back to almost what he started with. That's when Tom said the hell with it and started Development Unlimited."

"And Miss Wennersehn now works for him."

"So?"

"So nothing. Just a comment. How did the business community react to Pike's problem?"

"The way these things go, at first everybody was ready to believe the worst. People pulled their accounts. They said that while he was looking good with their money, he was piling up commissions. They said he'd been lucky instead of smart. Then it swang right around the other way when he was pretty well cleared. He was out of the brokerage business, and so what he did was move his big customers right out of the market, off-the-record advice, and put them into land syndication deals. Better for him because you can build some very fancy pyramids, using equities from one as security for loans on the next, and he can cut himself in for a piece by putting the deals together. He's moved very fast."

"Credit good?"

"He got past that iffy place when Doc Sherman's death fouled up some moves he was going to make. His credit has to be good."

"What do you mean?"

"He's got bankers tied into the deals, savings and loan, contractors, accountants, realtors. Hell, if he ever screwed up, the whole city would come tumbling down."

"Along with the new building?"

"All four and a half million worth of it. Land lease in one syndicate, construction loans and building leases in another."

"Very quick for a very young man."

"How old are the fellows running the big go-go funds? How old are the executives in some of the great big conglomerates? He's quick and tough and bold, and you don't know what his next move is going to be until it's all sewed up."

"Last item. How well do you know Hardahee?"

"More professionally than socially. Wint is very solid. Happens to be under the weather right now. Scheduled this morning at ten on an estate case where I represent one of the parties at interest and Stan Krantz appeared and asked for a postponement because Wint is ill and nobody else over there is up on the case. It's pretty complex. Jesus! All this work to do and I just can't seem to make my mind work. McGee, what are you after? What's this all about?"

"I guess it's about a dead nurse."

"That mean that much to you?"

"She was very alive and it was a dingy way to die."

"So you're sentimental? You're carried away because she was so sore at me she took you on? All she was, McGee, was——"

"Don't say it."

"You mean that, don't you?"

"Say it then, if you're sure you want to find out."

He looked at me and rubbed the back of his hand across his lips. "I think I'll take your word for it."

"You're mean in a curious way, Holton. Small mean. Like some kind of a dirty little kid."

"Go to hell," he said with no emphasis at all. He swiveled his chair. He was looking out at his little oriental garden patio as I walked out. The rain had stopped.

17

IT WAS FIVE when I got back to 109. I unlocked the door and leaned over and reached around it. No wad of paper anywhere near where it should be. I opened the door the rest of the way. The balled-up piece of stationery was five feet from the door, where it had rolled when somebody had opened the door.

It seemed a fair guess that if it had been a maid or a housekeeper, I would have found it in the wastebasket. I checked the phones first. I took the base plate off the one by the bed and found that my visitor was going first class. He'd put a Continental 0011 in there, more commonly known as a two-headed bug. It would pick up anything in the room and also over the phone and transmit it on an FM frequency. Effective maximum range probably three hundred feet. Battery good for five days or so, when fresh. It goes for around five hundred dollars. So he could be within range, listening on an FM receiver, or he could have a voice-activated tape recorder doing his listening for him. Or he could have a pickup and relay receiver-transmitter plugged into an AC outlet within range, and be reading me from a much greater distance. One thing was quite certain. The sounds of my taking the screws out of the base plate with the little screwdriver blade on the pocket knife would either have alerted him at once or would when he played the tape back.

So I said, "Come to the room and we'll have a little talk. Otherwise you're out five hundred bucks worth of playtoy." I took it out and thumbed the little microswitch to off. I then made a fairly thorough check of the underside of all the furniture and any other place I thought a backup mike and transmitter might be effectively concealed. The professional approach is to plant two. Then the pigeon finds one and struts around congratulating himself, but he's still on the air. If the same person, Broon, had checked me over the first time, then I had two more reasons to believe he wasn't much more than moderately competent.

I was finding a good place for the gun when Stanger phoned me. He said he hadn't been able to get a line on Broon as yet. He said the continuing investigation on the murder of Penny Woertz hadn't turned up a thing as yet. He had checked on Helen Boughmer and found they had her under heavy sedation.

I told him I had no progress to report.

I didn't actually. All I had was a lot more unanswered questions than before. I stretched out on the bed to ask them all over again.

Assume that Tom Pike had arranged that he and Janice Holton have their first assignation, in the full meaning of the word, in the apartment where Hulda Wennersehn lived. Janice couldn't get in touch with him to tell him she couldn't make it. So he had gone to the parking lot where they had arranged to meet and had finally realized she wasn't going to be there. Assume he went to the apartment alone and that he went to Penny's place in the late afternoon and she let him in and he shoved the shears into her throat. He tracked some blood into the Wennersehn apartment. He cleaned it up, cleaned up his shoes and maybe pants legs, and burned the rags.

But he had expected Janice to be there. He had changed his plan. What could the original plan have been? Janice certainly would have an understandable motive for killing her husband's girl friend. Having her nearby at the time of the murder could establish opportunity.

So if he planned to frame Janice Holton for the murder of Penny, and if Janice couldn't show up to be the patsy, why would he go ahead and kill Penny anyway? Lorette Walker had found out from the cleaning woman that somebody had stretched out on Hulda Wennersehn's bed.

So he had some thinking to do. He could cancel out and try to set it up another time. The death of the nurse would, of course, bust up the little duet of Penny and Rick, the two who had the unshakable belief Sherman hadn't killed himself. Did Penny have some random piece of information that she had not yet pieced into the picture and that made haste imperative?

Or it could have been some kind of sick excitement that grew and grew inside the brain of the man stretched out on the bed, until at last he got up and walked to Penny's place and did it because he had been thinking of it too long not to do it, even though the original plan was no longer possible.

Of course, it was possible that he might have at last decided to just go talk to the nurse and see if she did have the missing bit of information that he suspected she might have. Then, while he was with her, she might have made the intuitive leap, and suddenly he had no choice but to kill her, suddenly and mercilessly.

But my speculations kept returning to what the original plan could have been. What good would it do to knock Janice Holton out or drug her and set her up for the murder when under interrogation she would explain why she was at the Wennersehn apartment and who she was with? I tried to figure out how he could have planned to leap that hurdle. Kill them both and set it up as murder and suicide? That would have been a complex and tricky and terribly dangerous procedure.

Suddenly I realized that he could have framed her very safely, very beautifully, if she were unable to remember how she came to be there, in fact could not remember the assignation with Pike or even being in the Wennersehn woman's apartment or in Penny's apartment.

I found myself pacing around the room with no memory of getting off the bed. Suppose Pike had some way of making certain Maureen didn't remember a thing. No memory of suicide attempts. Couldn't Janice have no memory of committing a murder? Suppose she found herself in Penny's apartment with the dead girl, with no memory of how she got there?

Penny had been going to tell me something Dr. Sherman said about memory and digital skills. Digital? Skill with numbers or with fingers? Manual skills, maybe.

Maybe that Dormed thing fouled up memory. Electro-sleep. Portable unit, Biddy had told me.

I needed some fast expert opinions. I had no problem remembering the name of the neurologist in Miami. When your spine has been damaged by an angry man belting you with a chunk of two by four and your legs go numb, and somebody fixes what you were certain was a broken back and wasn't, you don't forget the name.

Dr. Steve Roberts. I got through to him in fifteen minutes. "Excuse me, Trav," he said. "This lady I live with has just handed me a frosty delicious glass. There. I have tested the drink and kissed the lady. What's on your mind? Back trouble?"

"No. Some information. Do you know anything about an electrosleep machine called a Dormed?"

"Yes, indeed. Nice little gadget. Very effective."

"If somebody used one a great deal, could it destroy their memory?"

"What? No. Absolutely not. Not enough current to destroy anything. If you keep hitting people with big charges, you don't destroy any particular process. You just turn them into a vegetable in all respects. Each series of shock treatments destroys brain cells. So do alcoholic spasms, if you have enough of them over a long enough period of time."

"How about convulsions? Like a woman might have if she had a kidney failure and lost a baby."

"Eclampsia, you mean? No, I doubt it. That sends the blood pressure up like a skyrocket, and before any brain damage could occur, you'd probably have a broken blood vessel in the brain. Where are you, anyway?"

"Fort Courtney."

"Practicing medicine without a license?"

"Practicing, maybe. But not medicine. Steve, can you think of any way you could make a person lose their memory?"

"*All* of it? Total amnesia?"

"No. Just of recent things."

"How long do you want this effect to last?"

"Permanently."

"Sometimes a good solid concussion will do it. Traumatic amnesia. Lots of people who recover after an accident lose a couple of hours or days out of their life and it seems to be gone forever. But there's no guarantee."

"Is there any chemical or medical way to do it?"

"Well . . . I wouldn't say that there's anything you could call a recognized procedure. I mean, there isn't much call for it, as I imagine you can understand."

"Is there a way?"

"Will you hold a minute. I think I can lay a hand on what I want."

I waited for at least two full minutes before he came back on the line. "Trav? I have to give you the layman's short course in how the brain works. You have about ten billion neurons in your head. These are tiny cells that transmit tiny electric charges. Each little neuron contains, among other things, about twenty million molecules of ribonucleic acid, called RNA for short. This RNA manufactures protein molecules—don't ask me how. Anyway, these protein molecules are related to the function we call memory. With me so far?"

"I think so."

"In certain experiments it has been shown that if you force laboratory animals to learn new skills, more RNA is produced in the brain, and thus more protein molecules are produced. Also, if you inject rats with magnesium pemoline, which doubles, at least, the RNA production, you have rats that learn a lot faster and remember longer. So they've tried reverse proof by injecting rats and mice with a chemical that interferes with the process by which the RNA produces the protein molecule. Teach a mouse to find its way through a maze, then inject it, and it forgets everything it just learned."

"What do they inject?"

"A substance called puromycin. At one university they've been treating goldfish with it, and they have some very stupid goldfish out there. Don't learn a thing and can't remember a thing."

"What would happen if you injected a person with puromycin?"

"I don't think anybody ever has. If it works the way it does on the lab animals, you'd wipe out the memory of what had recently happened, maybe forever. Personally, I'd rather be given magnesium pemoline. In fact, I don't know how I'm getting along without it. As to puromycin, I have no idea what the side effects would be."

"Could anybody buy it?"

"Any doctor could, or any authorized lab or research institute. What in the *world* have you gotten into?"

"I don't know yet."

"Will you tell me someday?"

"If it wouldn't bore you. Say, what about memory and digital skills?"

"What about it?"

"Well, make a comment."

"There seems to be a kind of additional memory function in the brain stem and in the actual motor nerves and muscles. We've discovered that a man can have a genuine amnesia, regardless of cause, and suppose he has been a jeweler all his life and you hand him a jeweler's loup. More often then not, without knowing why he does so, he will lift it to his eye, put it in place and hold it there, like a monocle. Give a seamstress a thimble, and she'll put it on the right finger. We had a surgeon here once with such bad aphasia he couldn't seem to make any connection to reality at all. But when we put a piece of surgical thread in his hand, he began to tie beautiful little surgical knots, one-handed, without even knowing what he was doing. Shall I go on?"

"No. That should do it."

"Don't turn your back on anybody holding a two by four."

"Never again." I thanked him and hung up.

An hour later I stood screened by the shrubbery on the grounds of a lake-shore house, empty and for sale, and saw the station wagon come out of the Pike driveway and turn toward me on the way to town. The two daughters of Helena, blond, dressed for the party, smiling, Biddy at the wheel and Maureen beside her.

I could reasonably assume that Tom Pike was already in the city, making certain of the arrangements, seeing that his guests would be taken care of. I moved through the screen of plantings, along the road shoulder, angled back along the property line to a point where I could look at the big house. Both cars were gone. Mosquitoes sang their little hunger note into my ears, and a bluejay flew to a pine limb directly over me and called me foul names and accused me of unspeakable practices.

I crossed the drive and the yard to the rear door and knocked loudly and waited. After the second try, with no answer, I tried to slip the lock, but there was too much overlap in the door framing, so I went along the back of the house and used a short sturdy pry bar on the latch of the first set of sliding glass doors. I had stopped en route at a shopping plaza and bought it, thinking of the sturdy construction of the steel cabinet I had seen in Maureen's bathroom. The metal latch tore easily and I slid the glass door and sliding screen open, glad that they had not yet adopted that most simple and effective device now being used more and more to secure sliding glass doors, one-inch round hardwood cut to proper length and laid in the track where the door slides.

I slid the foot-long pry bar back inside my slacks, the hook end over my belt, and went swiftly upstairs to Maureen's room. There was a party scent of perfume and bath soap in the still air, overlaying the constant undertone of medications. I knelt on the yarn rug in the bathroom and examined the lock on the metal cabinet. It was solid-looking, with such a complex shape of orifice for the key I could assume that trying to pick it would take too much time and patience. I bent the steel lip with the chisel-shaped end of the bar far enough so that I could work the curved nail-puller end into it. I held the cabinet with one hand and pulled slowly on the bar until suddenly the lock gave way and a flying bit of metal clinked against the tile wall.

There were all the usual bathroom nostrums and medications in the cabinet, things that could be harmful to children—iodine, aspirin, rubbing alcohol. There were syringes and injection needles laid out on a pad of surgical cotton. There was a box of disposable sterilized hypodermics. There was a little row of prescription medicines, pills in bottles and boxes, and there were only three small bottles of medication for injection, with a screw cap covering the rubber diaphragm through which the colorless solution was to be drawn into the hypo. Each had a prescription number, the same number. Two were full, one half empty. It seemed to be a very meager supply compared with enough needles for a nurse's station. The drugstore was Hamilton Apothecary, Grove Hills Shopping Center.

I knelt, pondering, automatically listening for any sound in the house. Biddy had said she had learned to give Maureen shots. So the prescription sedative could have been drawn off in whole or in part, and puromycin injected into the bottle. I took one of the two full bottles and the partially empty one. The twist caps on the full ones were still sealed. I realized that the placement of the three bottles bothered me. They were set out midway on the metal shelf, neither back against the rear, nor out at the edge. The other items on the other shelves were set back, taller items at the rear. So something could have been taken out, something that had stood behind the smaller bottles.

I got up and prowled and found a small flashlight on the nightstand in Biddy's room. I knelt again and shone the beam of light at a very flat angle against the metal shelf. There was a very, very faint coating of dust on the shelf, and I discovered that in the area behind where the three small bottles had stood there were four circular areas about the size of fifty-cent pieces where there was no dust. So four bottles or containers had rested there and had been removed very recently.

Deductive logic is self-defeating in that it is like the old-time taffy pull. Stretch it too far and too thin and it cools and sags and breaks. I had projected reasoning into an area where there were too many plausible alternatives.

Also I had the suspicion that all along I had been trying to make logical deductions on the basis of someone's actions and reactions who did not move in any reasoning predictable pattern.

If there had been something removed from the cabinet and if that substance was essential to keep Maureen Pearson Pike in her present childlike state, then either the necessity for keeping her in that condition had ended or she could not return to this house.

I reached my rented car in two minutes, no more. The sun was going down. A fat lady on hands and knees, grubbing in a flower bed, straightened up and stared at me from under the brim of a huge Mexican straw hat, her mouth a little round O as I went by at a full run, shoe soles whapping the suburban asphalt. I waved.

I made it into town in perhaps eight minutes, leaving a black spoor of rented rubber here and there. The new building was up on pillars, to provide parking room underneath. The earth around the building was still raw from construction efforts, the big sign listing prime contractor, architect, subcontractors, and future occupants still in place, portions of the sidewalk still fenced off, with temporary wooden walkways along the curbing. While still a half dozen blocks away I had seen, in the dusk, the lighted windows at the top floor. Perhaps forty cars were under the building, clustered in a casual herd over near the ramp and stairways that led up into the building. With no lights in the parking area, they looked like a placid herd of some kind of grazing creature, settling down for the night.

I started to park near them, then thought I might want to leave quickly, and latecomers might block me in. I swung around to the right, away from them, and parked, heading out, not far from the entrance I had used and off to the right of it. I got out and took my jacket off the seat and put it on. Revolver and pry bar were tucked away under the front seat, so I locked up.

Just as I took the first step toward the car cluster and the entrance up into the new building, I heard a faint cat sound, a thin yowl, then a thick, fat, heavy sound that ended the cat cry. It was a whomping thud, as if somebody had dropped a sack of wet sand onto the cat. There was a curious aftersound, a resonating, deep-toned *brong*, a vibration of the prestressed and reinforced structure overhead. I turned and went out that entrance driveway toward the sidewalk. The building was set back in that area, so that the roofing over the first part of the parking area was but one story high.

There were no pedestrians on the street. At the furthest corner cars were stacked waiting for the light to change. I went over to the temporary wooden walkway, roofed for pedestrian protection. I jumped and caught the wooden edge, pulled myself up onto the rough plywood roofing, and from there clambered up onto the permanent roof over that portion of the parking area underneath.

That roof portion was about fifty feet deep and a hundred and fifty wide. There was a long band of fading red across the western horizon, and the daylight had diminished everything to varying shades of gray. I could see from the construction thus far that doors opened out onto the roof area, and that it was designed to become some sort of patio, perhaps an outdoor dining area for a restaurant lease in the new structure.

Evidently large items of equipment had been derricked up onto that area and uncrated there and taken in through the double doors. The skeletal crates, pried and splintered, and various wrapping and packing materials were piled near the wall of the structure. That wall soared twelve stories straight up to the lighted windows of the top floor. I came upon the body of Maureen Pearson Pike just beyond the jumble of crates and packing materials.

She lay on her back about three feet from the side of the building and almost parallel to it. The upper part of her body was a little closer to the building than her legs were. She wore a gray-blue suit, a white blouse, one blue lizard pump. The other was nearby. I had seen the color of the suit when she and Biddy had gone driving by.

She was ugly, even though her face was undamaged. The impact had jellied her, inside the durable human hide. She was a long sack, roughly tubular, still enclosing all the burst meat and smashed bone, except where pink splinters came through the left sleeve of the suit near the elbow. Her mouth was wide open and unmoving. Her eyes were half open. She was flattened against the roof and bulged wrongly along the contours of her, so that the woman-shape was gone.

She had landed, as if with a purposeful neatness, with most of her on a crumpled sheet of heavy brown packing paper. It was that slightly waxy waterproofed paper they use to wrap pieces of heavy equipment when they are shipped in open crates, bolted down to heavy timber pallets. Where it was torn I could see that it was a sandwich of two layers of brown paper enclosing a black, tarry core.

I sat on my heels beside her. I touched the gloss of her hair, then closed her eyes. I smelled all those sharp familiar odors of sudden death. She was cooling meat, the spoiling process beginning. Still on my heels, I craned my neck and looked up. No row of heads up there, staring in sick fascination down the steep canyon drop to the disastrous impact.

I turned and looked at the building across the street. It was a much older building, an office building four stories high. All the windows were dark. I moved the edge of a crate that pinned the paper down. I gently moved her legs onto the paper. I brought a corner of it up and around her and tucked it under the flattened waist at the far side of her. I moved between her and the building and hesitated, then put my hands against the body and rolled it. That single piece was not big enough. I found another, bigger piece, big as a bed sheet, and swiftly straightened it out, put a corner under her and rolled her halfway up in it, then folded the top and bottom corners in, and rolled her up the rest of the way.

In the pile of crates I found some tangles of heavy hairy twine. I cut three pieces with my pocketknife and then I tied the long cylindrical bundle once around the middle and at points midway between the middle and each end.

I started to lose myself as I was doing the knots. I found myself making them too neat and making little throat-sounds of satisfaction at how neat and nice they were, and at what a splendid job I was doing. So I hauled myself back from that dark brink and made a quick search of the area and came upon a place a little better than I had hoped to find. It was a service hatch set into the side of the building, perhaps three feet square. Four big wing nuts held the metal plate in place. I took it off. The space was only about two feet deep behind it, ending at the grilled cover for some kind of big foam airfilters.

I went to her and looked up, looked at the windows across the street, and then picked her up. She was a stubborn, clumsy burden, improbably heavy. I had to stand it on end, lock my arms around it, and carry it in a straining, spread-legged waddle, across sixty feet of roof to the open service hatch. The paper was cracklingly heavy, the body somberly resistant. I forced it into a sitting position, pushed it back-first into the space, then bent the legs at the knee and pushed them in. The body lay tilted against the grillwork.

Parcel. All tied and stowed. Girl in a plain brown wrapper. Suddenly I realized that though I knew from the weight distribution which end was head and which feet, I had lost track of back and front. So either I had forced her into a sitting position or she was . . .

It was a sick horror, a viscid something that wells into the brain and stops all thought and motion. I shuddered and slammed the metal plate back on and turned the wing nuts down solidly. Only when I straightened did I realize I was soaked. I had sweated through my shirt, jacket, and the waistband of my slacks.

I went swiftly across the roof, made certain I would not be observed, then dropped to the plywood roof of the walkway and swung down and dropped to the sidewalk. As I started in, a car horn gave a warning beep and I moved aside. More guests for the party. I took my time and let them go up in the elevator first.

18 I STEPPED OUT of the elevator into party time. Gold rug, deep and resilient. Air conditioning laboring against too much smoke and too much body heat. Jabble and roar of dozens of simultaneous conversations. Two men in red coats at the bar set up in the impressive reception room of Development Unlimited.

Waitresses edging and balancing their careful way through the crush with trays of cocktails, trays of cocktail food with toothpicks stuck in each exotic little chunk. Girl in a cloth of gold mini-something and a gold cowboy hat and a golden guitar, wandering about with a fixed smile she had learned to wear while singing.

As I had come up alone in the elevator I had stared at myself in the mirror in the elevator. My face looked grainy and did not seem to fit. I had prodded at it with my fingers to make it fit. And I wondered if one eye had always looked bigger and starier than the other, and I had just never noticed. My lightweight jacket was dark enough so that it was not too evident how I had sweated it out. But it had been nervous sweat. It had turned ice cold. Not only did I feel as if I smelled somewhat like a horse, I felt that the exercise boy should trot me back and forth in front of the stalls for a time and rub me down or I'd catch the grobbles.

The guests were the business and investment community, the successful men of Fort Courtney and their women. Professional men, growers, bankers, merchants, contractors, realtors, brokers. Forties and fifties and sixties. Booming voices that spoke of confidence, optimism, low handicaps, capital gains. Many of their women had brittle questing eyes, appraising the hair, dress, and manner of their friends and acquaintances, checking to see who had come with whom.

It was easy to pick out the office staff. They were younger, and they seemed tense with the effort to be sociable and agreeable. I picked up a drink at the bar as protective coloration and moved along into what was apparently the largest area of the office suite, the bullpen, soon to be filled with girls, files, desks, duplicators, and electronic accounting equipment.

I saw Biddy Pearson in a small group at the far side of the room, talking animatedly. I worked my way over toward her, circling other conversation groups. She wore a little turquoise suit with a small jacket and short skirt. The jacket and the skirt fastened down the left side from shoulder to hip with five big brass old-fashioned galoshes-clamps, three on the jacket and two on the skirt. Her stockings were an ornate weave of heavy white thread with a mesh big enough for the standard seining net for bait.

She spotted me and looked flatteringly pleased and beckoned me over, introduced me to Jack and Helen Something, Ward and Ellie Somethingelse, and I moved in such a way as to block her out of the group just enough so that it dispersed. I did not trust my voice. I was afraid it would make a quacking sound. But it came out with reasonable fidelity as I asked her, "How are things going?"

"Beautifully! Tom is *so* pleased. Don't you think the decorator did a fabulous job?"

"Very nice."

"And Maurie is being an absolute dear! She seems to understand how important this is, really. And she's really being quite gracious." She went to tiptoe and lifted her chin to look about for Maureen.

So you take the gamble as you find it, and you make it up as you go along. "She certainly looks very, very lovely. That's a good color on her."

"Oh! You saw her already."

"Yes. Down in the lobby."

She was still looking for her, so it was a slow take. She turned toward me. "What? Where?"

"Down in the lobby."

"When?"

"I don't know. I've been here just long enough to get a drink. Five minutes ago? She got off the elevator when I got on."

She clamped her fingers around my wrist. "Was she alone?"

"Yes."

"My God, Travis, why didn't you stop her and bring her back up here?"

"Look, Biddy. She looked fine. She told me to go right on up and join the party. She said she had to get something out of the car. She said she'd be right back. Was I

217

supposed to grab her and bring her back up here, kicking and screaming?"

"Oh, she's so *sly!* Oh *damn* her, anyway. Just when everything was going *so* well. Tom was dubious about bringing her. But she seemed so . . . kind of better organized. Excuse me. I'd better find Tom. I thought she was still with him." She made a wry mouth. "And he probably thinks she's with me. He'll be sick, absolutely sick."

I found windows and oriented myself and went to a wide corridor that led past small offices to the big offices at the end. People were roaming up and down the corridor, being given the tour by some of the Development Unlimited staff. I turned a corner and went into an office and looked out and down and estimated I was not more than fifteen feet too close to the street side. I moved back toward the corner of the corridor and realized it had to be a room with a closed door. Almost all the others were open for inspection.

A pretty little redheaded woman came trotting along and stopped and stared up at me. She wore green and a pint of diamonds and a wide martini smile. "Well, hello there, darling! Are you one of *his* darling new engineers? Christ, you're a towering beast, aren't you? I'm Joanie Mace way down here."

"Hello, Joanie Mace. I'm not an engineer. I'm a mysterious guest."

"With a lousy empty glass? Horrors! Wait right here, mysterious guest. Don't move. Don't breathe. I'm a handmaiden."

She trotted away. My side of the corridor was empty. I heard voices approaching. I opened the door and stepped into a small office, unlighted. As I closed the door I saw that it was stacked with cartons of office forms and supplies. I made my way to the windows and found that the center window was fixed glass but that the narrower ones on either side cranked inward. A sliding brace stopped them when they were open perhaps eighteen inches. They were five feet tall, and the sill was a foot from the floor. The one on the left was open. I leaned and looked down.

It was the right one. I closed it, then pulled my jacket sleeve down across the heel of my hand and pressed the turn latch until it clicked into the fully latched position. As I turned, my toe came down on something soft. I could tell by the feel of it that it was a small leather evening bag. I shoved it into the front of my shirt and tightened my belt another notch.

I opened the door a careful fraction of an inch. A chattering group was approaching. When they had passed, I took the chance and walked out, perhaps too exaggeratedly casual, but there was no one there to fault the performance. I leaned against the corridor wall. Mrs. Mace brought me my drink, scuttling, holding it high, proud of her accomplishment. It was an extraordinarily nasty martini. I gave extravagant thanks. She said I should come by Sunday and swim in her pool. She would round up a swinging group. We'd all drink gallons of black velvets. Delighted. Yes, indeed.

We drifted along behind a group and ended up in the big room. Biddy came quickly to me and drew me aside. She looked determined and angry.

"Trav, I haven't told Tom and I don't intend to. Sooner or later he's going to find out she's missing and that will be time enough. I'm just not going to let my sister spoil the best part of it for him. She's done enough spoiling already. Would you please do me a very special favor?"

"Sure."

"Go down and start checking every bar you can find, and there are quite a few within three or four blocks of here. If you find her and if she isn't in bad shape yet, bring her back, please. But if she's had it, stay with her and put her in the station wagon down below. The tag is——"

"I know the car."

"Thanks *so* much! Poor Trav. Always doing stupid favors for the dreary Pearson family. And look, dear, do *not* ever let Tom know that I knew she was missing. He'd kill me. He would think I should have told him at once. But, darn it all . . . and . . . thanks again."

I started the slow journey through the crush of guests. I had to pass a group standing in respectful attention, listening to Tom Pike. He stood, tall, vital, dark, handsome, a little bit slouched, a little bit rustic and cowlicky and subtly aw-shucks about everything, his voice deep, rich, resonant as he said, ". . . job-creating opportunities in urban core areas, that's the answer if we're going to continue to have a viable center-city economic base here in Fort Courtney. The companion piece to this fine building should be—if we all have the guts and the vision—an enclosed shopping mall taking up that short block on Princess Street. Urban renewal to help tear down the obsolete warehouses and get the city to vacate the street, and I don't see why we couldn't have . . ."

I was by him, and a pack of ladies whooping at something that had just about tickled them to death drowned out the rest of the visionary address to the potential investors.

I rode down with a silent couple in the elevator. She stared with prim mouth and lofty eyebrows at the ceiling of the small machine. With clamped jaw and moody brow he stared at the blue carpeting underfoot. As we walked down into the parking area she did not realize I was as close behind them as I was. In a thin, deadly, indifferent tone she said, "Sweetheart, why don't you let me drive home alone while you go right on back up there and stroke Gloria's vulgar little ass all you want. She may be missing the attention."

He did not reply. I walked to my car and unlocked it and got in and clenched the wheel so tightly my knuckles made crackling sounds. I shut my eyes so tightly I could see rockets and wheels of fire. Little improvements come along, because the luck can go either way, and when you play the longer odds you open up the chance of the good luck and the bad. Her reaction helped. I had not expected it. I had wanted her to tell him that McGee had seen Maureen leaving by a route other than the one he knew she had taken, and so that would target him in on me, bring him in close enough for me to see what he was. But it was better the way she was doing it.

And I had to find Stanger, and find him fast.

I didn't get to Stanger until nine fifteen. I told him that it might save a lot of time and a lot of questions later if it went down on tape on the very first go-round.

"You look funny," he said. "You look spooked."

"It's been one of those days, Al."

"What's this all about?"

"When the tape is running."

"All right, all right!"

So he left Nudenbarger on traffic cruise by himself and rode down to headquarters with me in my car. I said I'd like to do it in the car if possible. He came out with a battered old Uher with an adaptor for the cigarette lighter. I found a bright white drive-in on Route 30 and parked at the far edge with the rear against the fence. A listless girl made two long walks to take the order and bring out the two coffees and hook the tray onto the car. Stanger had checked the recorder. It had some hiss but not too much. The heads needed cleaning and demagnetizing.

He rewound and started it again on record and established his identity, the date and time, and said he was taking a voluntary statement from one Travis McGee of such and such a place, said statement having some bearing, as yet unknown, on the murder by stab wound of Penny Woertz, and that said victim had been acquainted with said McGee. He sighed and handed me the mike.

As soon as I got into it, he stiffened and he boggled at me. As I kept on he wanted to interrupt so badly he began making little lunges and jumps, so I didn't give him an opening. At one point he bent over, hands cupping his eyes, and I could hear him grinding his teeth. I finished. I turned the remote switch on the mike and said, "Want me to turn it back on for questions?"

"No. No. Not yet. Oh, good Jesus H. Jumpin' Sufferin' Christ on the rocks! Oh you lousy dumb bastard! Oh, why did I ever think you had one brain cell to rub up against another. You silly bastard, I have got to take you in and shut the iron door on you. For God's sake, it is going to take me half the night just to write up the charges. And you have the gall, the nerve, the lousy . . . impertinence to ask me to sneak down there and grab that dead broad out of that crazy hidey hole and make like I found her in a ditch, and keep anybody from coming up with the ID and keep her the hell on ice as a Jane Doe until God only knows how. . . . No! Dammit, McGee. No!" It was an anguished cry.

"Why don't you ask me some questions. Maybe it'll calm you down, Stanger. You've got all night to go collect her."

He nodded. I turned the mike on.

"Are you absolutely certain she was dead?"

"She fell a hundred and twenty feet onto concrete."

"So all right! Did you realize when you touched the outside and inside knob on that office door and messed with the window and picked up the pocketbook, you were removing evidence of a crime, if there was one?"

"He wouldn't leave anything useful. I moved the body too. Jumped, fell, or pushed, it would look just the same."

"But what the hell do you expect to accomplish?"

I turned off the microphone. "Al, you won't play it my way?"

"I can't! It's such a way-out——"

"Who can make a decision to *try* my way? Your chief?"

"Old Sam Teppler? He's going to keel over in a dead faint if I try to tell him, even."

"How about your state attorney for this judicial district, Gaffney?"

"Gaffner. Ben Gaffner."

"Is there any chance he'd buy it? There's all kinds of prosecutors. What kind is he?"

Al Stanger got out of the car and slammed the door. He walked slowly around the car, scuffing his heels on the asphalt, hitching at his trousers, scratching the back of his neck. He came and looked down at me across the hook-on tray.

"Gaffner is on his fourth term. He gets a hell of a lot of respect. But nobody gets very close to him. He likes to

222

nail them. He drives hard. His record keeps him in. He isn't fancy. He builds his cases like they used to build stone walls in the old days. All I can say is . . . maybe. You'd have to sell him the whole thing. All the way down the line. He's straight and he's tough, and he likes being just what he is. But I'd even hate to try to explain to him why you're not behind iron right now, McGee."

"Let's give it a try."

He went to a public phone booth on the corner line of the gas station across the highway. I could see him in the floodlighted booth, talking for a long time. I could not tell from his dispirited pace as he came back what the answer had been.

He got in beside me and pulled the door shut. "He's based fifty-five miles from here. In Lime County. He'll leave in about ten minutes, he said, and bring two of his people. They'll make good time. They'll plan on me opening up one of the circuit court hearing rooms in the courthouse and we'll meet them there."

"What did you say to him?"

"Told him I had a nut here that wanted me to help him hide the body of a murder victim."

"What did he say?"

"He asked me why I'd called him, and I told him because I thought maybe the nut had a pretty good idea. So he said he'd better come over and listen. I don't think he'll buy it."

"No harm in trying to sell it."

"Why don't I just lock you up nice?"

"Because at heart you're a dandy fellow."

I blinked the lights and the girl came and got the tray and her money. Stanger checked in and said he was going off shift a little early instead of staying on until midnight. He told them to have the dispatcher tell Lew Nudenbarger. We went down to the courthouse. He located the night man and had him unlock the small hearing room next to the offices of the circuit judge on the second floor, and told him to stay by the side door near the parking lot, as Mr. Gaffner would be coming along.

The countersunk fluorescence shone down on a worn

red rug, a mahogany veneer table with ten armchairs aligned around it. The air was close and still, and the room had no windows. Stanger fussed with the thermostat until something clicked and cool air began to circulate. We laid out the various items on the oiled top of the table. The two prescription vials, one partially used. The two-headed bug. The recorder, now with AC line cord plugged in. One blue lizard envelope purse that matched the blue lizard pumps wrapped up with the dead wife of Tom Pike. Holton's revolver. The pry bar, which could be matched to the forced entry marks on the sliding glass doors and the metal medicine chest.

We waited for Gaffner, with Stanger wearing a tired little smile.

19 BEN GAFFNER sat at the middle of the long table. He directed me to sit opposite him, Stanger at my left. His two men sat at his right and his left. The thin, pale one named Rico was his chief investigator. The round, red one named Lozier was the young attorney who assisted him throughout the circuit.

Gaffner was an orderly man. He arranged in useful order in front of him a yellow legal pad, four sharp yellow pencils, glass ashtray, cigarettes, lighter. Rico had brought along a recorder, a Sony 800. He plugged it in, threaded a new tape, tested it, put the mike on top of a book in the center of the table, tested it again, changed the pickup volume, and nodded at Gaffner.

Only then did Gaffner look directly at me. The tape reels turned at slow speed. He had a moon face and his small and delicate features were all clustered in the center of the moon. His hair was cropped close except for a wiry tuft of gray on the top near the front, like a handful of steel wool. His eyes were an odd shade of yellow, and he could hold them on you without shifting them or blinking them or showing any expression. It was effective.

"Your name?" he said finally. Uninflected. No accent, no clue to area of origin. Name, age, address, occupation, marital status, local address.

"It is my understanding that you are making a voluntary confession, Mr. McGee. I must warn you that——"

"I am aware of my rights regarding self-incrimination, remaining silent, right to counsel, and so forth, Mr. Gaffner. I waive them freely and voluntarily, with no threats, promises, or coercion on your part."

"Very well. You will tell me in your own words your actions in regard to the alleged crime which you——"

"We're not going to do it that way, Mr. Gaffner."

"We are going to do it my way."

"Then, you had a long drive for nothing. Al, lead me to that iron door of yours."

Gaffner kept those yellow eyes on me for a long ten count. "How do you suggest we do this, McGee?"

"I want to start over five years ago and tell you how and where I met Helena Pearson Trescott and her daughters. I won't waste your time with anything not pertinent to the case I hope you will be able to take to the grand jury. Some of the subsequent events will be guesswork."

"I am not interested in your conjectures."

"I am not interested in how much or how little interest you have in my conjectures. I am going to give them to you, right along with what facts I have. Without the conjectures the facts won't hang together. You'll just have to endure it, Mr. Gaffner. Maybe you could just tell yourself you might get some leads out of them."

After another long yellow unwinking stare he said, "Proceed, then. Try not to ramble. When I hold up my hand like this, please stop, because I will want to write a note on this pad. When I stop writing, continue, and try to continue where you left off. Is that clear?"

"Perfectly."

It took a long time. It took both sides of a five-inch reel of tape and half of another before we were done. He wrote many pages of notes, his writing swift, neat, and very small.

My chain of motive and logic went thus:

Dr. Stewart Sherman had indeed killed his wife, and in the course of his investigation the special investigator for Courtney County, Dave Broon, had come up with something that, if he reported it or turned it in, would have been enough to give a reasonable assurance of an indictment by the grand jury. A practicing physician would be far more useful to Dave Broon than a man indicted for murder. A man of Broon's shrewdness would probably lock it all up very carefully, perhaps by trading cooperation and silence for a written confession which could be tucked away.

Next consider Tom Pike's narrow escape when he was being investigated for unethical practices while working as a stockbroker. The intervention of Miss Hulda Wennersehn was almost too opportune. One might detect here the possibility of Dave Broon stepping in and doing Pike a great favor. It would be profitable to help Pike. Maybe he dug up information on the Wennersehn woman to use as leverage, or maybe he already had something and was waiting for a good chance to use it. This would give Broon a certain hold over Pike as well. Pike was becoming more and more successful, and possibly overextended.

Then we have Helena Pearson Trescott, before her first operation for cancer, telling her daughters the terms of her will and the surprising size of her estate. Maureen would certainly have told Tom the terms. Then we have the surgeon, Dr. Bill Dyckes, telling Tom Pike, but not the daughters, that Helena will not recover from the cancer of the bowel. Suddenly the expected baby is a potential source of loss compared to (under the terms of the will) the optimum solution. The ideal order would be for Helena to die first, then for Maureen to die without issue, and for Tom Pike to marry Bridget.

The family doctor is, by accident or plan, Dr. Sherman. One can assume that through a mutually profitable relationship Pike and Broon have become confidants. Trust could be guaranteed by putting various damaging pieces of information in a safe place, available only upon the death of either conspirator.

So pressure is put on Sherman to induce spontaneous abortion of the child Maureen Pike is carrying. There are drugs that can be given by injection that will dangerously inhibit kidney function. Do it, or face complete exposure and disgrace and perhaps a life term. It works almost too well, making Maureen dangerously ill.

Here there is an area of pure guesswork. Why was it so necessary to wipe out Maureen's memory of the immediate past? Did she suspect the shot Sherman gave her had killed the child? Or, more probably, when she appeared to be comatose, she could have heard too much of some quiet bedside conversation between Dr. Sherman and her husband. Nothing could make a woman keep her mouth shut about that. If memory could not be wiped out, she would have had to be killed, in spite of the money loss it would mean. Sherman had been doing animal experimentations on memory, on the retention of skills once learned, of retraining time when such skills were forgotten. As the doctor on the case, he could easily give Maureen a massive dose of puromycin. When it wiped memory clean of all events of the previous several days, one can assume Pike would soon realize how useful that effect could be. It could help him lay the groundwork for her death, which would have to come after Helena had died, and it would be a way of keeping Bridget there in the house, with the two of them, where she could fall in love with Tom Pike.

Once she is home from the hospital, Tom Pike, with Biddy's unwitting cooperation, keeps his wife on puromycin. Her day-by-day memory function is fragmented. Her learning skills are stunted. A side effect is a kind of regression to childhood, to sensual pleasure, to the naughtiness of running away. But this helps keep Biddy near. She cannot leave her sister. So while Helena still lives, he sets the stage for eventual successful suicide. There is no risk in feeding her the sleeping pills and waiting a seemingly risky length of time before taking her in. She will have no memory of it. No harm in putting her in the hot tub, making the hesitation marks on her wrist, then one cut deep enough, and waiting, then breaking down the unlocked door. She will not remember. She will not know that it was he who fashioned the clumsily knotted noose instead of she.

But he was not aware of the way potential suicides stay usually with one method and never more than two. But here we have four.

The reason Dr. Sherman became ever more troublesome seems clear. He would slowly come to realize that there was a very small chance of their ever using the evidence of his wife's murder against him, because if indicted, he would certainly be expected to tell of the induced abortion performed at the request of Pike, with leverage by Broon, and tell of the drug that he had been supplying Pike to inject into Maureen, the drug that had caused the mental effects that baffled the neurologists and the psychiatrists. Meanwhile he had been induced to invest everything in Pike's ventures, even to cashing in his insurance policies and investing the proceeds.

Maybe Sherman began to talk about confession. Maybe he began to gouge money out of Pike in return for supplying the puromycin.

How was that murder done? A week before she died, Penny Woertz had a dream that reminded her of something. A trap door in Sherman's forehead, a little orange light like the one that winks on the face of the Dormed control. Count the flashes. Could she have remembered some casual comment that Sherman made about some trouble with the electrosleep device he had supplied for Maureen Pike and taught Biddy to operate?

A careful check might reveal that on the night the doctor died the daughters and Helena might have driven down to the Casey Key house. And it might reveal that Pike was out of town, in Orlando or Jacksonville. There he could have rented a car, gone home, gotten the Dormed and put it in its case and taken it down to Sherman's office to be tested. It was portable. The case was pale. The machine was heavy. A tall man had been seen leaving Sherman's office. Tall is relative. Pike was fairly tall. Six feet almost? Height is such a distinctive thing that a pair of shoes with extreme lift is a very efficient disguise. I have a pair of shoes with almost a four-inch lift. It takes my six four up to six eight. With them I wear a jacket a couple of inches longer than my normal forty-six extra long. People remember the size. They remember seeing a giant. They remember little else about him.

Simplest thing in the world to take it in for Sherman to check. "Maureen says it hurts her. Biddy and I have tried it. There are little sharp pains at first. Try it and see."

In moments the doctor is asleep, with the impulses set at maximum. Take the key out of the pocket. Unlock the drug safe. Roll the sleeve up. Tie the tubing around the arm. Inject the lethal shot of morphine. Untie the rubber tubing. Go and collect all the puromycin out of the back-room supplies. Wait a little while and then take the headpiece off, unplug the machine, repack it in its case, and leave.

Helen Boughmer promises trouble. Tell Broon to find a way to shut her mouth. Broon has no trouble.

Holton and Nurse Woertz begin to make a crusade of the whole matter. Nothing they can find out, probably. Broon discovers and reports to Pike that Holton and the nurse have become intimate. Then whisper the news to Janice because, disloyalty being contagious, she can be a good source of information about Holton's progress in his independent investigation. Make the casual contact with her. By being sympathetic, play upon her hurt and discontent. Keep it all on a platonic basis, but be as cautious and discreet as though it were a physical affair—because were Biddy to learn of it, some unpleasant new problems would arise.

Helena dies. Perhaps the new source of funds, a large lump sum from her estate, is becoming more and more imperative. Broon had gained a lot of leverage with the murder of Sherman and could become increasingly expensive to Tom Pike.

Enter McGee, a worrisome development to Tom Pike

229

when he learns that Helena has been writing to McGee. He does not know if Helena suspected anything. The story of tracing the *Likely Lady* seems implausible. Then he gets the little query from Penny Woertz. Did you tell the doctor you were having trouble with the Dormed? Did he check it for you?

Put Broon onto McGee. Then Broon reports that Holton has asked him to check McGee's room. Puzzling. Then, Broon reports, Holton and the nurse and McGee spent quite a bit of time together in 109 and then Holton left. The nurse stayed with McGee all night. But by then Pike has arranged how to take care of Penny Woertz. He has already arranged the Saturday date with Janice. He has temporarily transferred the Wennersehn woman to Jacksonville and has the key to her apartment, two doors from Miss Woertz.

At that point something made me aware of Stanger and I glanced at him and saw him glaring at me in anger and indignation.

"Sorry, Al. When he missed connections with Janice, I think he went to the apartment alone. Had he met her and had she followed him there in her car, I think that he would have spent a good part of the afternoon making love to her. After all, it wasn't going to be anything she could talk about later. Then, perhaps, when she napped, he would go over to Penny's place. She would let him in. He would kill her with whatever weapon came easiest to hand. Go back and perhaps pin down the sleeping woman and inject her with a massive shot of puromycin. Lead her in her dazed condition over to Penny's apartment. Shove her in and close the door. Drive away. She would not recall having any date, any assignation. She would be in the dead nurse's apartment, with the shears in the dead throat of the woman who was sleeping with her husband. Traumatic emotional amnesia. Not a terribly unusual thing.

"But he lay there for a long time thinking it over and maybe decided it was a risk he could accept. Blood spattered on his shoes and pants legs. He went back to the Wennersehn apartment and cleaned himself and the floor and burned the rags in the fireplace. The maid swept the fireplace out on Monday."

"Who will verify that?" Gaffner asked.

"It better be Tom Pike. My source is not available. I completely forgot who told me."

"We can give you a long time to sit and think."

"I have a terrible memory."

Yellow stare. Small shrug. "Continue."

I told them that investigation would probably prove that Tom Pike landed in Jacksonville Sunday morning in plenty of time to direct-dial Rick Holton and whisper to him about the note, knowing that bullheaded Holton would track it down. And, having done so, because of the contents that Tom had conned out of Nudenbarger, might solve the McGee problem suddenly and dramatically, which would take Holton out of the play too.

When that didn't work, Pike had put Broon back to work on me. I mentioned that Broon could well own over forty rental houses in Southtown, and it might be interesting to find out how he could live so well and afford to buy real estate too.

"And that brings me up to the point where I burgled the Pike house and picked up this stuff. It's in detail on Al's tape, so I suggest you listen to that."

We all did. I was glad of the break. My throat felt raw.

One of the group was missing. When I had told of the letter and the check for twenty-five thousand forwarded to me by D. Wintin Hardahee, and how he had been cooperative at first and then had brushed me off completely, Gaffner had sent Mr. Lozier, who knew Hardahee, out to bring him in, with instructions not to tell him what it was all about.

Lozier came in alone and sat down quietly and listened to the balance of the tape I had made in the car.

Gaffner turned to Lozier and said, "Well?"

"Well, sir, that is just about the weirdest——"

"I was asking about Hardahee."

"Sir, I didn't tell him what it was about. He came willingly. And all of a sudden, halfway here, he started crying. I pulled over, and when he could talk, he said that he had promised Dave Broon he would cooperate and Broon had promised not to turn him in."

"For what?"

The young lawyer looked very uncomfortable. "Apparently, sir, Mr. Hardahee has been having . . . uh . . . a homosexual affair with his tennis partner, and Dave Broon bugged the cabin where they've been meeting for over a year."

"How was he asked to cooperate?"

"Broon wanted to know the contents of the letter Mrs. Trescot wrote to Mr. McGee. He convinced Broon he had never had a chance to read it. He told Broon about the check to Mr. McGee. Mr. Broon asked him to give Mr. McGee no advice or cooperation at all. Broon told him that he might hear from Mr. Pike about an investment opportunity, and when he did, it might be a good thing to go into it, substantially."

"Where is Hardahee?" Gaffner asked softly.

"He's sitting down in the car, sir."

"Well, Larry, suppose you go down and drive the poor sad silly son of a bitch home. Tell him we'll have a little talk someday soon. Tell him that in the absence of a complaint, there's no charge."

As Lozier left, Gaffner turned to Stanger. "Would it be asking entirely too much to have you go out and come back here with Broon, Lieutenant?"

"I swear to God, I have been hunting that man here and there and up and down the whole day long, and he is plain gone."

He shifted his unwinking stare to me. "And it is your thought, Mr. McGee, that Mr. Pike will suddenly crack under the strain and start bleating confessions at us all?"

"No, sir. I don't think he will ever confess to anything at all. I don't think he feels any guilt or remorse. But you see, if Maureen disappears, there is no proof of death. He can't bail out by marrying the younger sister. If he's in a tight spot, he'll have to make some kind of move." It astonished me a little to hear myself call him "sir." It is not a word I use often or loosely.

"Don't you think, Mr. McGee, that you are assuming

232

that a very intelligent man like Pike has committed some very violent and foolish acts?"

"Right now they seem violent and foolish because we all have a pretty good idea of the things he's done and why he's done them. But when things get more and more complex, Mr. Gaffner, it leaves more room for chance. For luck, good and bad. Where would we be with all this if I hadn't come into the picture? Not that I've been particularly bright about any part of this. I was something new added to the mix and I guess I've been a catalytic agent. His luck started to run the other way. The biggest piece of bad luck was when I decided not to park over by the other cars. When she hit the overhead, it was a hell of a sound. I didn't know what it was. I knew it was something right over my head. One hell of a smack to make the whole prestressed roof ring like a drum. Okay. No workmen around. Building empty except for the party on the top floor. So I had to find out what made that noise. Maybe I knew what it had to be. Maybe my subconscious fitting things together in a single flash of intuition. What if I hadn't found her?"

"He doesn't know you found the body."

"And so he's handling it according to plan. She ran off again. Big search. Worry. Then in the morning the workmen find it, and it fits with her recent history of suicide attempts and her condition. He's going through the motions now. He thinks he's home free. Violent, yes. Foolish, however, is another word. I think he's legally sane, but I think he's a classic sociopath. Do you know the pattern? Superficially bright, evidently quite emotional, lots of charm, an impression of complete honesty and integrity."

"I have done the necessary reading in that area, Mr. McGee," Gaffner said.

"Then you know their willingness to take risks, their confidence they can get away with anything. They're sly and they're cruel. They never admit guilt. They are damned hard to convict." He nodded agreement.

I told him about the couple who had worked for the Pikes. I told him of the golf club incident. Then I described Tom Pike's bedroom, the strange sterility and neatness of it, how impersonal it seemed, without any imprint of personality.

Gaffner asked Stanger if he could add anything. "Not much on him," Al said, examining the sodden end of a dead cigar. "Florida born. Lived here and there around the center of the state, growing up. His folks worked the groves, owned little ones and lost them, took over some on lease, made out some years and crapped out other years. Don't know if there's any of them left or where they are now. Tom Pike went off to school up north someplace. Scholarship, I think. Came here a few years ago, just married, had money enough to build that house out there. I guess there must have been credit reports on him for the size loans he's got into and I guess if they turned up anything out of line, he wouldn't have got the loans. The people that don't like him, they *really* don't like him a damn bit, but they keep their mouths shut. The ones that do, they think he's the greatest thing ever walked on two legs."

After a silence Ben Gaffner said softly, "Ego. The inner conviction that everybody else in the world is soft and silly and gullible. Maybe we are, because we're weighted down with excess baggage the few Tom Pikes of this world don't have to bother with. Feelings. The capacity to feel human emotions, love, guilt, pity, anger, remorse, hate, despair. They can't feel such things but don't know they can't, so they think our insides are just like theirs, and they think the world is a con game and think we fake it all, just as they have learned to do."

I said, "You've done your reading, sir."

"What have we got right now? Let's say we could open Broon up and make him the key witness for the prosecution. If he confirms what you think he can confirm, McGee, then I'd take a chance on going for an indictment. But Pike is going to be able to get top talent to defend him. The jury is going to have to either believe Broon or believe Pike. Circumstantial case. Pike is likable and persuasive. And I'm saddled with a story to present that sounds too fantastic and I'm saddled with medical experts who'll be contradicted by his medical experts. One long, long trial, a lot of the public monies spent on it, and I would say four to one against a conviction."

"About that," Stanger agreed unhappily.

"So what if there's no way to open Broon up? Or what if he's gone for good? Nothing to go on. I'd be a fool to go after an indictment."

"Gone for good?" Stanger asked. "Little cleanup job by Pike?"

"Only if Pike could be sure Broon wouldn't leave anything behind that might turn up in the wrong hands. Otherwise, on the run. Cash in the chips and leave for good, knowing that sooner or later Pike would want to get rid of the only link to all the rest of it."

"So where does that leave us, Mr. Gaffner?" Stanger asked.

"I think you and Rico better start moving. What time is it? Three fifteen. Best get a panel delivery. We'll have to make sure Pike isn't in that area anywhere. Get that body out of there at first light. Drive it back over to Lime City. Is that old phosphate pit on the Hurley ranch dry at the bottom?"

"Since he cut through, it runs off good."

"About eighty-foot drop down that north wall. Get hold of that big matron with the white hair."

"Mrs. Anderson."

"She can keep her mouth shut. I want the fancy clothes off that body, tagged and marked and initialed by both of you and put away in my safe, Rico, and I want her dressed in something cheap and worn out. Put her at the bottom of that drop, then, soon as you can, you get her found. You could tell Hessling to go check a report of kids messing around there last night. Then I can come in on it through normal channels and we'll process an autopsy request, and I'll make sure I have somebody come in to backstop Doc Rause and run a complete series on the brain tissue."

He turned toward me with the slow characteristic movement of his round head, moon face. "It isn't all that big a risk, in case we get nowhere. She kept wandering off and had to be found. So she wandered off and hitched a ride maybe, and ended up dead in the bottom of a phosphate pit."

Stanger said, "Won't Pike make sure she's listed as missing, and won't she fit the description enough so that he might come over to make the identification?"

"We'd better make a positive on her. We can change our mind later on. Who do you think, Rico?"

The pale, mild investigator said, "That drifter girl that jumped bond on that soliciting charge four, five months back? If the prints matched, it could be a screwup in the filing system that we could catch later on."

"I like it," Gaffner said. Lozier had returned. He said Hardahee had pulled himself together. Gaffner said they would decide later on if they wanted an affidavit from Hardahee.

Then Gaffner swiveled his head slowly and nailed us each in turn with the yellow appraisal. "All of you listen carefully. We are engaged in foolishness. You do not have to be told to keep your mouths shut. I do not buy all of McGee's construction. I buy enough of it to continue the idiocy he started. We are all going to remember that our man won't get jumpy. He won't become superstitious and fearful. Psychos are notoriously pragmatic. If a body is gone, somebody took it. He'll wait to find out who and why, and while he is waiting he'll make the perfectly normal and understandable moves of the alarmed husband with a missing wife. Stanger, you and Rico better get going. And after Rico is loaded and gone, Stanger, your job is find Broon for me. Lozier, wait in the hall out there while I have a word with Mr. McGee."

The table had been cleared of gear. All that remained were the overflowing ashtrays. Gaffner looked as fresh and rested as when the session had begun.

He stood at attention and looked up into my face. "You're the bait, of course. When the woman is not found, Miss Pearson is going to feel more and more guilty. She is going to blame herself. And so she will confess to her brother-in-law that she knew Maureen was gone and didn't tell him. She will say that you saw Maureen leaving. Then you are the key, because you can supply the information about the body. No body, and the whole scheme is dead."

"So he has to talk to me."

"And he is still wondering what's in that letter Mrs. Trescott wrote you."

"And what he says to me, that's what you have to know. That's what you need so you can move. What if he decides to accept his losses, write this one off, go on from here? What if he can squeak through, assuming he is in a little financial bind?"

"As soon as the working day starts, Mr. McGee, I am going to make some confidential phone calls to some of the more important businessmen I know over here in Fort Courtney. I'll tell them it's just a little favor. I can say that as a matter of courtesy I was told that the Internal Revenue people are building up a case against Pike for submitting fraudulent tax returns, and it might be a good time to bail out, if they happen to be in any kind of joint venture with him. I think he might feel a lot of immediate pressure. You could provide the answers that would relieve it. I think we can hurry him along."

"So how do you want me to handle it?"

"I think the thing he would respond to best, the attitude he'd most quickly comprehend, would be your offer to sell him the body for a hundred thousand dollars. But I don't want to move, to set it up, until we have a good line on Broon. I'd like him in custody first. Additional pressure. So we'll get you back to your motel, and I want you to accept no calls and have your meals sent in until I instruct you further. Can you . . . ah . . . suppress your natural talent for unilateral action?"

"I bow to the more devious mind in this instance, Mr. Gaffner."

There was no trace of humor in him. "Thank you," he said.

20 *I SLEPT UNDISTURBED* until past noon. The door was chained, the DO-NOT-DISTURB sign hanging on the outside knob.

The first thing I remembered when I awoke was how, about an hour before first light, I had driven by the new building, with Gaffner beside me and Lozier following in the car they had arrived in.

I drove by knowing she was still up there, behind the metal plate of the service hatch, waiting out the first hours of forever, leaning against the interior grill, firmly wrapped, neatly tied.

Helena, I didn't do very well. I gave it a try, but it was moving too fast. Dear Tom sidled her into the little office past the boxes, perhaps kissed her on the forehead in gentle farewell, opened the window as wide as it would go, and told her to look down, darling, and see where the lovely restaurant will be. She would turn her shoulders through the opening and peer down. Then a quick boost of knee in the girdled rump, hand in the small of the back. Her hand released the purse to clutch at something, clutch only at the empty air of evening, then she would cat-squall down, slowly turning.

I showered, shaved. I felt sagging and listless. I had the feeling that it was all over. Odd feeling. No big savage heat to avenge the nurse, avenge the big blond childish delicious wife. Perhaps because nothing anyone could do to Pike would ever mean anything to him in the same sense that we would react to disaster.

He was a thing. Heart empty as a paper bag, eyes of clever glass.

As I was reaching for the phone, there was a determined knocking at my door. I called through it. Stanger. I let him in. He seemed strange. He drifted, in a floating way, as if happily drunk. But he wasn't. His smile was small and thoughtful.

He looked at his watch and sat down. "We've got a little time to spare."

"We have? That's nice."

"I did a better job of bugging Mr. Tom Pike than I did on you. Was it that wad of paper on the floor?"

"Lieutenant, I'm disappointed in you. Bugging people on your own team. Shame!"

"My only team is me. I had a lot of thoughts about you. One of them was you were smokescreening the fact maybe Tom Pike brought you in here for some reason or other. Was it something about that paper on the floor?"

I said it was and told him how it worked, then said, "So why didn't you let me know last night?"

"Wanted you to have all the window trimming there was. The more you could come up with, the better chance you had of selling Gaffner. You did good with that man."

"That was an expensive piece of equipment you planted on me, Al. City property?"

"Personal. It wasn't like planting it on a stranger. I knew I'd get it back. You might as well think it was Broon did it. But he didn't because the very last time anybody saw him at all was a little before noon, Monday. He went to the Courtney Bank and Trust and opened his deposit box, and it gave me the ugly feeling he was gone for good. So it was mighty comforting to hear I'm going to meet up with him."

"You keep looking at your watch."

"So I do. But there's still plenty of time. Don't you want to know how I bugged old Tom?"

"You're going to tell me anyway."

"Why, so I am! Who else can I tell? I went right to a fellow who happens to be the second oldest of those six brothers of Penny Woertz and who happens to work for Central Florida Bell, and I told him I was in need of a little illegal help, and first thing you know, we had a nice tap on both Pike's private unlisted lines. Nothing I can ever take to court, naturally."

"Naturally."

"Lord God, that man has had trouble this morning! Between keeping people busy hunting all over for his missing wife and trying to calm down the people who want to take their money out of his little syndicates and corporations, I bet you ol' Dave Broon had to try a lot of times before he got through. About ten of eleven when he did. Had to put in thirty-five cents for three minutes."

"So?"

"So thank God when Tom said they could meet at the usual place, Dave didn't want any part of it. Saves a lot of trouble. Dave Broon picked the place. Six miles southwest of town. I just got back from there, checking it over, getting something set up. Pretty good place to meet. Big piece of pastureland. Used to be the old Glover place. Pike and some people bought it up a while ago to turn it into something called ranchettes. Two-acre country estates. There's a gate with a cattle guard near the west side and a lot of open land and just one big old live oak shade tree smack in the middle, maybe a quarter mile from the nearest fence line."

"When do they meet?"

"Two thirty. But I left Nudenbarger staked out. We can swing around and go in the back way and cut across to where I left him. Less chance of running into either of them."

"You seem very contented, Mr. Stanger."

"Sure. Broon told him to bring a big piece of money. They haggled some. Pike said thirty thousand was absolute tops. Broon said it would have to be an installment. Broon told him not to get cute. It's sure empty out there. Bugs, buzzards, and meadowlarks. They'll meet by the tree and have a nice talk."

"And you bugged the tree."

His face sagged and his mouth turned down. "You take the pure joy out of things, McGee. I'm sorry I decided to bring you along for the fun."

240

"I'm sorry I spoiled your fun. I haven't had anything to eat yet. Is there time?"

"Fifteen minutes."

Stanger drove the city's sedan hard. He took a confusing route through the back country, along small dirt roads. At last he stopped and got out at a place that looked like any other. He extended the aerial of a walkie-talkie and said, "Lew? You read me?"

"I read you, Al. No action yet. Nothing. Hey, bring that bug dope out of the glove compartment."

"Okay. We'll be coming along now. Let me know if either one shows up before we get there."

He told me that he'd left Nudenbarger staked out with binoculars, a carbine, and the receiver-recorder end of the mike-transmitter unit he'd tied in the oak tree. He said we had a mile to go. He hadn't wanted to put the car on any directly connecting road for fear Broon or Tom Pike would drive a circuit around the whole ranch to see if everything was clear before driving in.

We had to crawl under one fence and climb over another. The air was hot and still, but there was a hint of coolness whenever the breeze stirred. Stanger seemed to be plodding along listlessly, but he covered ground faster than one would think.

We came out onto a dirt road, crossed it, leaped a watery ditch on the other side. I followed Stanger into a clump of small pines, thick ones, eight to ten feet tall. He motioned me down, and we crawled the last dozen feet to where Nudenbarger lay on his belly close to the fence, staring through the binoculars. He turned and looked with a certain distaste at me and said, "Nothing yet, Al. Maybe they called it off, huh?"

Stanger ignored him. He said to me, "Ringside. Like it?"

We were sheltered on three sides by the pines. We could look under the bottom strand of wire and see the big oak tree about five hundred yards away. Stanger pointed out the gate they'd drive through. "Five after

241

two," he said. "Ought to get some action along about now."

And we did. A dusty beetle-green Ford two or three years old appeared in the distance, trailing a long plume of dust. The rain of yesterday had dried quickly and completely.

"Broon," Stanger said. The car slowed as it approached the open gate with the cattle guard steel rails paving the entrance, and then went on past, accelerating slightly. In a tone of approval Stanger said, "Took a look to see if Pike was early and now he'll swing around the place. About four miles to go all the way around it. He'll come right down this here dirt road behind us."

We waited. It stirred old instincts, old training. Terrain, cover and concealment, field of fire. The brown pine needles underneath me had a faded aromatic scent. Skirr of insects. Piercingly sweet call of meadowlark. Swamp-smell of the ditch water nearby. Sway and dip of the grasses in the breeze. The motor sound became audible, grew, and it went by behind us, shocks and springs chunking as it hit the potholes in the clay road base. Faded off. A drift of road dust filtered the sunlight for a few moments.

Long minutes later we saw, far across the flat pasture-land, distant glints as he drove along the opposite road, the one that paralleled the road behind us. He was behind the hedgerow of scrub pine and palmetto, chrome winking through the few open places.

When he returned to the gate, he slowed and turned in and drove across the open pastureland, through the grass that had grown to over a foot high since the stock had been moved. The car rolled and bounced and he made a swing, a half circle and parked perhaps fifty feet beyond the lonely live oak.

When he got out, Stanger reached and took the binoculars away from Lew Nudenbarger. "Not now, you damn fool! He'll be looking every direction, and you pick up the sun just right on a lens, he's gone."

"Sorry, Al."

We watched the man walk slowly over to stand in the

242

shade of the oak. Five hundred yards was too far for me to get much more than an impression of a smallish man with a trim and tidy way of moving, pale hair, brown face, white shirt, khaki trousers.

I thought I saw him raise a hand to his mouth, and was suddenly startled by a small, dry coughing sound that came from the monitor speaker of the receiver. It stood on a level place between Stanger and Nudenbarger, a few feet back from the small crest.

"Do the talking right there," Stanger pleaded in a low voice. "Right there. Don't, for God's sake, set in the car and talk. We want you right there, you slippery little scut."

Minutes passed. And then a red car appeared far away, pulling a high-speed dust tower. It braked and turned into the gate. It was the red Falcon wagon, and the last time I had seen it in motion, Helena's daughters had been in it.

It followed the same route through the grass that Broon had taken. It made a wider circle around the tree, in the opposite direction, and stopped on our side but not in the line of vision.

Stanger was looking through the glasses. He lowered them and hitched down and turned on the old Uher recorder, now functioning on battery pack and jacked into the receiver. He took another look through the glasses. "Dave got a gun in his hand," he said.

Broon's voice came over the speaker, resonating the diaphragm as he shouted across the sunlit space. "Whyn't you turn off the motor and get out?"

Pike was so far from the mike his answer was inaudible.

"Talk in the shade, brothers," Stanger pleaded. "Go talk in the shade of the nice big tree."

"I wanted you to see the gun right off, Tom," Broon called out to him. "So you wouldn't get cute until I told you something. If I don't make a phone call tonight to a certain party, an eight-page letter gets mailed special delivery to the state attorney. I spent half the night writing

243

that letter. Now I'll toss this here gun in my car and we can talk things out."

We watched the distant scene and saw them both walk slowly into the shade of the big oak. "Real nice," Stanger whispered.

Broon's conversational voice over the speaker had a startling clarity and fidelity. His tone was mild. "I give you credit, Tom. You suckered me good. Never occurred to me there was something in that bottle different from what you were sticking into your wife. What the hell was it?"

"Mostly nitric acid. I estimated it would eat through the lead stopper in about twenty-four hours."

"What made you so sure I'd put it in my lock box when you told me to keep it safe?"

"I wasn't sure. If you hadn't, I was no worse off, was I?"

"You sure to God made me worse off. Turned everything in my box to a mess of dirty brown stinking mush. Papers and tapes and photos and one hell of a lot of good cash money. It even et a corner out of the box. That bank woman was real upset about the stink. Thing is, Pike, it ruined a lot of stuff that didn't have a damn thing to do with you and me."

"You forced me to do something, Dave."

"How do you figure?"

"You got too expensive. I couldn't afford you."

"With folks standing in line to hand you their savings?"

"But with you taking so big a cut, I couldn't show a return. Then the supply dries up. I had to cut down on your leverage."

"It didn't work. I've got a good memory. I got a lot of facts in that letter I wrote. They can be checked out. Pike, you just made it harder on yourself, because I got to collect all that money you burned up with that damned acid stunt, and we're starting with that thirty thousand you better damn well have brought along."

"Things are too tight. I didn't bring it."

"Then I'm going to pull the stopper, boy, and let you go right down the drain."

"I don't think so."

"Now, just what gives you reason to think I won't?"

"Because you're only half bright, David. But you're bright enough to understand the way things are now. And you're going to keep right on working for me. But your rates have gone down."

"The *hell* you say!"

"If you were bright, you wouldn't have left so suddenly. I knew from the way you acted that I'd destroyed the actual proof. You'd have made me believe you still had the edge. Now, letter or no letter, all you've got is your naked word against mine. Who will be believed, you or me? Think it over. With the Sherman tapes and the signed statement, you could destroy me, possibly. Now you're only a potential annoyance. I brought along thirty-five hundred dollars for you, to show good faith. You're bright enough to know I'm going to be a pretty good source of income for you. Nothing like before, of course. You'll accept it."

"You sure of that? You sure I'll settle for a little bit here and a little bit there?"

"As opposed to nothing at all, why not?"

"It won't pay for the risk."

"What risk?"

"Maybe I'm only half bright, like you say, but I'm bright enough to know you're not going to last. They're going to grab you, and when they do, you'll put me in it right up to the eyeballs."

"Grab me for what?"

"For killing folks. Maybe with Doc Sherman it was your only way out. But I think you liked doing it. You told me they'd grab Janice Holton for stabbing that nurse. But it went wrong somehow and you went ahead anyway, without any real good reason. Pretty soon you're going to set up that suicide deal on your wife and enjoy that too. Then you'll start thinking about somebody else. Maybe me. No, thanks. You've turned into a bug, Pike. I've seen them like you and seen what happens. Maybe it makes you feel so big you have to keep doing it."

"My poor wife threw herself out a twelfth-story window last evening, David."

"What! What the hell are you saying? There wasn't a thing in the paper about——"

"Believe me, she went out the window. I heard the sound of the impact and I know she didn't walk away. I thought the workmen would find the body, but it seems to be gone."

"What the hell do you mean—gone?"

"Today I learned from Biddy that her old friend, Mr. McGee, told her at the party that he saw Maureen sneaking out alone. Assume he knows the terms of the trust funds. So I think he'll get in touch with me to sell me a little information. Your next job is to get to him first, David, and see if you can encourage him to tell you all about it."

Broon did not respond. I found it hard to relate the voices that came over the little speaker to the two men standing under a distant tree across the sunny pastureland.

"You poor damn fool," Broon said.

"It's really quite imperative to get going on it," Tom Pike said, "because even if he hadn't interfered, it will take several months before they'll close out the trust and transfer the principal directly to Bridget."

"Somebody steals a body and you think it's some kind of an inconvenience! You damn fool!"

"Why get in an uproar, Broon? Body or no body, nobody can ever prove a thing."

"You don't even realize it's all over, do you? I'll tell you, there's only one way I can walk away from this one, partner."

Quite suddenly there was a grunt of effort, a gasp of surprise, over the speaker. The distant figures had merged abruptly, and as they spun around it looked, at that distance, like some grotesque dance. The taller figure went up and over and down, and we heard the thud of impact. Both of them were down and invisible. The grass concealed them. Dave Broon stood up, stared down for a moment. Stanger lowered the binoculars quickly. Broon made a slow turn, all the way around, eyes searching the horizon.

"Shouldn't we——"

"Shut up, Lew," Stanger said.

Broon trotted out of the shade and across the sunlit grass to his car. He opened the trunk. Stanger put the glasses on him as he came back.

"Coil of rope," he said. "Tie him up and tote him away, maybe."

"But if he drives off——" Nudenbarger started to say.

"If I can't punch that engine dead at this range with that there carbine, Lew, I'm not trying."

Broon squatted over Tom Pike for a little while, then straightened and took Pike under the armpits and dragged him about fifteen feet. He dropped him there and went quickly to the tree, jumped and caught a limb, quickly pulled himself up and out of sight in the leaves.

"Son of a gun!" Stanger said.

"Why is he climbing the tree?" Lew asked plaintively.

"He took the end of the rope up with him. What do you think?"

Nudenbarger looked baffled. I comprehended the shape and the sense of it. And soon it was confirmed when Tom Pike sat up in the grass quite slowly, slumping to the side in an unnatural way.

Then he rose slowly up from a sitting position.

"Oh, God!" cried Nudenbarger.

"Keep your damned voice down to a soft beller!" Al snapped.

Over the speaker came a strange sound, a gagging, rasping cry. Pike ran a few steps in one direction and was snubbed to a halt. He staggered back. He tried the other direction and did not get as far.

Stanger said, not taking his eyes from the glasses, "Got the fingers of both hands into that loop now, holding it off his throat."

"Broon!" the deep voice cried, cracked and ragged.

He seemed to run in place and then he moved up a little bit. Straight up. And a little bit more. His legs made running motions. He began turning. Then his shoes were above the highest blades of grass. Dave Broon dropped abruptly into view. Nudenbarger raised the carbine and Stanger slapped the barrel down.

Broon got into the red wagon and swung it in a quick turn and parked it close to where Pike hung.

He got out, backed off, looked at Pike, and then ran for his car.

"Now!" Al Stanger said. He snatched up the carbine and vaulted the fence with an agility that astonished me. By the time we were over the fence, he had a twenty-yard lead. As the green Ford began to roll, picking up speed, Stanger stopped, went down onto one knee, and fired four spaced, aimed shots. At the fourth one the back end of the car bloomed into a white-orange poof of gasoline, and as the car kept moving, Broon tumbled out the driver's door, somersaulting in the grass. He got up and started to run at an angle toward the far side of the pasture but stopped quickly when Stanger fired his fifth shot.

He turned, hands in the air, and began to walk slowly toward the tree. The car had stopped in tall grass, tinkling, frying, blackening. He walked more quickly. And then he began to run back toward the tree.

"Head him off, Lew. Grab him."

Lew had good style. He loped in that loose deceptive stride of a good NFL end getting down for the long bomb. Stanger and I headed for the tree. He jogged. I started to run by him and he blocked me with the barrel of the carbine extended.

Thus we all got to the red wagon at about the same time. Nudenbarger was taking no chances with Dave Broon. He had one meaty hand clamped on the nape of Broon's neck and had Broon's arm bent back up and pinned between Broon's shoulderblades by his other paw.

Broon was hopping up and down, grunting, struggling, yelling, "Cut him down! Al! Hey, Al! Cut him down!"

We looked up at Tom Pike. He turned slowly toward us. His clenched fists were on either side of his throat, fingers hooked around the strand of rope that crossed his throat. He looked like a man chinning himself, face blackening with total effort.

I saw that I could swing him over and up onto the roof of the station wagon and get the pressure off his throat immediately. As I moved toward him quickly, Stanger clanked the carbine barrel against the back of my skull. The impact was exquisitely precise. It darkened the day without turning the sun out completely. It loosened my knees enough to sag me to a squat, knuckles against the turf, but not enough to spill me all the way. I turned and stared up at Al, blinking away darkness and the tear-sting of skull pain.

"Don't go messing with the evidence, boy," he said.

"Don't *do* this to me, Al!" Broon begged. "Please, for God's sake, don't do it like this."

Nudenbarger, with Broon firmly in hand, was staring slack-mouthed at Tom Pike. "Jesus!" he said softly. "Oh, Jesus me!"

And Tom Pike continued the slow turn. He lifted his right leg slowly, the knee bending. Classic shoes, expensive slacks, navy socks of what looked like brushed Dacron. The leg dropped back.

"See him twitching any, Lew?" Stanger asked mildly.

"Well . . . that leg moved some."

"Just reflex action, Lew boy. Posthumous nervous twitch, like. Doesn't mean a thing."

Broon said, "You're killing me, Al. You know that."

"You're all confused. You killed Tom Pike, Davey."

"You're miserable, Al. You're a mean bastard, Al Stanger."

Slowly, slowly, Tom Pike turned back to face us. He had changed. The look of muscular tension had gone out of his fists and wrists. They were just slack hands, pinned there by the loop, fingers pressing into the flesh of the throat. His chin had dropped. His toes pointed downward. His face had become bloated and the eyes no longer looked at anything at all.

"See now how it was just the nerves twitching some?" Al asked gently.

"You were right, Al. He's dead for sure," Lew said.

I pushed myself up and fingered a new lump on the back of my head. "How long would you say he's been dead, McGee? All things considered."

"I'd say he must have been dead by the time Broon started to drive away, Al. All things considered."

"Guess we shouldn't touch a thing. Get a reconstruction by the lab people to match up with the eyewitness account." He handed me the carbine and went over and took handcuffs out of a back pocket. He snapped one around Broon's wrist, told Lew to bend him over a little, and snapped the other around Broon's opposite ankle. Lew let go and Stanger gave Broon a push. Broon sat in the grass, knees hiked up.

"Lew, you cut across and get the car and bring it around in here. Might as well stop and pick up our gear over there on the way. We'll be waiting right here."

With a last look at the body, Nudenbarger hurried off.

The body had stopped turning. Stanger stared into the distance, sighed, spat. "Sorry I had to rap you like that."

I looked into his small dusty brown eyes. "I guess it was the quickest way to stop me, Al."

"Feel all right?"

"Just a little bit sick to my stomach."

"Funny. So do I."

21

I STAYED AROUND and did what I could to help Bridget Pearson through the worst of it. In a conference about strategy, Ben Gaffner had accepted my suggestion that nothing would be gained by opening up the actual way in which Maureen had died.

It could bring down on us a lot of awkward questions from high places.

Better to make it an identification error over in Lime County and let the phosphate pit story stand.

He agreed that there was so little to go on that Dr. Sherman's death might as well remain on the books as suicide. But the Penny Woertz murder had to be taken out of the active file, and properly closed. That meant some acceptable explanation of motive. Dave Broon came in handy. He was smart enough to have started talking about strangling Tom Pike in a fit of anger and then, upon discovering he was dead, trying to string him up to make it look like suicide.

That gave Gaffner a choice—to play ball with Broon or to go for murder first. Murder first would need only the eyewitnesses to state that they had seen Pike trying to get free as Broon was slowly hauling him clear of the ground. Gaffner had Broon brought in for a private play-back of the tape of the conversation under the live oak. Broon then said it was his certain knowledge that Pike was having an affair with the nurse and had killed her out of jealousy. Gaffner, out of respect for the reputation of the deceased Miss Woertz, edited it down to Pike's pursuit of her, with the crime of passion occurring doubtless when his advances were repulsed. All this cooperation earned Broon the chance at a plea of guilty to murder second, with, whether the sentence was ten, fifteen, or twenty, a chance at parole in six.

Even though by funeral time—a ceremony for two, for Mr. and Mrs. Pike—the swarm of auditors and examiners were beginning to find that Tom Pike had been distributing newly invested capital to previous investors and calling it a distribution of capital gains, Fort Courtney was full of people who could not, and would never, believe that such a brilliant and warm and considerate and handsome and well-mannered man could have ever juggled a single account in any questionable manner, to say nothing of *stabbing* anyone.

No, it all had to be some kind of vicious and clever conspiracy, engineered by *Them*. *They* were the subtle, hidden enemy, hiring that Broon person, making some kind of intricate deal with him, and then probably taking over the wonderful properties Tom Pike had such great plans for at the time of his death.

So the funeral was well-attended. Biddy knew that all the allegations were so absurd as to be grotesque. And so did Janice Holton. Biddy was so certain, that I could not risk the slightest slur or shadow of doubt to color anything I said to her, or she would never have let me try to help her in any way. She kept going on tranquilizers and raw courage. I helped her close up the house. It would be sold once all estate and inheritance matters were straightened out, and the funds would go to the unfortunate who had invested in Development Unlimited. Fortunately, as there was no doubt of Maureen's having died first, the trust fund would go directly to Bridget. Because Maureen had signed certain papers in connection with her husband's enterprises, had he died first, it was possible the monies might have been diverted to the creditors of Development Unlimited.

She said she was going to drive on down to Casey Key and open up the old house and stay there for a time, quite alone. She said she would be all right. She would walk the beach, get a lot of painting done, sort herself out.

The morning I was packing to leave the Wahini Lodge, Lorette Walker stopped by and said she heard from Cathy I was checking out. I asked her to come on in. She leaned against the countertop and lit a cigarette and said, "Stayed you a long time, huh?"

"I couldn't tear myself away from this garden spot."

"Lot of things happened. Always like that wherever you go?"

"I'm happy to be able to say no."

"That's no good way to fold a shirt! Mess it all up for sure." She came over and took the shirt back out of the bag, spread it out on the bed, folded it quickly and deftly, and put it in the bag. "Best way," she said, backing off. "Sorry I couldn't do you much good on what you wanted me to find out."

"You did a lot of good. You'll never know how much."

"But nobody come hard-nosing around to try to make me say it twice."

"I told you I'd leave you out of it."

She said wistfully, "Could be better for me if you never did keep your word."

"How do you mean?"

"I told myself, back there when I wanted to trust you some, I said okay, gal, you just go ahead and he'll mess you up good. Be a good lesson. Stop you from ever going soft again for any whitey."

"That's why you did it?"

She put on a look of owlish innocence. "Well, then there was that chance of the airplane ride you mentioned. I figured on Paris. Anyway, here's the change from that two hundred. I spent eighty of your dollars on people that didn't have anything worth telling."

"So let's split what you've got left there."

She flared immediately. "So it means I got no right to tell myself I ever did a damn thing for you just for a favor? You buying me for this sixty dollar, you think?"

"Right off the slave block, woman. You did a favor, but I've got no right to do a favor, according to you. I know you didn't expect a dime, but by God you'll take that sixty dollars and you'll buy yourself a pretty suit, something tailored, maybe a good medium shade of blue, and you will wear that damned suit, and you will accept it as a gesture of friendship and trust."

"Well . . . I guess you don't need no lessons in coming on mean, mister. I . . . I guess I can take it like it's meant. And thank you very much. You're sure? The only thing I got a right to do with it is buy a winter suit?"

"That's how it has to be," I said, putting the sixty left over into my wallet.

She shrugged and smiled. "Well, then . . . got to get on back up to those rooms. We run pretty full last night."

I held my hand out. "You helped a lot. And a pleasure to get to know you, Mrs. Walker."

After a moment of wary hesitation she shook hands. "Same to you. Good-bye."

She opened the door and turned back, her hand on the knob, and looked at me and moistened her lips. "McGee, you have a nice safe trip back home, hear?" She bolted out and closed the door. My last glimpse and last impression of her was of the slender and vital brown of her quick legs. Another lady in a plain brown wrapper. No, that was not a good analogy, because there was nothing very plain about that sleek wrapper. It was special— flawless, matte finish and inordinately lovely.

I went back knowing that whatever had been wrong with me, any restlessness, irritability, mooniness, had come to an abrupt end. Seeing him hanging and turning so slowly had brought me back to the fullness of life, probably just because his was so evidently gone. I was full of offensive cheer, bounding health, party plans.

Three months later, on a windy gray afternoon in January, Bridget Pearson appeared. She apologized for showing up at Bahia Mar without any advance notice at all. She said it had been an impulse.

She came aboard *The Busted Flush* and sat in the lounge and took neat small sips of her drink and seemed to smile too quickly and too often. The weeks had gaunted her down and in some eerie way she had acquired that same slightly haggard elegance that Helena had evidenced at the time we sailed away in the *Likely Lady*. The long legs were the same, and the way she held her hands, and I knew that all of her was so much the same that it would be like an old love revisited.

She told me that she was restless, wondering what to do with herself, thinking maybe she might go on a trip of some sort. She said she kept coming up with strange little inconsistencies in her memories of Tom Pike. They bothered her. As if there had been something warped and strange that she had been too close to. Was everything the way she believed it had been? Could I help her understand?

Why, now, don't you trouble your purty little head about a thang, little sweetheart. Why, for goodness sake, ol' Uncle Trav will take you on off a-cruisin' on this here comfortable and luxurious ol' crock houseboat, and he'll just talk kindly to you and comfort you and love you up good, and that'll put the real sunshine back in your purty little smile.

I thought of what it would do to her eyes and to the shape of her mouth if I ever told her how it had been for her mother and me aboard the *Likely Lady* in that long-ago Bahama summertime. I tried to sort out the intervals. I am X years older than this lovely young lady and I was X years younger than her lovely mother.

No, thanks. It was too late for me to take a lead role in a maritime version of *The Graduate*. And even had it been possible under my present circumstances, I did not want to astound myself with the unavoidably queasy excitements of an incestuous sort of relationship.

I let too many long moments pass. I could sense that she had thought it all over quite carefully and had come with the definite purpose of opening the door a little way, thinking that I would take over from there. The half-stated offer was withdrawn. We made a little polite talk. I told her I had not seen anything particularly inconsistent about Tom Pike. And that was the truth. She said she was going to meet some friends in Miami and she had better go. I told her I was sorry she couldn't stay longer. She turned when she was halfway along the dock and gave me a merry wave and went striding on, out of my life.

I went back below and freshened my drink and mixed some Plymouth with some fresh grapefruit juice for the lady.

She was sitting on the side of the big bed in the master stateroom, filing her nails. She wore a big fuzzy yellow towel wrapped and tucked around her. She lifted her head sharply to toss her dark hair back and looked at me with a twisted and cynical smile.

"A wealth of opportunity, McGee?"

"Or it never rains but it pours."

"Let me see. Finders keepers, losers weepers. How did she seem?"

"Gaunt. Haunted. At loose ends."

"Wanting comforting? How sweet! And did you tell the poor dear thing to come back some other day?"

"Any show of jealousy always comforts me," I said, and gave her her drink. She sipped it and smiled her thanks and reached and put it on the top of the nearby locker. I stretched out behind her and propped my head up on a pair of pillows.

"Sorry I was here?" she asked.

"Been the same thing. I would have had to go with my instinct. And it said no dice."

"She's very pretty."

"And rich. And talented."

"Hmmm!" she said. The file made little rasping sounds. I sipped my drink. "Mr. McGee, sir? Which really surprised you most? Her showing up or me showing up?"

"You. Definitely. Looked down from the sundeck and saw you standing there and nearly choked to death." I reached an idle finger and hooked it into the back of the wrapped and tucked towel. One gentle tug untucked it and it fell, pooling around her. She slowly straightened her long, slender, lovely back. She reached and picked up her drink and took half of it down, then replaced it.

"May I assume you are quite serious, Mr. McGee?"

"It is crummy weather out there, and you have an extraordinarily fine back, and you were pleasantly bitchy about Miss Pearson, so I am serious, my dear."

"Shall I bother to finish these last three fingernails?"

"Please do, Mrs. Holton."

"I shall try to finish them, Mr. McGee. I think it would be good for my character, what little I have left."

So I listened to the busy little buzz of the nail file and admired her, and sipped the drink, and thought about the way she had looked that day I had watched her spray-painting that old blue metal chaise.

And then I heard the wind-blown January rain move in from the sea and across the beaches and the boat basin and roar softly and steadily down on the weather decks of my houseboat.